Blockchain and Ethereum Smart Contract Solution Development

Dapp Programming with Solidity

Weijia Zhang
Tej Anand

Apress®

Blockchain and Ethereum Smart Contract Solution Development: Dapp Programming with Solidity

Weijia Zhang
Austin, TX, USA

Tej Anand
Chappaqua, NY, USA

ISBN-13 (pbk): 978-1-4842-8163-5
https://doi.org/10.1007/978-1-4842-8164-2

ISBN-13 (electronic): 978-1-4842-8164-2

Managing Director, Apress Media LLC: Welmoed Spahr
Acquisitions Editor: Aaron Black
Development Editor: James Markham
Coordinating Editor: Jessica Vakili

Distributed to the book trade worldwide by Springer Science+Business Media New York, 233 Spring Street, 6th Floor, New York, NY 10013. Phone 1-800-SPRINGER, fax (201) 348-4505, e-mail orders-ny@springer-sbm.com, or visit www.springeronline.com. Apress Media, LLC is a California LLC and the sole member (owner) is Springer Science + Business Media Finance Inc (SSBM Finance Inc). SSBM Finance Inc is a **Delaware** corporation.

For information on translations, please e-mail booktranslations@springernature.com; for reprint, paperback, or audio rights, please e-mail bookpermissions@springernature.com.

Apress titles may be purchased in bulk for academic, corporate, or promotional use. eBook versions and licenses are also available for most titles. For more information, reference our Print and eBook Bulk Sales web page at http://www.apress.com/bulk-sales.

Any source code or other supplementary material referenced by the author in this book is available to readers on the Github repository: https://github.com/Apress/-Blockchain-and-Ethereum-Smart-Contract-Solution-Development. For more detailed information, please visit http://www.apress.com/source-code.

Printed on acid-free paper

To our students at the University of Texas at Austin, Columbia University in the City of New York, and the University of Maryland in College Park.

Table of Contents

About the Authors

Dr. Weijia Zhang teaches a smart contract development course at the University of Texas. He has extensive R&D knowledge and engineering experience in blockchain, cognitive sciences, mental modeling, computational fluid dynamics (CFD), software modeling, computer technologies, and industrial standards. Weijia has published over 30 research and technical papers and is named as an inventor for over 20 patents, granted and pending, in computer and digital technology. He has also served as a technical committee voting member to publish the Solution Deployment Descriptor (SDD) by the Organization for the Advancement of Structured Information Standards (OASIS).

Dr. Tej Anand is a Clinical Professor at the Smith School of Business, University of Maryland, and a visiting lecturer at the School of Professional Studies, Columbia University. Tej spent the first part of his career working in AI/Data research at Philips Research, Nielsen, and NCR/Teradata, and the second part of his career as a business-technology executive at Golden Books, CA Technologies, MedcoHealth, and CareCentrix.

ABOUT THE AUTHORS

Tej's research interests include blockchain governance, firm-wide analytics maturity, and business leader traits for successful technology adoption.

Tej was previously an Assistant Clinical Professor at McCombs School of Business at the University of Texas in Austin.

About the Technical Reviewer

 **Prasanth Sahoo** is a thought leader, an adjunct professor, a technical speaker, and a full-time practitioner in blockchain, DevOps, cloud, and Agile working for PDI Software. He was awarded the "Blockchain and Cloud Expert of the Year Award 2019" from TCS Global Community for his knowledge share within academic services to the community. He is passionate about driving digital technology initiatives by handling various community initiatives through coaching, mentoring, and grooming techniques.

Prasanth has a patent under his name, and to date, he has interacted reaching over 50,000 professionals, mostly within the technical domain. He is a working group member in the Blockchain Council, CryptoCurrency Certification Consortium, Scrum Alliance, Scrum Organization, and International Institute of Business Analysis.

Acknowledgments

This book is partially based on the courses we taught at the McCombs School of Business at The University of Texas at Austin, the School of Professional Studies at Columbia University, and the Smith School of Business at The University of Maryland in College Park.

We would not be writing this book if Prof. Prabhudev Konana, Prof. Sriram Vishwanath, and Dr. Caryn Conley did not work extremely hard to get our course approved at the University of Texas at Austin. Prof. Arthur Langer was instrumental in getting the course approved at Columbia University, enabling us to expand the content to technology management professionals. Prabhudev Konana and Prof. Pallassana Kannan gave us the opportunity to further refine our content to reach business executives by allowing us to create an executive education offering at the University of Maryland.

Sriram Vishwanath, Dr. Karl Kreder, Mr. Vijay Rathna, and Prof. Anand Anandalingam have co-taught this course with us at different times and our learnings from them are reflected in this book.

This book has benefited from the excellent work of the creative, knowledgeable, and hardworking teaching assistants across all the courses. These teaching assistants have included Alan Orwick, Yihe Liu, Parikshit Hegde, Cody Morton, Joseph Dowdall, Shubhangkar Jain, Roque Martinez, Ajay Nyamati, Denzell Ford, and Nicholas Khami. Shubhangkar spent a lot of time helping us with the quiz questions for Part 1.

We have also benefited from innovative instructional design support from Matthew Vaughan, Jennifer Hoeritz, and Joshua Shannon-Chastain. Several of the diagrams in this book are easy on the eyes due to the graphical design expertise provided by Nicholas Bonneau and Dr. Shohreh Anand.

ACKNOWLEDGMENTS

We also want to thank industry experts who provided helpful academia-industry connections to enable our teaching to be up to date with cutting edge blockchain technologies. Ron Resnick has been instrumental in pioneering token taxonomy concepts which we mentioned in the tokenization chapter. Conor Svensson has provided good discussions on Enterprise Ethereum Architecture which we discussed in Chapter 6; Jack Lu, Peter Robinson, Chaals Nevile, and Dan Reecer have provided their insight on crosschain technology which we believe will connect both public and enterprise blockchains. We also want to thank Dr. Dan Burnett, Ken Fromm, James Harsh, Brittany Mauck for organizing numerous blockchain seminars and conferences which sharpened our knowledge on blockchains and blockchain education.

We believe that writing blockchain educational books are tedious tasks that cannot be accomplished without unconditional support from our families. We appreciate their forbearance, continued support, and love.

PART 1

The Context for Blockchain

In the first part of this book, we describe the context that gives blockchain (please note that throughout this book, we will spell blockchain with a lowercase "b" to stress its mainstreaming) technology its enormous disruptive potential.

It is quite possible that many of you have heard of blockchain through its association with Bitcoin,[1] a cryptocurrency, so we start with a brief history of money and describe the complications associated with exchanging money. We then generalize the discussion beyond money to **value** and explain how value exchange is the driver of our economy. Value exchange between parties requires **trust**. This trust is inherently absent, and this has resulted in the creation of several mediating parties (also known as third parties) who guarantee trust for a fee. In some cases, the mediating parties have wittingly or unwittingly amassed power in the economy with unforeseen unintended consequences. These unintended consequences are a source of many inefficiencies in our economy, and we describe these inefficiencies in detail. We then pose the question

---

[1] We have taught six blockchain classes since January 2019, and we can attest that enrollment in our class is correlated with the price of Bitcoin.

whether a system that can create trust between parties who do not trust each other has the potential for decreasing the inefficiencies in our economy. We believe that blockchain is such a technology with enormous disruptive potential. Our focus in this book is how you can design and create enterprise applications using blockchain technology (distributed applications) with the goal of increasing value, driving productivity, and unleashing growth across entire economic sectors.

We believe a clear-eyed understanding of blockchain is necessary to create pragmatic solutions. This understanding requires a high-level, quasi-technical understanding of the core technologies that are used to implement blockchain. These technologies are cryptology, distributed systems, and peer-to-peer networks. We provide a brief overview of these technologies in Chapter 2. This overview will help you understand the design trade-offs that are necessary to implement blockchain applications. This overview will also provide an understanding of the research challenges that are currently being worked on and need to be solved before blockchain can achieve its full potential.

With an understanding of the core technologies, we will be in a position to understand conceptually how blockchain works, its core components, and architecture. This will be our focus in Chapter 3. A conceptual understanding of blockchain will provide the business semantics for the technical capabilities of blockchain.

In Chapter 4, we provide guidelines on how use cases for building enterprise blockchain business applications should be selected. We also discuss the design decisions and trade-offs that need to be considered for a blockchain application and the systems integration effort that will be necessary for business adoption and success.

We end Part 1 of this book with a comprehensive and concise overview of Bitcoin, the first blockchain implementation, in Chapter 5. We also discuss the rationale for the design trade-offs that were made during the implementation and describe the current debates within the Bitcoin community, concluding with a peek at the economics of Bitcoin.

CHAPTER 1

Business and Economic Motivation for Blockchain

In our society, it would be difficult to imagine any business process that wasn't either supported, mediated, or completely automated by the combination of computer hardware, software, and networks. In this book, computer hardware, software, networks, and the related disciplines of data and process analysis, user experience design, and system design are all collectively referred to as information technology. Studies have established the wide-ranging positive impact of information technology on business productivity (Loveman, 1993, Brynjolfsson 1991). In this chapter, we start by providing an enumeration of the information technology innovations since the mid-1960s that have all contributed to improving business productivity with the purpose of understanding those aspects of a business that have not yet been impacted because these are the areas that blockchain has the potential to impact.

© Weijia Zhang and Tej Anand 2022
W. Zhang and T. Anand, *Blockchain and Ethereum Smart Contract Solution Development*,
https://doi.org/10.1007/978-1-4842-8164-2_1

Introduction

We deem the release of the IBM mainframe in April 1964 (Cortada, 2019) as the event that started the process of information technology becoming the dominant force propelling business. This was followed by the invention of the relational database management system in 1970 (Codd, 1970), the invention of the Ethernet in 1976 (Metcalfe and Boggs, 1976), and the creation of the personal computer in 1981 (Baldwin, 2019). In the 1990s, two technologies that had been under development since the mid-1960s started becoming viable for widespread adoption in the business world. The first of these technologies was Enterprise Resource Planning (ERP) software with the release of the R/2 system in 1992 and the R/3 system in 1999 from SAP (Thomson, 2020). The second technology is what we now ubiquitously call the internet. The term "internet"[1] was formally defined in 1995 (Leiner et al., 1997) even though the internet was already being commercialized. Some noteworthy early innovative companies that commercialized the internet were Yahoo and Amazon (both founded in 1994), Netflix (founded in 1997), and Google (founded in 1998).

From a business standpoint, these collections of technologies provided two competing thrusts. The mainframe, relational database management systems, and ERP software appeared to create value by standardization and centralization. On the other hand, the personal computer and the internet appeared to create value by decentralization. As businesses adopted these technologies, they made design trade-offs that fit their worldview and culture to find the optimal point on the centralization-decentralization continuum. The business value for firms successfully adopting ERP software came from clarifying the strategic intent of a business and then relentlessly reengineering business processes and systems to match this strategic intent (Treacy and Wiersema, 1995). The

---

[1] Throughout this book, we will spell internet with a lowercase "i" to stress its mainstreaming.

business value for firms successfully adopting the internet came from also clarifying strategic intent and then relentlessly digitizing, streamlining business processes (akin to reengineering), and globalizing to increase margin, reduce costs, and increase share of wallet (Porter, 2001).

We have been working with these technologies across several businesses for the last 30 years, and even after all these years, successful adoption for ERP software and the internet is still a work in process. These two technologies are also rapidly converging with ERP software increasingly available as a Software as a Service (SaaS). During our time working with companies to adopt these technologies, there are a few "truisms" that we have come to understand about these technologies.

First, these technologies have achieved success by either preserving the existing power structures or by creating new sources of power that started off as egalitarian but ended up becoming highly centralized and controlling. For example, both ERP and internet implementations did very little to change the power dynamic between a business and its suppliers or customers. ERPs were usually internally focused, and to obtain executive sponsorship and deal with change management issues, they tended to strengthen existing power centers within a firm. The internet initially created a sense that power would shift to customers by creating transparency and access to information; however, it ended up creating new sources of power with centralized platforms such as Facebook, Amazon, Google, Uber, and Airbnb. We are only now beginning to grapple with the unintended consequences of these new sources of power.

Second, it is not clear if these collections of technologies improved productivity by reducing work. It is clearer that productivity was improved by shifting work to settings where it could be done cheaper, or by streamlining (and even automating) the flow of information, or by shifting work to customers by making them feel that they had more control.

Third, the goal of these technologies was data sharing and information exchange ostensibly to eliminate information silos, promote interoperability, and optimize business planning. While this was a laudable goal and drove operational efficiency, the benefits flowed disproportionately to the most powerful firms in the supply chain since they dictated the formalisms of information exchange. The context of this goal was also bereft of any trust among the parties. The lack of trust led to firms creating pipelines for data sharing that were silos in themselves while hoarding their own proprietary information semantics. In the best case, this created localized benefits for some firms, and in the worst case, this increased work and costs for all except the already-dominant firms.

Fourth, and perhaps most importantly, the lack of trust among firms led to a preservation of the current payment mechanisms used by businesses albeit with greater connectivity among parties and a marginal improvement in settlement time. The role of government, banks, and clearinghouses has remained unchanged and continues to be a barrier to improved productivity and leads to increased costs for non-value-added activities. Whenever we hyperbolically make the claim that the internet has really not improved payment efficiency, our students challenge us with the improvements enabled by firms like Venmo, PayPal, and Square. There is no doubt that these firms have made incremental improvements; however, if we look behind the curtain, these firms are relying on the same clearinghouses and banks that have always existed. The reason that firms like Venmo can create a perception of significant improvement is because these firms are subsidizing consumer fees. We contend that these subsidies will go away once these firms are large and profitable and have consumer capture.

We believe when we look at blockchain, we should keep the four "truisms" discussed earlier front and center in our mind. The Bitcoin system (Nakamoto, 2008) introduced the Bitcoin currency, the first digital currency with a viable solution for the "double-spend" problem (Chohan, 2021), a payment mechanism among parties that lacked trust where settlement did not require a trusted third party, and a distributed ledger that gave all parties a complete copy of all transactions. While much attention has been paid to the price of Bitcoin, it is the integration of all the three features of Bitcoin that together have the potential of addressing the "truisms" that the ERP and internet have collectively failed to adequately address.

In this chapter, we start with a brief history of money. This will help us understand why currencies such as Bitcoin[2] are not as outlandish a concept as they might be perceived and what are the sources of complications in the exchange of money. We will then abstract our discussion to cast the entire economy as the exchange of value. This will help us understand the sources of complications in value exchange across global supply chains. These complications directly drive the inefficiencies in our current economic system that have not yet been adequately addressed by ERP software and the internet. We end this chapter by considering why blockchain has the potential to address these economic inefficiencies and thus usher in a new era of productivity that some refer to as Web3.

A Brief History of Money[3]

To understand the notion of money and how it has evolved over time, we start with the situation where a person (individual #1) has a surplus of one good and a scarcity of another good. Let's assume that there is another individual (individual #2), known to individual #1, who has a surplus of the good that is scarce for individual #1 and a scarcity of the good that individual #1 has in surplus. Now, in order to address their scarcity, individual #1 would be willing to exchange some units (say, x) of the surplus good with some units (say, y) of the scarce good with individual #2. This exchange in our terminology constitutes a **transaction**, and the conditions for consummating this transaction are considered a **contract**

---

[2] We will refer to digital currencies such as Bitcoin as cryptocurrencies in this book.
[3] A good reading reference for this section is Menger, 1892.

between individual #1 and individual #2. The x units of one good for y units of another good is the **exchange rate**. The transaction we have described here is called a barter.

Let's consider, for example, if I am individual #1 and have several loaves of bread but no butter and a friend of mine is individual #2 and has several sticks of butter but no bread. We would be both better off and come out ahead if I gave some of my surplus bread to my friend in exchange for butter – let's say I give half a loaf of bread to get a quarter stick of butter. The exchange rate of a half a loaf of bread for a quarter stick of butter then represents the perceived and agreed relative value of bread and butter between my friend and me, and the exchange rate is the only condition that makes up the contract. As soon as I have the butter and my friend has the bread, our transaction has been settled.

Let's build this example further. My friend now has a craving for tea. My friend knows another person (individual #3) who has a surplus of tea. Individual #3 has no need for butter, but individual #3 is willing to exchange half a pound of tea for a loaf of bread. So my friend exchanges butter for bread with me and now has a surplus of bread that can be exchanged for tea with an exchange rate of half a pound of tea for a loaf of bread. This is an example of a multiparty exchange. The respective exchange rates are the only conditions that make up the contracts between me and my friend and my friend and individual #3. Now we could make this more complex, if I adjusted the exchange rate based on my perception of my friends' need for tea, but for now, we will not do that. Table 1-1 summarizes the transactions and the change in ownership of goods assuming I started with 4 loaves of bread, my friend started with 4 sticks of butter, and individual #3 started with 4 pounds of tea.

Table 1-1. *Simple exchange transactions (barter)*

	Time: t = 0 (starting point)	Time: t = 1 (first transaction has settled)	Time: t = 2 (second transaction has settled)
Goods owned by individual #1	4 loaves of bread	3.5 loaves of bread ¼ stick of butter	2.5 loaves of bread ¾ stick of butter
Goods owned by individual #2	4 sticks of butter	½ a loaf of bread 3 ¾ sticks of butter	½ a loaf of bread 3 ¼ sticks of butter ½ a pound of tea
Good owned by individual #3	4 pounds of tea	4 pounds of tea	3 ½ pounds of tea 1 loaf of bread

Now, given how the transaction with individual #2 transpired, it would be reasonable for individuals #1, #2, and #3 to conclude that bread was a far more acceptable good for exchange than butter or tea. With this judgment, it would also be reasonable to assume that all individuals would consider it worthwhile to have surplus bread, because bread can be exchanged for something else. In general, if a good was scarce and it was valued by people, then it would be more likely to be accepted as a medium of exchange. If we could find such a good that everyone would accept as a medium of exchange, then we would call this good a **universally acceptable medium of exchange**. This is how we get to the definition of money. In society, money is that good which is universally accepted as a medium of exchange.

A few other points to note about our rather simplistic example:

1.   The exchanges were happening between individuals– these were peer-to-peer exchanges (more about the technical implications of this in Chapter 2).

2. There was no third party involved, and therefore, no fees were paid to settle the transactions.

3. It would be reasonable to assume that the peer-to-peer exchange without fees was possible because individuals #1 and #2 knew and trusted each other and individual #2 and #3 knew and trusted each other.

Various societies have been on a quest for goods that can serve as money. Different societies have used commodities such as gold, silver, and other precious metals as money. Yet other societies have used grains and other crops or shells as forms of money. In the prisons in the United States, cigarettes and ramen noodles get used as money. An interesting story about money comes from the island of Yap in the South Pacific, where a quartz like crystal, called rai, was used as money (Bryan, 2004). Rai were mined from a neighboring island, and the people of Yap judged the value of rai based on how difficult and dangerous they thought it was to mine and transport the rai. People have referred to rai as the "original" Bitcoin (Dockrill, 2019).

There are several challenges or drawbacks with money that is based on commodities. For one, commodities can be heavy and cumbersome to transport, making it difficult for parties to "send" money to each other. Commodity-based money can also be difficult to produce with production costs dependent on a host of factors such as weather, geography, and the cost of labor. All of these costs will vary over time and be different for different societies. Access to the commodity (or the level of scarcity) that is being used for money will also not be uniform across different societies,[4] leading to the possibilities that different societies end up using

---

[4] We have chosen to use the word "societies" instead of countries to avoid any nationalist undertones. It might be easier for the reader's understanding to think of societies as countries.

different commodities as their basis for money. Commodities can also be difficult to measure or evaluate in real time and on the spot. Over time, many countries settled on gold as a basis for money. Gold was scarce, it was highly desired, and it could be evaluated by its weight and purity by people with tools and expertise. However, gold has the other drawbacks of commodity money, so political authority by nations was used to create denominations of money (currency), in paper and coins. The value of the total amount of money in circulation was guaranteed by reserves of gold held by that nation. Over time, this backing of the gold reserve was removed,[5] and money was guaranteed merely by the centralized political power of the nation that created the currency. We call currency backed by the political power of a nation as "fiat"[6] currency. So does the US government really decide what the value of a dollar is? Please see the sidebar[7] "What is $1 worth?" for discussion on this topic. Is a nation the only institution that issues fiat currency? Please see the sidebar - "Alternate Currencies" for a discussion on this topic.

The discussion up to this point has equipped us to define the three fundamental properties of money now more formally:

1. **Medium of exchange** – Money is something that is acceptable by everyone as a medium of exchange of transactions. This usually implies that money can be used repeatedly and has a long life (durable) and it can be carried and transported easily (portable).

---

[5] In the United States, the backing of the gold reserve was removed in a two-step process. In 1933, President Roosevelt announced that the United States would no longer commit to convert dollars to gold. In 1971, President Nixon announced that the United States would no longer convert dollars to gold at a fixed price.

[6] Fiat – from Latin meaning determination by authority.

[7] In our teaching, we use the content in the sidebars for interactive, experiential class discussions.

2. **Store of value** – People can assume that the value of their money will be stable; that is, it will not change or only change predictably over time. One way for achieving this goal is to ensure that the amount of money in circulation (the money supply) remains relatively constant over time. High rates of inflation tend to reduce the confidence people have in a currency.

3. **Unit of account** – This is the name of the currency and the value or "units" assigned to different denominations of that currency. A dollar is a unit by which we can accurately represent the worth of goods, services, assets, and liabilities in an economy. For a unit of account to inspire confidence, it should be a good store of value. In addition, every instance of the same denomination should be uniform in terms of its purchasing power. For example, every $1 bill has the same purchasing power. It should also be fungible; that is, there is no difference between two $1 bills, they are completely interchangeable. Finally, money should be divisible; that is, a $10 bill can be broken down into two $5 bills, ten $1 bills, or five $2 bills.

With this definition of money, based on our current knowledge about Bitcoin, can we say whether it can be categorized as money?

At this stage of its evolution, the answer to this question is a resounding no. Bitcoin cannot be considered a medium of exchange because even though it is scarce, there are not yet enough people or businesses who are willing to accept Bitcoin as a medium of exchange. Bitcoin also cannot be considered a store of value since its value fluctuates greatly day to day when compared to fiat currency. In some aspects, Bitcoin can be considered a unit of account, it is fungible, and it is divisible. However, Bitcoin cannot accurately represent the worth of goods, services, assets, and liabilities because of its volatility.

Most exchanges of currency in the economy today are not settled by the direct exchange of paper currency (also known as cash). In the next section, we will see how this creates the necessity for third parties and government regulations. Let us, however, end this section by looking at the similarity of transactions conducted using cash with transactions conducted using Bitcoin.

- Both cash and Bitcoin transactions are anonymous and privacy preserving.

- Both cash and Bitcoin if lost cannot be recovered.

- Cash and Bitcoin usually belong to whoever has possession, though the meaning of possession is different.

- Cash and Bitcoin are both difficult to counterfeit.

We hope that the understanding of money from this section clarifies for you that Bitcoin, while unique in its implementation, is conceptually in line with the evolution of money, even if in its current state, we cannot categorize it as money.

In the next section, we will broaden our aperture and look at value exchange in the economy as a whole, how and why third parties are needed, how and why government and other organizations impose regulations, and how collectively this creates a range of inefficiencies in the economic system.

Economy As Value Exchange

To understand how value exchange is the basis of all economic activity, let us revisit an old monetary riddle (Henderson, 2012).

It's a slow day in some little town …

The sun is hot … the streets are deserted.

Times are tough, everybody is in debt, and everybody lives on credit.

On this particular day a rich tourist from back west is driving thru town.

He stops at the motel and lays a $100 bill on the desk saying he wants to inspect the rooms upstairs in order to pick one to spend the night.

As soon as the man walks upstairs, the owner grabs the bill and runs next door to pay his debt to the butcher.

The butcher takes the $100 and runs down the street to retire his debt to the pig farmer.

The pig farmer takes the $100 and heads off to pay his bill at the feed store.

The guy at the Farmer's Co-op takes the $100 and runs to pay his debt to the local prostitute, who has also been facing hard times and has had to offer her services on credit.

She, in a flash, rushes to the motel and pays off her room bill with the motel owner.

The motel proprietor now places the $100 back on the counter so the rich traveler will not suspect anything.

At that moment the traveler comes down the stairs, picks up the $100 bill, states that the rooms are not satisfactory, pockets the money & leaves.

NOW, … no one produced anything … and no one earned anything … however the whole town is out of debt and is looking to the future with much optimism.

This is interesting, isn't it?

From an accounting standpoint, everyone had a debt, but they also had a credit. For example, the motel proprietor had a debt with the butcher and a credit with the prostitute, and so on. In aggregate, none of them had a debt even without the sequence of exchanges triggered by the rich traveler. We just needed the first exchange to trigger the domino. Exchange of value keeps our economy humming and allows us to take on additional debt against perhaps offsetting credit we might have.

In general, the economy includes four atomic types of exchange (see Figure 1-1). Exchange can happen between two individuals. An individual is a producer, and another individual is the consumer. This is the type of exchange we have described so far in all our examples. The second type of economic exchange can happen between a firm and an individual. Here, the firm is a producer, and an individual is a consumer. This is the classic exchange between a manufacturer producing a good and a customer purchasing that good. This is also referred to as a business-to-consumer exchange. The third type of economic exchange can happen between two firms. Here, one firm is a producer, and another firm is a consumer. An example could be one firm producing a part that is used by another firm in creating their product. This is also referred to as a business-to-business exchange. The fourth type of economic exchange can happen between an individual and a firm. This is the classic exchange between an employee who provides service to their employer and the employer providing compensation in terms of wages, bonus, equity, and benefits.

Figure 1-1. *Four atomic value exchanges*

Most exchange transactions in the economy are a combination of one or more of the four atomic transactions. The parties in a transaction do not have to be geographically proximate, and the transactions do not settle immediately, as we have described in our simplified examples. Figure 1-2 characterizes the exchange of value among the transacting parties into three types: Currency, Goods, and Services.

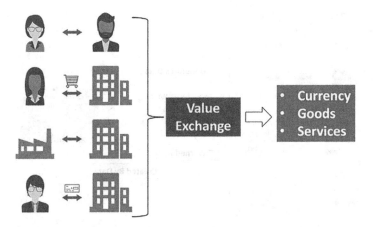

Figure 1-2. *Type of value*

Currency (or money, or cash) is involved in all transactions. Parties can exchange Currency with each other, either to make change or to change the unit of the currency (cross-border transactions), or parties can exchange goods for money or services for money. The parties usually transact by creating credit or accounts receivables and debit or accounts payables. The timing of payments for the transactions and penalties associated with late payment are all determined by stipulated contracts between parties. The parties exchange money through banks or other financial institutions since it is not possible to physically give money. Sometimes, firms need cash to fund operations so they borrow money by pledging collateral. Since transactions do not settle immediately, involve multiple parties, and include the tracking of credit and debit, all transactions need to be recorded. This is usually done by a party in a ledger. This creates the importance of data in all exchange transactions. Figure 1-3 shows three critical roles played by data.

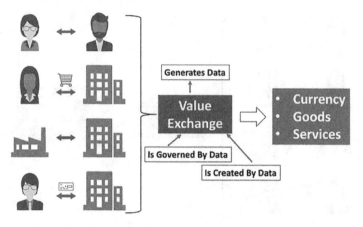

Figure 1-3. *The role of data in value exchange*

- First, all exchange transactions create data. These data
  serve as a record of the transaction and are used for
  auditing, monitoring, analysis, and planning.

- Second, all exchange transactions are governed by
  data. These are data that set the parameters of the
  contract that stipulate the conditions for the settlement
  of the transaction.

- The third role played by data expands the definition of
  value to include the exchange of data as an inherent
  source of value. This role played by data is still nascent,
  and the underlying contracts are still evolving.

With this understanding of the involvement of third parties, let's
drill down further into value exchange transaction between two firms.
Figure 1-4 shows the involvement of financial institutions as discussed
previously.

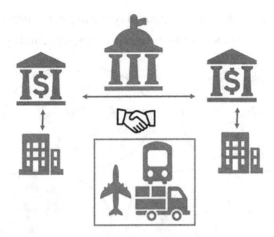

Figure 1-4. *The role of third parties in value exchange*

Cash between firms is exchanged through their respective financial institutions. Each financial institution charges fees. In addition, the government gets involved by regulating exchange transactions between the financial institutions. Multiple governments can be involved if the firms are in different countries and the exchange transactions are cross-border transactions. Governments also get involved with regulations that are purportedly put in place to fairly adjudicate potential disputes between the transacting parties. Regulations such as these are rarely neutral and usually are biased to the more powerful and politically connected firm in the transaction. We would categorize the involvement of the government and financial institutions as adding very little or no value to the exchange transactions. In addition to financial institutions and the government, Figure 1-4 also shows the involvement of another type of firms. These firms are referred to as "third-party logistics" (TPL) providers. These firms assist in the exchange of goods between firms by helping with transportation, storage, scheduling, and distribution. TPL providers add value in the exchange of goods and execute tasks that the principal firms involved in the exchange delegate to them.

We already know the key role data play during value exchange. Figure 1-5 shows how this manifests itself among transacting firms.

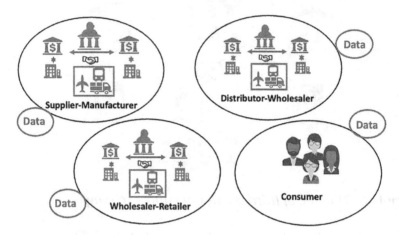

Figure 1-5. *Proprietary data among transacting firms*

Each firm creates data to record the transaction and manages data that governs the transactions between the firms. We would naively expect that (1) these two firms are capturing the same or similar data, (2) the data at the two firms is equivalent, and (3) the two firms can interrogate and understand each other's data. Our expectations are likely to be dashed. Each firm uses different processes and different systems and has varying objectives that result in the creation of data that only people in that firm can understand. You would be correct if you surmise that this lack of understanding of each other's data causes difficulties in conducting business. We will see in the next section that this proprietary data is the cause of economic inefficiencies.

We end this section by looking at the complexity of all the exchanges that are necessary for goods from a manufacturer to make their way to a consumer. Figure 1-6 depicts this supply chain. You can see that there are several business-to-business exchanges between firms before there can be an exchange between a firm and a consumer. Raw material or part suppliers exchange their goods with manufacturers for cash payment. Manufacturers create their product and then exchange it with Distributors, who then exchange it with Wholesalers, who in turn exchange it with Retailers. Retailers then exchange the product with a consumer. Figure 1-6 now shows the wide range of third parties involved – several financial institutions whose value add is dubious at best, and several TPL providers whose services are essential for the efficient functioning of the supply chain. You will also notice the role of government is more pervasive and far-reaching. You will also notice that with each firm, there is another proprietary data set produced by the systems and processes within a firm that results in only people in a firm having the capability to make sense of their data. The economic inefficiencies that we alluded to with one exchange are now multiplied across all the exchanges within a supply chain. Supply chains in our globalized world are worldwide, and therefore, most transactions cross national political borders, increasing the complexity of the exchange.

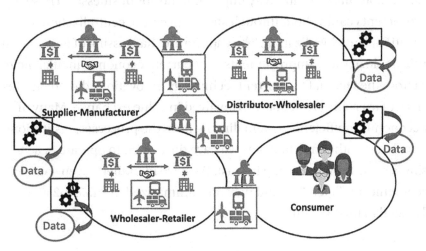

Figure 1-6. *Complexity in the supply chain caused by third parties and proprietary data*

In this section, we have seen how value exchange is the foundation of our economy. For the economy to function with firms that do not trust each other, third parties and government regulations proliferate. Third parties charge fees without adding commensurate value, slow the process, and become power centers with inordinate influence. We also elaborated on the role of data, specifically proprietary data about the exchange that nontrusting parties involved in value exchange begin to create.

In the next section, we will delve deeper into the economic inefficiencies that are created by our current *modus operandi*. We will end this chapter by describing at a very high level why and how blockchain can reduce the current economic inefficiencies.

Current Economic Inefficiencies

We started this chapter with the assertion that the arc of technology innovation that led to the creation of ERP software and the internet has led to extraordinary productivity improvements for businesses. These improvements came about through standardization, centralization, digitization, and globalization. The capture and harnessing of data played a critical role in these improvements. Our current economic inefficiencies stem from the fact that the current technology innovations did not address the lack of trust among the parties involved in value exchange. Many of our economic inefficiencies stem directly from the processes, institutions, protocols, and other mechanisms we have developed to operate in a business environment lacking in trust. We have identified seven sources of economic inefficiencies, and they are summarized in Table 1-2 and elaborated in this section.

Table 1-2. *Seven sources of economic inefficiency*

Economic inefficiency	Brief description
1. Time to settle transactions	In the current business environment, transactions can take days, weeks, or months to settle.
2. Fees paid to third parties	Financial institutions such as banks and credit card processors charge fees to process currency exchange transactions.
3. Data-related redundant work, rework, and reconciliation work (the three R's)	Since each party involved in a business maintains proprietary data, they incur unnecessary costs creating, maintaining, and reconciling these data.
4. Constraints from government regulations and rules from nongovernmental organizations	Government regulations, created ostensibly to help, lead to increased unnecessary costs. In some industries, firms voluntarily agree to adhere to rules imposed by nongovernmental industry groups that can also add costs and stifle innovation.
5. Fraud	The complexity in our current systems for value exchange and the lack of transparency create opportunities for fraud.
6. Privacy trade-offs	To transact in our current system, individuals have to part with identifying data that negates the privacy of cash-based fiat currency transactions.
7. Data security risks	Proprietary centralized data stores are inviting targets for malicious actors to breach and harness.

Time to settle transactions – Depending on the type of transaction and industry, transactions can take days, weeks, or even months to settle. For example, cash transfers within the United States can take 1 to 3 business days to settle. Similarly, credit card transactions can also take 1 to 3 business days to settle. Cross-border cash transfers can take 5 to 14 business days to settle depending on the amount of money being transferred, the originating country, and the destination country. It is also not uncommon for some healthcare transactions to take as much as six months to completely settle from the point of value exchange. Similarly, it is not uncommon for some supply chain–oriented transaction between firms to take at least three months and sometime up to a year to completely settle. These long settlement times create inefficiencies by requiring companies to have more cash flow to "float" their business than necessary, unsettled money is an idle asset that cannot be productively deployed, exchange rate fluctuations cause uncertainty in the value being exchanged, and some transaction end up not being successful due to unforeseen technical (or other) reasons. These issues with long settlement times also drive firms to invest in labor to track the transactions while the settlement is in process.

Fees to third parties – Credit card processing firms such as Visa, Mastercard, and American Express charge in the range of 1.3% to 3.5% of the value of the transaction to process the exchange (Daly, 2021). According to Statista (2021), in 2019, the total value of credit card transactions in the United States was $3.96 trillion. These are not the only fees firms pay. They also pay a cut to the payment processor, interchange fees, assessment fees, and processing fees (Daly, 2021). Most firms pass this cost back to the consumer in terms of higher prices, and in some cases, firms show these fees as an additional charge on a transaction. There are similar fees associated with wire transfers (Napoletano, 2020) and other bank-to-bank transfers. Consumers might not have transparency on all these fees. In addition to the obvious expense associated with the fees, firms also incur additional costs associated with the maintenance of contracts and contractual relationships with the third parties, labor to track and reconcile the fees, setup and maintenance of data transmission infrastructure, and the management of the security and confidentiality risks associated with sharing of data. While we can consider the facilitating of exchange in an economy to be a net value add, we can also assert that from a strict utility perspective, these firms are only adding value because the available exchange mechanisms do not allow firms that do not trust each other to transact with surety.

Data-related inefficiencies – Previously, we have described the reasons that our current economic system results in firms creating and maintaining their proprietary data. Here, we will describe the resulting economic inefficiencies. To make these economic inefficiencies memorable for the students to remember, we have coined the three "Rs" to label these inefficiencies. The three R's are redundant work, rework, and reconciliation work.

Proprietary data makes several parties who are going to engage in a transaction duplicate the same work, wasting effort that could be spent on something else to drive productivity. Let's look at a few examples of redundant work. In the healthcare system, all health systems need to verify the credentials of the clinicians that have privileges to work at that health system. A clinician usually collects all their credentials from parties that can certify the authenticity of the credentials. The clinician then submits these credentials to the health system where they want privileges. This health system now goes to third parties (sometimes the same third parties that the clinician had gone to in the first place) to verify the authenticity of these credentials. This work is duplicated for every health system where the clinician seeks privileges. If there is any change in the credentials of the clinician, then this wasteful process with redundant work is repeated. Keep in mind the data exchanges in all these cases are electronic, so the ERP software and the internet have done their job. The lack of trust resulting in proprietary data has created this redundant work. Let's look at another example of redundant work. In a supply chain, it is customary for a firm to issue a purchase order for the goods that are being ordered, a notification of when goods are shipped, an invoice for the amount owed, and then a payment for the goods received. Data in the supply chain for all these transactions are exchanged electronically, and the format of the data being exchanged has been agreed to among all parties. Yet when data is received by the firm, redundant work is conducted. This redundant work in the best case might simply involve double checking everything and in the worst case will involve the manual reentry of data – with a whole lot of options in between.

While we can go on with examples of redundant work, let's move on to rework. Rework is often the result of redundant work that is not done according to the norms and contracts that have been agreed upon by the parties. When the same work is done at different firms, there is a high likelihood that one of the firms will do their work incorrectly. If the error is caught in a timely manner, then we will have rework, and that will remedy the situation. Let's take for example the situation when a firm receives payment for goods. The data that accompanies the payment usually includes which specific transactions this payment is related to. However, when this payment is received and the redundant work of applying this payment to different transactions is done, an error can be committed, and the payment can be applied to a different transaction than the intended transaction. If someone (or some process) catches these errors, then rework is done to correct the error. Please keep in mind data is still being transmitted electronically using protocols that the parties have agreed to mutually. So the ERP software and the internet have done their part. The rework is directly a result of the lack of trust between transacting parties and the existing systems and economic environment not overcoming that lack of trust.

The third R refers to wasteful reconciliation work. If the errors created by redundant work amidst proprietary data and business processes are not caught and fixed with rework, then over time the transacting parties will be greatly out of sync with each other, resulting in the parties engaging in *ad hoc* reconciliation work to get back in sync. A real-world example of this reconciliation work comes from the processing of healthcare claims. A small family-owned creator of custom wigs for patients with cancer submits claims to a large national health insurance company.

Unfortunately, the health insurance company denies the claims leading to cash flow issues for the small provider. Unable to address this issue, as a last resort, the small provider stops accepting patients covered by the insurance company. The patients are understandably upset, and they complain. The large insurance company is annoyed and calls the small provider demanding to know why their patients are not being accepted. The small provider then shares their predicament that the insurance company owes them $2M, for example, and the majority of this amount has been owed for over 90 days. The insurance company representative follows up by looking at their proprietary data and comes back with a completely different take on the money that is owed. The representative asserts that the insurance company owes the provider only $200K and all of it is current; that is, it has been owed for less than 30 days. This starts the reconciliation dance. Several people from the insurance company get on a conference call with two people from the small firm to understand the discrepancy. After two hours of heated conversation, people are no closer to understanding the issue. They then decide to exchange data in spreadsheets representing their proprietary understanding of the situation. After a few rounds of exchanging data and conference calls with multiple people, the two parties decide to settle with the insurance company paying the provider $1.5M. Both parties are upset. The small provider feels cheated out of $500K, and the large insurance company feels cheated out of $1.3M. Their trust is further frayed. To top this all, their proprietary systems are still out of sync and only artificially reconciled. We can conceive of several more similar examples of the wastefulness and pointlessness of reconciliation work. Please note once again that the data exchanges were electronic and used protocols that had been agreed to mutually. The issue was the lack of understanding in each other's proprietary data that had been created due to a lack of trust between the transacting parties and the inability of the economic system to overcome the lack of trust.

Regulations and rules constraints – As we described earlier, an economic system that makes the role of third parties with dubious value add prominent and depends on fees paid to these third parties to overcome the lack of trust invites government regulations to deal with conflict and competing interests. These business regulations invariably are tilted toward larger firms with political power and unintentionally create inefficiencies for the economic value chain as a whole. In addition to the regulations from the government, there are many nongovernmental organizations, such as the American Medical Association (AMA), the American Institute of Certified Public Accountants (AICPA), and the American Bar Association (ABA) (to name only three American organizations out of thousands of such advocacy organizations across the world), that set rules and governance for their membership. While the purpose of these rules is codifying ethical practices, these rules are again necessary because the economic system does not inherently overcome the lack of trust among transacting parties. These rules end up acting as powerful forces for protecting the *status quo*, increasing the power of those who are the most powerful members, and in general stifling innovation. All these regulations and rules lead to overall economic inefficiency in the value chain. In addition to this, firms are required to sink labor and capital to set up and maintain a compliance framework to track adherence to all these rules and regulations, and firms also incur expense to pay fines related to witting or unwitting compliance failures. More importantly, smaller firms have to constantly deal with the costs of uncertainty caused by not having control on how the regulations and rules may change in the future, stifling innovation. Larger firms, on the other hand, incur large expenses for advocacy and lobbying to exert influence and wrest a measure of control. To imagine the efficiency that would flow in the absence of constraints from regulations and rules, we can look at the innovation that has spurred economic productivity from technologies such as the internet that were initially spared from regulation. However, since the internet itself did not overcome the inherent lack of trust among transacting parties, we are now seeing the outcry for increased regulation, most of it well intentioned, but history tells us that the eventual consequences for the increased regulation will end up having unintended consequences that are contrary to our desired purpose.

Fraud – Up to this point, we have described an economic system that is rife with fee-charging third parties that add little or no value, rules and regulations that end up stifling innovation and preserving the *status quo*, parties transacting with each other using proprietary data and business process, and transaction settlement terms with ambiguity that the parties to a transaction do not fully understand. Another way of characterizing our economic system is that it is complex and opaque – a veritable black box. This is an ideal situation for fraudsters, hucksters, and criminals to find and exploit loopholes. Fraud takes a big bite out of many industries. For example, fraud in healthcare is estimated to be 3% to 10% of total healthcare spend (Simborg, 2008)[8]; the US Chamber of Commerce has estimated that 10% of insurance claims contain some fraud (Hoyt, 1990); based on a survey of supply chain employees in manufacturing, median losses due to interorganizational supply chain fraud were estimated to be 9% of a firm's total revenue (DuHadway, Talluri, Ho, Buckhoff, 2019).

In addition to the obvious economic loss associated with fraud as illustrated earlier, firms also invest in labor and capital costs to establish and maintain an infrastructure to prevent fraud, and an indirect consequence of fraud is the enactment of new rules and regulations to protect the public from fraud (we have already seen the unintended consequences of rules and regulations).

Privacy trade-offs – Our current economic systems for enabling transactions require all parties to disclose their private data to multiple

---

[8] The Centers for Medicare and Medicaid Services(CMS) estimates that healthcare spending reached $3.8 trillion in 2019 (`www.cms.gov/Research-Statistics-Data-and-Systems/Statistics-Trends-and-Reports/NationalHealthExpendData/NationalHealthAccountsHistorical`).

parties, multiple times with little or no safeguards or control for how this data will be maintained and used after the underlying transaction is settled. Consequently, data sovereigns have lost control of their data. While economic studies have been attempted to quantify what value consumers put on their data (Acquisti, John, Loewenstein, 2013), we have not found studies that quantify the direct cost for data sovereigns for losing control of their data.

Indirect costs for data disclosure include agreements that parties negotiate with each other to protect their data and shield themselves against liability if the data were to be disclosed inappropriately, labor and capital invested to set up and maintain infrastructure to ensure compliance with these agreements, and the usual costs associated with regulations and rules that are being promulgated by governments to ostensibly protect customers against unauthorized data disclosure or data loss.[9]

Data security risks – Proprietary data stores that underlie our economic system are magnets for hackers to breach and pilfer valuable data. The Institute for Applied Network Security (IANS) estimates that technology firms tend to spend 10.4% of their overall Information Technology (IT) budget on security (Williams, 2021). The equivalent percentage for the finance and insurance firms is 9.7%, and for healthcare firms, it is 7.3% (Williams, 2021). With increasing IT budgets, this is a large investment that is theoretically completely defensive and not driving innovation and productivity in a firm. This investment has also not prevented firms from having high-profile breaches, and a single security breach can cause significant economic and reputational harm to a firm,

---

[9] We often ask our students if the Health Insurance Portability and Accountability Act (HIPAA) was put in place to shield healthcare consumers. Students are surprised when we tell them that HIPAA defined the parties and standardized the practice of sharing our healthcare data.

not including job loss for senior executives, sometimes including the Chief Executive Officer.

Indirect costs related to data security are the significant dampening of innovation and growth due to the slow and costly process of obtaining all requisite security approvals. The indirect consequence also includes the inevitable rules and regulations to protect the public from data breaches. By now, we know the unintended consequences of rules and regulations.

In this section, we have discussed at length the economic inefficiencies that are inherent in our value exchange systems. Our current systems have benefited by technology innovations that have culminated in the standardization and business process streamlining from ERP software and the digitization and globalization created by the internet and innovations associated with the internet. The current systems have not overcome the innate lack of trust among transacting parties, leading to the creation of proprietary data stores and business processes, powerful fee-charging third parties, and governmental regulations and rules from membership-based professional and advocacy organizations. In the next section, we will examine at a very high level if blockchain has the potential to positively impact the economic inefficiencies in our current exchange systems.

Blockchain's Potential to Address Current Economic Inefficiencies

We have not yet described the capabilities of blockchain technology, what underlying technologies enable these capabilities, the current limitations of these capabilities, or the implementation details of how these capabilities can be harnessed. We will elaborate this in the forthcoming chapters in the book. In this chapter, we will ask you to take at face value the core capabilities of blockchain[10] that create its promise to address the inefficiencies in our current economic system.

Blockchain creates a *distributed ledger* of cumulative transactions. All transacting parties have an authentically identical copy of this ledger, and as transactions are consummated, these copies stay in sync and identical. Transacting parties do not need to trust each other and can settle transactions *peer to peer* without the involvement of third parties. Transacting parties also do not have to share information about their identity that will be meaningful outside the context of an individual transaction and for parties who are not involved in the transaction – blockchain transactions are designed to be privacy preserving through the use of *encryption* and *hashing*. Before transactions are consummated and committed to the distributed ledger, all transacting parties have to arrive at a consensus. This *consensus protocol* is agreed to by all transacting parties, it is well understood by them, and it cannot be changed by any centralized authority without the agreement of transacting parties. Once a transaction is committed to the distributed ledger, it is almost impossible to alter or tamper with this transaction (*immutable*). Transacting parties can create software-based contracts that represent the terms for the execution of transactions – these software-based contracts are referred to as *smart contracts*. Lacity (2018) described eight sources of business value from blockchain capability where parties transact directly and have visibility on the status of the transaction, with no need for reconciliation, a reliable audit trail (*provenance*), automatic execution of contract terms, reduction in transaction fees, control over one's data, and fault tolerance.

Table 1-3 summarizes how the blockchain capabilities that we have described can address the inefficiencies in our current economic system.

---

[10] Here, we describe blockchain capabilities without caveat or nuance. In reality, there are many caveats that collectively represent the limitations of the current technology. These will be elaborated in the forthcoming chapters.

Table 1-3. *Potential of blockchain capability to impact economic inefficiencies*

Economic inefficiency	Blockchain capability
1. Time to settle transactions	The automatic execution of the agreed-upon well-understood consensus protocol with the peace of mind that transactions once committed cannot be altered reduces the time to settle transactions.
2. Fees paid to third parties	Peer-to-peer transactions eliminate powerful, centralized third parties, reducing fees. Fees in blockchain are designed to incentivize transacting parties to maintain the working of the consensus protocol and the synchronization of the distributed ledgers.
3. Data-related redundant work, rework, and reconciliation work (the three R's)	Authentically identical copies of the distributed ledger, well-understood consensus protocol, and software-based smart contracts will greatly reduce the inefficiency.
4. Constraints from government regulations and rules from nongovernmental organizations	The ability for parties that do not trust each other to transact without the facilitation of third parties reduces the necessity of government regulations and rules from membership and advocacy nongovernmental organizations.
5. Fraud	The transparency of the consensus protocol and smart contracts reduce the opportunity of fraud.
6. Privacy trade-offs	Privacy-preserving encryption and hashing make it possible for parties to transact without losing control of their data.
7. Data security risks	The lack of centralized proprietary data sources reduces security breach targets, encryption, and hashing, and the ability to reconstruct the distributed ledger reduces the impact of a security breach.

At a very high conceptual, perhaps even aspirational, level, we see that the core capabilities of blockchain have the potential to positively impact the inefficiencies in the current economic system. Blockchain can continue the positive impact to economic productivity that was started by the collection of technologies that we have labeled as ERP software and the internet.

This book is all about how to operationalize these aspirations with a clear-eyed understanding of the limitations of the current capabilities and where the arc of research and development within blockchain is headed. While, Bitcoin, the first blockchain implementation was released in 2008 (13 years ago), we are still in the early innings of the business adoption of this technology.

Chapter Summary/Key Takeaways

Key takeaways from this chapter are as follows:

- Since the mid-1960s, technology innovation has been rapid, creating a collection of technologies that we have labeled as ERP software and the internet. These collections of technologies have had a very high positive impact on the economy based on standardization, business process streamlining, digitization, and globalization.

- Money acts as a medium of exchange to facilitate transactions within the economy. The value assigned to money represents a consensus between transacting parties. The mechanisms of money have evolved over time in different societies culminating in sovereign national governments seizing control. The widespread prevalence of alternative forms of money in concert with government money provides one possible path and rationale for digital or cryptocurrency.

- The current economic system is based on the value exchange between transacting parties. The lack of trust among transacting parties is not overcome by the underlying economic system leading to fee-charging, powerful, and centralized third parties that add little or no value, government-imposed regulations and nongovernmental organization-imposed rules, and proprietary data and processes.

- The current economic system has inefficiencies that limit productivity improvements. These economic inefficiencies can be categorized as time to settle transactions; fees paid to third parties; data-related redundant work, rework, and reconciliation work (the three R's); constraints from government regulations and rules from nongovernmental organizations; fraud; privacy trade-offs; and data security risks.

- The core capabilities of blockchain include a distributed ledger, peer-to-peer transactions, a well-understood consensus protocol, privacy-preserving encryption and hashing, immutable transactions, and software-based smart contracts.

- The core capabilities of blockchain have the potential to positively impact the inefficiencies in the current economic system by enabling peer-to-peer transactions between parties that do not trust each other without the facilitation of third parties. The blockchain distributed ledger can reduce proprietary data, and smart contracts can provide the transparency that transacting parties need.

In the next chapter, we will begin our journey in understanding the core underlying technologies that enable the capabilities of blockchain that hold so much promise. These core underlying technologies are cryptology, distributed systems, and peer-to-peer networking. While these technologies have been around for some time, and they continue to be enhanced, it is their ingenious integration that gives blockchain its incredible capabilities.

Sidebars

Sidebar 1: What is $1 worth?

If money is not backed by a commodity such as gold, how do we determine the value of money? When we ask this question, we get varying answers ranging from "well the government decides" to "it depends on what I am trying to buy and what I consider its worth to be."

Both these answers are partially correct.

We as consumers decide what a $1 is worth by choosing to buy or not buy goods at the offered price. If enough of us refuse to buy a good at a certain price, then the seller will have to lower the price, and if more of us want to buy a good at the price that it is offered, a seller can either make more of that good or raise the price. In this manner, we are collectively and directly determining the worth of $1.

The government, however, also has tools that allow it increase or decrease the supply of money, and this indirectly controls the worth of a $1. In the United States, these tools are exercised by the Federal Reserve and include setting interest rates, purchasing/selling certain types of assets, and determining that certain denominations of currency are valid/invalid.

Several governments have abused their power and corruptly manipulated the value of their currencies, causing hardship to ordinary individuals. Examples of this abuse include runaway inflation in several countries that destroys the value of money and arbitrary demonetization of certain denominations of money in other countries.

Sidebar 2: Alternate currencies

While we most often transact with government-issued money (also known as fiat currency), we also transact with several alternate currencies that are not issued or guaranteed by the government. These alternate currencies include the following:

- **Frequent flier points** – These are issued by airlines for using their service or services from their partners. We can convert these points to goods and services. (Of course, we trade the ability of the airline and its partners to track our activities in return for the frequent flier points.)

- **Membership rewards** – These are similar to frequent flier points and issued primarily by credit companies for transacting using a credit card issued by them. The issuing company controls the amounts of rewards available for different types of transactions. The issuing company also controls the value assigned to each reward and how this value can be redeemed. Usually, the issuing firm reserves the right to unilaterally change the value assigned to each reward.

- **S&H green stamps** – These used to be issued by a company called Sperry and Hutchinson in the days before electronic reward systems. They worked similar to frequent flier points and membership rewards. A shopper received S&H green stamps for shopping in specific retail outlets, and these stamps could be exchanged for specific goods.

- **Gift cards** – These are cards for specific value purchased by a party and sent to another party. The receiving part can exchange the gift card for goods and services. Transaction fees are usually involved.

- **Traveler's checks** – These can be purchased for specific amounts and then can be exchanged for goods and services in currencies different than the currency used to purchase the traveler's check.

Quiz Questions

1. The mainframe, relational database management systems, and ERP software appeared to create value by _____ and _____.

2. The personal computer and the internet appeared to create value by _____.

3. Which of these is not a current economic inefficiency?

    1. Time to settle transactions

    2. Fees paid to third parties

    3. Fraud

    4. Transparency

4. Describe the three R's of economic inefficiency.

5. Explain briefly how blockchain will help with time to settle transactions.

6. Explain briefly how blockchain will reduce fraud.

7. Explain what makes some good an universally acceptable medium of exchange.

8. Which of these is a fundamental property of money?

    1. Medium of exchange

    2. Store of value

    3. Unit of account

    4. All of the above

9. Which of these is not a similarity between cash and Bitcoin?

    1. Anonymous

    2. Nonrecoverable if lost

    3. Meaning of possession

    4. Difficult to counterfeit

10. Credit card firms charge _____% of the transaction value to the merchant.

11. Explain the role and functionality of third-party logistics providers briefly.

References

Loveman, Gary W. 1993. "An Assessment of the Productivity Impact of Information Technologies." In Information Technology and the Corporation of the 1990s: Research Studies, edited by Thomas J. Allen and Michael S. Scott Morton, 84–110. Oxford: Oxford University Press, 1993

Brynjolfsson, E. 1991. The Productivity of Information Technology: Review and Assessment. CCS TR #125. MIT. http://ccs.mit.edu/papers/CCSWP130/ccswp130.html

Cortada, J. W. 2019. Building the System/360 Mainframe Nearly Destroyed IBM. IEEE Spectrum. https://spectrum.ieee.org/building-the-system360-mainframe-nearly-destroyed-ibm

Codd, E.F. 1970. A relational model of data for large shared data banks. Comm. of the ACM 13, 6, June 1970

Baldwin, C.Y. 2019. Design Rules, Volume 2: How Technology Shapes Organizations Chapter 15 The IBM PC. Working Paper 19-074. Harvard Business School. www.hbs.edu/ris/Publication%20 Files/19-074_7cff5546-df6a-4dee-b581-e51751053159.pdf

Metcalfe, R. and Boggs, D. 1976. Ethernet: Distributed Packet Switching for Local Computer Networks. Communications of the ACM, volume 19 number 7, 1976

Thomson, P. 2020. The complete history of ERP: Its rise to a powerful solution. www.g2.com/articles/history-of-erp

Leiner, B., Cerf, V., Clark, D., Kahn, R., Kleinrock, L., Lynch, D., Postel, J., Roberts, L. and Wolff, S. 1997. A brief history of the Internet. Internet Society. www.internetsociety.org/internet/history-internet/brief-history-internet/

Treacy, M. and Wiersema, F. 1995. The discipline of market leaders: Choose your customers, narrow your focus, dominate your market. Addison-Wesley

Porter, M. 2001. Strategy and the internet. https://hbr.org/2001/03/strategy-and-the-internet

Nakamoto, S. 2008. Bitcoin: A Peer-to-Peer Electronic Cash System. https://bitcoin.org/bitcoin.pdf

Chohan, U. 2021. The Double Spending Problem and Cryptocurrencies. https://doi.org/10.2139/ssrn.3090174

Menger, K. 1892. On the origin of money. The Economic Journal. Vol. 2, No. 6 (June 1892), pp. 239–255 (17 pages) Published By: Oxford University Press. https://doi.org/10.2307/2956146 www.jstor.org/stable/2956146

Bryan, M. 2004. Island Money. Federal Reserve Bank of Cleveland. www.clevelandfed.org/Research/commentary/2004/0201.pdf

Dockrill, P. 2019. The "original Bitcoin" was this giant stone money on a tiny Pacific island. www.sciencealert.com/the-original-bitcoin-still-exists-as-giant-stone-money-on-a-tiny-pacific-island

Henderson, D. 2012. An answer to a monetary riddle. www.econlib.org/archives/2012/01/an_answer_to_a.html

Daly, L. 2021. Average credit card processing fees and costs in 202. www.fool.com/the-ascent/research/average-credit-card-processing-fees-costs-america/

Statista. 2021. www.statista.com/statistics/568554/credit-debit-card-transaction-value-usa/

Napoletano, E. 2020. All about wire transfers. Forbes. www.forbes.com/advisor/banking/all-about-wire-transfers/

Simborg, D. 2008. Healthcare fraud: Whose problem is it anyway? Journal of the American Medical Informatics Association, 15 (3), pp 278–280, https://doi.org/10.1197/jamia.M2672

Hoyt, R. 1990. The effect of insurance fraud on the economic system. Journal of Insurance Regulation. 8 (3), pp 304–316

DuHadway, S., Talluri, S., Ho, W., Buckhoff, T. 2019. Light in dark places: The hidden world of supply chain fraud," in IEEE Transactions on Engineering Management, doi: 10.1109/TEM.2019.2957439. https://ieeexplore.ieee.org/stamp/stamp.jsp?tp=&arnumber=8948004

Acquisti, A., John, L., Loewenstein, G., 2013. What is privacy worth? The Journal of Legal Studies, 42 (2), pp. 249-274. doi: 10.1086/671754

Williams, B. 2021. Establishing the cybersecurity budget: It's a balancing act. www.unionbank.com/commercial/insights/fraud-prevention/cybersecurity-budget-considerations-for-businesses-a-balancing-act

Lacity, M. 2018. Enterprise blockchains: Eight sources of business value and the obstacles in their way. https://walton.uark.edu/enterprise/downloads/blockchain/LacityBlockchainsExplained.pdf

CHAPTER 2

Overview of Core Technologies Supporting Blockchain

The promise of blockchain is achieved by innovatively integrating existing technology concepts from distributed systems, cryptography, and peer-to-peer networking. These technologies also impose limitations that drive engineering design decisions for blockchain implementations.

Introduction

We ended Chapter 1 by asking you to take at face value the core capabilities of blockchain that, we believe, create a potential for enormous business benefits:

- A distributed ledger of cumulative transactions

- Computers with identical copies of the distributed ledger communicating with each other and staying in sync

© Weijia Zhang and Tej Anand 2022

W. Zhang and T. Anand, *Blockchain and Ethereum Smart Contract Solution Development*,

https://doi.org/10.1007/978-1-4842-8164-2_2

- Privacy-preserving transactions that limit sharing of identity with only those who need to know

- Software-based encoding of the terms and conditions underlying value exchange transactions.

In this chapter, we will describe the technology concepts that enable these capabilities. We believe it is important to have a business-level understanding of these technology concepts to make design decisions regarding the applicability of blockchain to address the business problems related to the seven economic inefficiencies that we described in Chapter 1.

The technology concepts related to distributed systems and peer-to-peer network architectures will help us understand how blockchain maintains a digital ledger of cumulative transactions in sync across multiple computers connected through the internet. Distributed systems will also help us understand the design trade-offs that blockchain systems have to make and the implications of these design trade-offs. The technology concepts related to cryptography and digital signatures will help us understand how blockchain implements privacy and security for its transactions. The integration of cryptography, digital signatures, distributed systems, and peer-to-peer networks makes it possible for blockchain to enable value exchange between geographically dispersed and untrusting parties without the centralized coordination provided by third parties. This integration makes it possible to abstract the terms and conditions underlying the value exchange and represent them in software that can be executed on multiple computers.

In this chapter, we start by reviewing technology concepts of cryptography and digital signatures, followed by the concepts of distributed systems and peer-to-peer network architectures. We then describe how these concepts are integrated to create the core capabilities of blockchain.

Cryptology and Digital Signatures

In this section, we will describe the basics of cryptology and digital signature. It is very important for businesses who want to leverage blockchain to understand these basics.

Figure 2-1 shows a high-level illustration of the encryption-decryption process of cryptology. We start with plain text that everyone can read, and then we encrypt the text into text that everyone cannot read. We call this cipher text. When this cipher text is decrypted, we get our original plain text back.

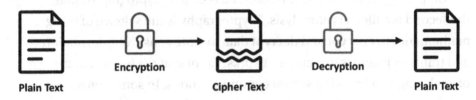

Figure 2-1. *High-level encryption-decryption process*

Figure 2-2 is an illustration of the encryption-decryption process. Let's start with the plain text HELLO. We can encrypt this using an algorithm called offset the alphabet. In this example, we will offset the alphabet by four letters, so H becomes L, E becomes I, L becomes P, L becomes P again, and O becomes S. Encrypting HELLO using this algorithm results in the cipher text LIPPS. To make sense of the cipher text, LIPPS, a recipient will need to know how it was encrypted, that is, if a recipient that does not have this knowledge will not be able to make meaning from the cipher text. When we decrypt LIPPS, we will apply the algorithm in reverse and get HELLO. L will become H and I will become E and so on. This is a simple description of the encryption-decryption process.

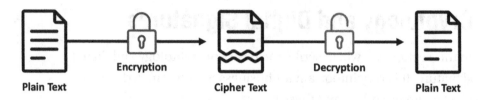

Figure 2-2. Encryption-decryption illustration

Cryptology consists of two fields. One is called cryptography, and the second is called cryptanalysis. Cryptography is the science of using mathematics to encrypt and decrypt data to store sensitive information and transmit it across insecure networks. Cryptanalysis is the science of analyzing and breaking secure communications. In some sense, cryptanalysis is the science of "cracking the code." Strong cryptography results in ciphertext that is very difficult to break. Strong cryptography is what we are interested in.

At a very high level, cryptography works as follows: we take plain text and pass it through a cryptographic algorithm, a cipher, and the cipher working with a key converts the plain text into ciphertext (Figure 2-3). In our previous example, our cipher was "offset the alphabet," and our key was 4. Figure 2-4 depicts this process.

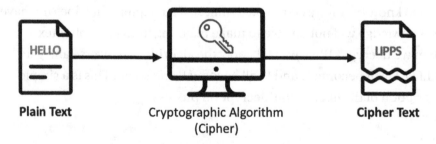

Figure 2-3. Cryptography in action

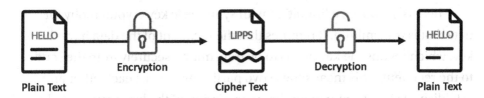

Figure 2-4. *Cryptography in action illustration*

Let's now look at a specific type of cryptography called symmetric key cryptography. In symmetric key cryptography, the key used to do the encryption is the same as the key used to do the decryption (Figure 2-5). Obviously, the algorithm is the same, but here, the key is also the same. That means the recipient of ciphertext needs to know the key that was used to do the encryption.

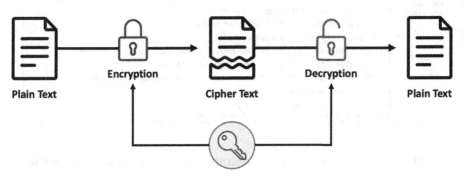

Figure 2-5. *Symmetric key cryptography*

Symmetric key cryptography is fast, simple, and high performing. Symmetric key algorithms can be implemented either in hardware or software. This is the preferred method for encrypting data when it is not transmitted and is kept in one place (also known as "data at rest").

There is, however, a limitation with symmetric key cryptography for data that is transmitted. It requires that the recipient of the data have the key, which means the key needs to be transmitted securely from the sender to the recipient. This means these two parties must trust each other and establish a trusted channel for the transmission of the key. Setting up this trusted secure channel can be expensive. Due to this limitation, symmetric key cryptography gets limited to parties who know one another and who can afford to invest in setting up a trusted channel infrastructure.

Table 2-1 provides a summary of some of the popular algorithms that are used for strong symmetric key cryptography.

Table 2-1. *Summary of strong symmetric key algorithms*

Advanced Encryption Standard (AES)	• Considered the best symmetric encryption algorithm • Block cipher with three keys: 128-bit, 192-bit and 156-bit • Encrypts data by blocks rather than by bits • Encrypts blocks in rounds – 10 for 128-bit key, 12 for 192-bit key and 14 for 156-bit key
Triple Data Encryption Standard (3DES)	• Replaced the DES algorithm because hackers learned how to crack it • Symmetric block cipher with three individual 56-bit encryption keys creating a 168-bit key • Much slower than other encryption algorithms • Easy to decrypt data since it encrypts short blocks
Blowfish	• Designed in 1993 and still not defeated • Flexible data encryption used for payment security and in password management tools • Block cipher with encryption keys from 32 bits up to 448 bits • Splits data into 64-bit blocks and encrypts each block individually in 16 rounds
Twofish	• Free successor to Blowfish – not patented • Block cipher with 128-bit, 192-bit and 156-bit keys and encrypts data in blocks of 128 bits in 16 rounds

Next, let us review another cryptography method, called asymmetric key cryptography, or public/private key cryptography. In this method, there are two keys. There is a public key that can be shared and a private key that is not shared. Both the sender and recipient of data have a public key and a private key. Let's look at an example. Helen wants to transmit a message to Marco securely. Marco's public key is known to Helen, so Helen will encrypt the message using Marco's public key. When Marco receives the message, they decrypt the message using their private key that is only known to them. When Marco is successful in decrypting the message, they know that the data was intended for them. Please note that in this method, unlike symmetric key cryptography, only the encrypted message is transmitted. No key is transmitted.

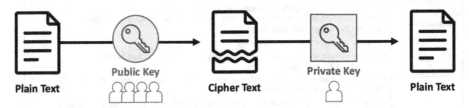

Figure 2-6. *Asymmetric or public/private key cryptography*

In asymmetric key cryptography, there is no need to set up a trusted secure channel. This now makes it possible for more people and parties to use cryptography – parties no longer have to know one another, and they do not need to invest in setting up infrastructure to securely share keys.

While asymmetric key cryptography resolves the limitation with symmetric key cryptography, it has its own limitation. This limitation is as follows: Marco knows that they have received a message intended for them because they have successfully decrypted the message with their private key. Marco, however, cannot be certain that the message was sent by Helen. The message could have been sent by anyone who knew Marco's public key. While Helen can communicate to Marco that they sent the message, Marco does not have a foolproof guarantee. Marco could have received the message from anyone. We will discuss later how to address this limitation with asymmetric key cryptography.

Table 2-2 provides a summary of some of the popular algorithms that are used for strong asymmetric or public/private key cryptography. These are all very efficient algorithms that result in strong cryptography and are unlikely to be broken for many years, even perhaps with the advent of quantum computing.

Table 2-2. *Summary of strong asymmetric key algorithms*

RSA (Rivest–Shamir–Adleman)	• RSA enables safely sharing data over an insecure network and use a public and a private key • RSA public and private encryption keys can be 1024-bit, 2048-bit, 3070-bit or 4096-bit • As the key size increases encryption slows, but also becomes more secure
Diffie-Hellman	• Invented in 1976, using discrete logarithms in a finite field - two parties exchange a secret key over an insecure medium without any prior secrets – secure protocol when the generator element has a high order exponent • Usually, not implemented on hardware
DSA (Digital Signature Algorithm)	• Federal Government standard or FIPS for digital signatures proposed in 1991, adopted in 1993 and revised in 1997 • Main problem with DSA is the fixed subgroup size (the order of the generator element), which limits the security to around 80 bits
ElGamal	• Public key cipher – an asymmetric key encryption algorithm for public-key cryptography wbased on the Diffie-Hellman key agreement • ElGamal is the predecessor of DSA

One way to address the limitation of not having a foolproof guarantee of the identity of the sender with asymmetric key cryptography is to use digital signatures.

Let's look at an example: Helen wants to send a message to Marco. This time, Helen is actually going to send the same message twice. The first message is encrypted by Marco's public key, and Marco can decrypt this message with their private key (asymmetric key cryptography shown in Figure 2-6). The second message will be encrypted by Helen's private key, and Marco can decrypt this message with Helen's public key. The second message is Helen's digital signature (private key) as shown in Figure 2-7. Marco now gets two messages: One message is decrypted by their private key (Signature Verification in Figure 2-7), and the second message is decrypted with Helen's public key. When these two decrypted messages match, Marco has a foolproof guarantee that they are the intended recipient of the message and Helen was the sender of the message.

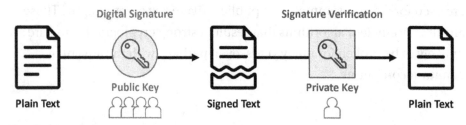

Figure 2-7. *The process of digital signatures*

So far in this section, we have discussed how asymmetric key cryptography solves the limitation of a trusted secure channel requirement by symmetric key cryptography and how digital signatures solve the limitation of the lack of a foolproof guarantee of the identity of the sender of asymmetric key cryptography.

We are not yet done though!

Digital signatures as we have described them so far also have a limitation. They are slow, and they create an enormous amount of information. We are sending double the amount of data, and our networks and transmission are not free. If digital signatures are implemented as we have described them so far, they will be expensive and slow and result in delays due to network latency.

Hashing is a technique that can help us address this limitation with digital signatures. To get a good sense of what hashing is, let's start by looking at mathematical functions.

In general, a mathematical function works like this: You give an input x to a function f, and you will get output y. We say y is equal to f of x. If the function was square root, we would get the square root of x. If x equals to 9, then f of x, where f is square root, will lead to y being 3 (actually, + or - 3).

Figure 2-8 provides a classification of functions into two types. They can be two-way maps or one-way maps. Two-way maps are functions where given x, we can get y and given y, we can get x. For one-way functions, given x, we can get y, but given y, we cannot get x. Functions like Sum and Average are examples of one-way functions.

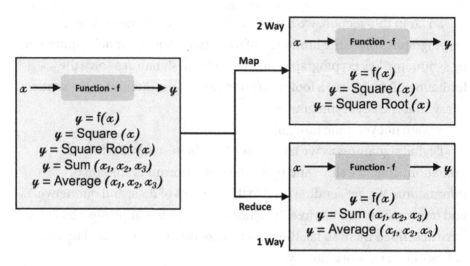

Figure 2-8. *Types of functions*

One-way functions are also called reduce functions because the output represents a reduction of several inputs into one output. Encryption and decryption are two-way map functions where we can take plain text, encrypt it to get ciphertext, and then decrypt the ciphertext to get back the plain text. Hashing is a one-way reduce function. What hashing does is reduce the data volume and storage of the input. No matter the length of input, a hash function will produce a fixed length output. Relational databases, for example, have hashed indexes, and these indexes speed up search, inserts, updates, and deletes in the database.

The best thing about hashing is that it is an extremely scalable high-performing function. We say that these functions have a complexity $O(1)$, pronounced as Big 0-1. Big 0-1 means that the hashing algorithm is going to perform at the same speed no matter the size of the input.

Let's take a simple example of a hash function. Let's say we have three strings – ABC, DEFG, and GHI. You can see that these strings are not of equal length. For our hashing function, we are going to map A to 1, B to 2, C to 3, and so on. We will add the numbers that our letters are mapped to in a string and then apply the mod function. The mod function takes two numbers as input and returns the remainder when the first number is divided by the second number. So a mod (6,5) will return 1 – when 6 is divided by 5, we get 1 as a remainder. For our example strings, to hash ABC, we are going to sum ABC to get 6, and then we will do a mod (6, 5) to get a 1. So the hash of ABC is 1. The hash of DEFG is 2 – DEFG sums to 22, and mod (22, 5) gives us 2. Similarly, the hash of GHI is 4. Table 2-3 is a summary of the hashed values.

Table 2-3. *Hashed values using the mod function*

0	1	2	3	4
	ABC	DEFG		HGI

As you can see in Table 2-3, no matter the length of the input string, the output is a fixed length string.

We are sure by now you can tell that there is a problem with hashing. This problem is called collision. ABC and CBA are going to result in the same hash, and that's not good.

Computer scientists have developed sophisticated hashing algorithms that minimize the chance of collision. They don't guarantee that we will never have a collision, but these hash algorithms have proven that the probability of having a collision is not something we need to worry about. Table 2-4 provides a summary of two hash algorithms that guarantee collision is minimized to such an extent that for all practical purposes, we can operate as if there are no collisions.

Table 2-4. *Summary of two hashing algorithms*

SHA2 (Secure Hashing Algorithm)	• SHA2 takes strings of arbitrary length and generates a unique and irreversible 256 (SHA256) or 512 (SHA512) bit strings (SHA2 is the successor to SHA1 that generated 160 bit strings) • SHA1 was derived from MD4
MD5 (Message Digest)	• MD5 is also a "child" of MD4 and produces a 128 bit output string • MD5 works by chaining a "compression function

With this background on hashing, we will revisit digital signatures.

This time rather than sending two messages to Marco (one encrypted by Marco's public key and the second encrypted by Helen's private key), Helen sends the message once encrypted with Marco's public key. Then Helen takes the original message and hashes it to get a reduced set of data (also known as a message digest). Helen then takes the hashed message, signs it with their private key, and sends it to Marco (see Figure 2-9). By hashing the message, Helen has greatly reduced the volume of data that is sent to Marco.

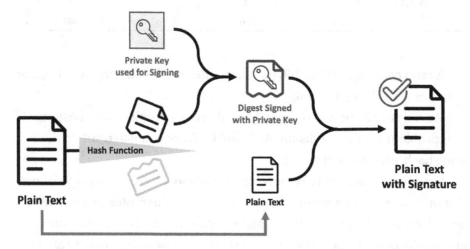

Figure 2-9. *Hashed digital signatures*

Marco will now take the message they got that was encrypted with their public key and decrypt it with their private key and retrieve the original message. They will then take the encrypted hashed digital signature and decrypt it with Helen's public key and get the hash of the original message. Next, Marco with take the original message (decrypted by their private key) and hash it. When this hash matches the decrypted hash, Marco has a foolproof guarantee that Helen was the sender of the message.

The previous discussion shows that hashing can address the limitation of excessive amount of data transmission of digital signatures.

In summary, in this section, we have reviewed symmetric key cryptography and understood its limitation related to secure data transmission (parties needed to know each other and invest in infrastructure to securely transmit the key). This limitation was resolved by asymmetric key cryptography where each party had a public and a private key and messages were encrypted by a party's public key and decrypted by the party's private key, eliminating the need to transmit the key. Asymmetric key cryptography itself had a limitation that there was no foolproof guarantee of the identity of the sender. This limitation was resolved by digital signatures, where two messages were sent, one encrypted by the public key of the recipient and the second encrypted by the private key of the sender. Digital signatures had the limitation that they doubled the amount of data that needed to be transmitted for each message. This limitation was resolved by hashing digital signatures.

Before concluding this section on cryptography, let's review three states of data – data at rest, data in transit, and data in use – and how data can be secured in each of these three states.

- Data at rest means data are stored on a computer or more precisely the nonvolatile storage managed by a computer. Symmetric key cryptography is ideal for data-at-rest encryption. Storage in laptops, personal computers, and servers used for databases are encrypted using symmetric key cryptography. This is what makes it possible for us to not worry about data theft when we lose a laptop.

- Data in transit means data are being communicated from computer A to computer B using a computer network such as the internet. Asymmetric or public/private key cryptography with hashed digital signatures is ideal for data-in-transit encryption. To secure data in transit, we need to guarantee that when data arrives, it has not been tampered with; it is confidential; that is, it has not been seen by anyone; and we have a foolproof guarantee of the identity of the sender. Asymmetric or public/private key cryptography with hashed digital signatures ensures that all these conditions can be guaranteed.

- Data in use means we are using the data in an application. To secure data in use, we want to make sure that data is only accessed by people with a need to know. To accomplish this, we use policy safeguards in conjunction with technology. Policies include rules for access to systems and authorization based on the need for access to data. Technology solutions include data masking and data redaction.

In this section, we have reviewed at a very high business level the concepts of cryptography and digital signatures. We will review in the last section of this chapter how the cryptography concepts from this section are pertinent to blockchain implementations. In the next section, we will review concepts related to distributed systems.

Distributed Systems

Blockchain systems are distributed systems; that is, computation and data related to a blockchain system are distributed across multiple computers that can communicate with one another through a computer network. In this section, we will review the benefits of distributed systems and the design issues and trade-offs that should be kept in mind when dealing with distributed systems.

Definitionally, we can think of a distributed system as composed of multiple independent computers that all coordinate among themselves to fulfill a common goal. For these multiple independent computers to coordinate their work, they have to be able to communicate with one another through some form of network connectivity. The common goal that these multiple independent computers are trying to achieve is determined by the software that they are running.

There are two views of distributed systems:

1. The optimists think of a distributed system as a collection of independent computers that to anyone using that system appear to work as one single coherent computer.

2. The pessimists, on the other hand, think of a distributed system as a collection of computers when the crash of a computer you have never heard of before prevents you from completing your work. This was described by Leslie Lamport, a computer scientist associated with a great deal of seminal work around distributed systems, in an email archived at `https://lamport.azurewebsites.net/pubs/distributed-system.txt`.

We will further our understanding of distributed systems by reviewing three real-world issues that distributed systems are designed to mitigate.

1. **Complexity** – Our systems are becoming increasingly complex. The software that powers our systems has more lines of code and increased functionality evolved over many years with changing teams of software developers. These software systems generate increasingly vast amounts of data of varying types. Our software systems are used by a large number of people ("users"), and often, it is difficult to predict the number of users who will use the software at the same time (concurrent users).

To mitigate the real-world issue of complexity, the goal of distributed systems is *scalability*. We want to scale our systems so that they can function correctly with complex software that is changing all the time, large volumes of data with data types such as numbers, structured text (known format), unstructured text (unknown format and length), audio, video, images, spatial (related to location), and temporal (related to time), and a large number of unpredictable concurrent users.

One way distributed systems achieve the goal of scalability is by "partitioning" the data and the computation handled by the software into special processes. We call these lightweight processes because each process is simple to understand, but together, they can deliver complex functionality. To get to lightweight processes, we take a complex task and break it into many simple tasks that can then run independently of each other on independent computers. Once each simple task has been completed, we can combine their output to complete our complex task. This is one of the most common ways of achieving scalability in distributed systems.

In order for a distributed system to be scalable, they have to overcome expensive network coordination so that we're not sending a lot of data back and forth among networked computers that can result in systems waiting for one another.

2. **Failures** – Similar to how we expect and plan for our automobiles and home appliances to break down, we need to expect and plan for the computer

systems, computer networks, and software systems to break down. However, unlike automobiles and home appliances where we can probably carry on with alternatives while repairs are being conducted, failures related to computer systems, computer networks, and software systems can be catastrophic since these systems are now embedded into the critical infrastructure that our society depends on. This puts an onus on prevention to a much larger extent than repair. Preventing failures is the second real-world problem that distributed systems are designed to accomplish.

To address the real-world issue of preventing failures, the goal of distributed systems is *fault tolerance*. We make the assumption that faults, or failures, will inevitably occur, and we want to design and implement systems such that they continue to function even when failures occur; that is, we are able to tolerate faults in our system. Fault-tolerant systems keep functioning in spite of faults, they are always available to users, and the data that they hold is not lost or corrupted. They are able to deal with the uncertainty of when and where system faults might occur.

One way distributed systems achieve the goal of fault tolerance is by "replication" where multiple computers have copies of the same software and data and these computers are available to perform the same function as any computer that has a failure. This is also referred to as building redundancy into the system. A rather contrived analogy of redundancy would be having an extra automobile available to you whenever your primary automobile fails.

This solution adds costs, and professionals weigh the benefits of these costs against the losses from occasional failures and ensure that the costs for failure mitigation are commensurate with the business impact of the occasional failures. Continuing with the automobile analogy from the previous example, while purchasing a car and having it available might not be cost-justified, purchasing insurance that pays for renting an automobile when your automobile needs to be repaired might be acceptable.

For distributed systems, where multiple computers coordinate to accomplish a specific goal, the concept of fault tolerance is more complex. Instead of dealing with failure as a binary yes or no that is immediately ascertainable, we also need to consider if all computers in a distributed system know if other computers are available and functioning accurately. A computer in the distributed system could have been hacked and compromised and thus no longer "trustworthy" for exchanging information.

Thus, there are two types of uncertainty that a fault-tolerant distributed system needs to overcome. First, every computer in a distributed system does not know if the other computers in the system are functional or not. They might be down; they might be up; they might be partially functional. Second, every computer in a distributed system does not know if all the other computers on the network are trustworthy. Are they working as designed or have they been compromised? Are they sending messages that are malicious and deceptive?

The problem of overcoming these two uncertainties is referred to as achieving Byzantine Fault Tolerance[1] or BFT.

Most distributed systems achieve Byzantine Fault Tolerance through algorithms that are called consensus protocols. Consensus protocols help computers in a distributed system ensure the veracity of communication from other computers. Several BFT algorithms ensure accurate functioning of the system if at least 51% of the computers in the distributed system are functioning as expected. If 51% or more computers maliciously collude, they can hack the distributed system for their own nefarious purpose. Since distributed systems are made up of independent computers, the larger the number of computers, the more difficult it would be for 51% of the computers to collude. For example, if a distributed system had only three computers, then we needed two computers to collude. However, if a distributed system included 1,000 computers, then we would need 501 computers to collude. It is much easier for 2 people to collude and conspire than for 501 people to collude and conspire.

3. **Consistency** – The third real-world issue that distributed systems need to mitigate arises directly from the approaches to mitigating the

---

[1] Byzantine Fault Tolerance alludes to the problem that Byzantine Generals need to overcome when they are coordinating an attack on a city that they have surrounded. They can only communicate by messenger, and each general does not know if they have received the message that was sent, if a message was indeed sent, or if the message they are receiving is from a general who had decided to betray the cause (Lamport, Shostak, and Pease, 2019).

issues of complexity and failures – partitioning and replication. When computation and data are partitioned for scalability and data and computation are replicated for fault tolerance, then ensuring consistency among all these replicas or partitions is important, but difficult.

How do you make sure that these computers connected over a network are consistent with one another not only syntactically but also semantically?

One way distributed systems achieve the goal of consistency is through rigorous agreements as to how and at what frequency they will all make sure they have synchronized. These agreements are designed into the system ahead of time and consist of messages that are exchanged and algorithms that can ensure the veracity of the messages. Checksum can be considered a very simple example of such a mechanism. With checksum, each piece of data is assigned a checksum value that can be the sum of the bits in the message, or the number of bits in the message, or a hash of the data being transmitted. The checksum is transmitted in addition to and separately from the data that was transmitted. Computers who receive the data have the algorithm to compute the checksum, and if the checksum that they compute does not match the checksum that is transmitted, then they know that there was an error in the transmission.

The mechanisms used for consistency create constraints on performance (speed) and add costs (sometimes, significant) to distributed systems implementation. Therefore, consistency mechanisms that are implemented represent design trade-offs that are engineered based on the business problems that are being addressed by the distributed system. Over time, two distinct approaches related to consistency have been researched, designed, and implemented. These are known by their acronyms, ACID and BASE.

When we are designing and implementing systems with mission-critical real-world data where precision and accuracy of the data are of paramount concern, the ACID approach is preferred. ACID stands for **A**tomicity, **C**onsistency, **I**solation, and **D**urability. Atomicity means that when an operation is performed on data – irrespective of if the data is in one place or partitioned and/or replicated across many computers – that operation will either be completely successful or will completely fail. The importance of atomicity is usually illustrated with a bank transfer example. When we transfer money from one bank account (Account A) to another account (Account B), this operation is made up of several components: the withdrawal from Account A, the updating of available balance from Account A, the deposit into Account B, and the updating of available balance from Account B. If any of these components fail, then the entire transaction fails; we cannot ever be left in a state where the money is withdrawn from Account A but not deposited in Account B. Consistency means that once an operation has successfully completed on data – irrespective of whether this operation is on one computer or spans multiple computers with data on one computer or multiple computers – it is guaranteed that all of the data across all of the computers will be the same. Isolation means when multiple operations are concurrently being executed, each operation is independent and is not impacted by the other operation (or the intermediate state of another operation). Atomicity, consistency, and isolation are intertwined; you cannot possibly have one without the other two. The final component of ACID is durability, which means that once a write operation has been successfully completed, data will persist indefinitely. By the way, if the write operation is deleting data, then the data is gone forever. Distributed database relational management systems invest much effort in the implementation of ACID capabilities (or semantics) because more often than not, relational database management systems support business processes where the accuracy of data needs to be guaranteed. Implementing ACID semantics in centralized systems – where the computation and data are all within a single physical computer – is a lot simpler than implementing ACID semantics across a distributed system.

The BASE semantics are quite different from ACID. BASE stands for **B**asically **A**vailable, **S**oft State, and **E**ventually Consistent. These semantics are appropriate when systems are dealing with data that are not mission critical and all the data need not be always precise. "Basically Available" means that some of the components of a system might be down, but as far as the users are concerned, they perceive the system as available even though not all functionalities might be always available. Soft State means that the state of the system may change over time, and it might change even without any user input. Eventually Consistent means that given enough time, and enough time with no input, we guarantee that all the various replicas will become consistent. What we are finding out is that in content-driven web-based architectures, where we are not necessarily dealing with mission-critical data all the time, implementing BASE semantics meets our business requirements, so BASE semantics have become acceptable for such systems. The word "acceptable" here is key. While we would not accept our bank balance changing without specific actions initiated by us, we accept content on websites changing from time to time.

Figure 2-10 provides a summary of the real-world issues that distributed systems are designed to mitigate, the goal distributed systems try to achieve in mitigating those real-world issues, and the most common approaches that are considered to implement the goals.

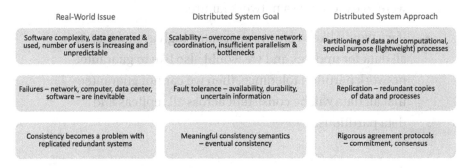

Real-World Issue	Distributed System Goal	Distributed System Approach
Software complexity, data generated & used, number of users is increasing and unpredictable	Scalability – overcome expensive network coordination, insufficient parallelism & bottlenecks	Partitioning of data and computational, special purpose (lightweight) processes
Failures – network, computer, data center, software – are inevitable	Fault tolerance – availability, durability, uncertain information	Replication – redundant copies of data and processes
Consistency becomes a problem with replicated redundant systems	Meaningful consistency semantics – eventual consistency	Rigorous agreement protocols – commitment, consensus

Figure 2-10. *Summary of issues, goals, and approaches for distributed systems*

Sidebar provides a list of distributed systems terms and their definitions that are essential as a reference when designing blockchain applications.

The last concept regarding distributed systems relevant for blockchain that we need to understand is the CAP theorem. The CAP theorem was postulated by computer scientist Eric Brewer. For more information and discussion, please see Brewer (2012). The CAP theorem states that a distributed system can only achieve two of the three goals of strong consistency, high availability, and network partition tolerance[2] with respect to data. Please note that the theorem makes no claims regarding the performance of a system. The implications of this theorem are as follows:

- If we would like to guarantee high availability of all data all the time for updates and we would also like to guarantee that all data are consistent across all replicas and data partitions, then we cannot guarantee network partition tolerance; that is, we would not be able to guarantee availability of the system and its data if we were to experience a network failure.

- If we would like to always guarantee high availability of all data for updates and we would also like to guarantee network partition tolerance, then we cannot guarantee that all data will be consistent across all replicas and data partitions.

---

[2] A network partition means that there are computers that are supposed to be connected to one another but there is no working network path connecting these computers – we say that there is a partition. Not that this use of the term "partition" is different from our earlier use of partition where we partitioned the computation and data so that it could be executed on multiple computers – we shall refer to this as a data partition.

- If we would like to guarantee that network partition
  tolerance and we would also like to guarantee that
  all data are consistent across all replicas and data
  partitions, then we cannot guarantee that all data will
  be available all the time for making updates.

No system designer wants to completely give up on any of the three properties of high availability, strong consistency, and network partition tolerance. The CAP theorem forces system designers to think through the trade-offs that they can afford to make and at the same time meet all, or the majority of, the business requirements. Distributed systems are engineered to balance high availability of data for updates, strong consistency of data, and network partition tolerance.[3]

In this section, we have reviewed at a very high business level the concepts of distributed systems that will be important for us in the design of blockchain applications. We will review in the last section of this chapter how blockchain implementations make the design trade-offs necessitated by the distributed system concepts that we have reviewed in this chapter. In the next section, we will review concepts related to peer-to-peer networking.

Peer-to-Peer Networking

Blockchain systems are made up of computers, also known as compute nodes, or simply nodes, connected to one another in a peer-to-peer network. In this section, our focus will be to identify and understand the differences between traditional computer network architectures and peer-to-peer network architectures.

---

[3] In this sense, there are no purely distributed systems. Most distributed systems have some components that are centralized.

Figure 2-11 represents an illustrative traditional computer network architecture. The cloud in Figure 2-11 represents the computer network, which makes it possible for the computers connected to the network to communicate with one another through some type of networking path. In Figure 2-11, we are showing two types of computers. Let's call the computers in red as client computers. Client computers are usually looking for something. They want to be serviced. Let's call the computers in black as servers. They respond to requests for service from clients, and if a client is authorized to request that service, then the server fulfills the request. We can think of many types of servers based on the types of service they provide. Database servers, for example, respond to requests for creating, reading, updating, and deleting data. Domain name servers (DNS) provide a phone book–type service, given the name of a website they provide the network address of the server that hosts that website. Web servers receive requests for specific web pages, and they "serve up" those pages. We also have firewalls that act as servers and servers that do specialized computations, and so on.

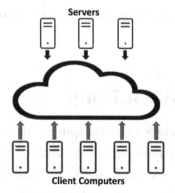

Figure 2-11. *Traditional computer network architecture*

In a traditional computer network architecture, we have two types of computers: the clients and the servers. The servers in some sense have power over the clients. They control who is authorized to access their services, what services they will provide, what are the semantics of the service, what is the syntax for requesting the service, when they will provide the service, and the speed at which they will provide the service to different types of clients. If a server is not available, for any reason whatsoever, then the clients will not receive any of their services, and in fact, the clients might not even know that the server is not available. A server can also unilaterally change any aspect of the service they provide, even though in practical terms, a server is not likely to do that because the value proposition and utility of any server depend directly on how many clients use their service.

In many cases, there is also centralized ownership of the servers; that is, even though there can be multiple computer servers that all provide the same type of service, they could all be owned by the same party. This centralized ownership of the servers and their specialization can introduce constraints in the performance, cost, and functionality of the overall network.

Let's now turn to peer-to-peer networks.[4] Figure 2-12 represents an illustrative peer-to-peer network. In this figure, the cloud once again represents the network, and you can see that all computers are connected to one another through the network represented by the cloud; that is, all computers can communicate with one another through some network path.

---

[4] Perhaps we should make clear that a peer-to-peer network is a specific case (or topology) of a distributed system.

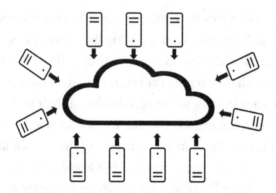

Figure 2-12. *Peer-to-peer network architecture*

In Figure 2-12, all the computers have the same color, and we can either say that they are all clients or that they are all servers. In some sense, all computers are the same. They can provide the same function. Each computer might not be connected to another computer with a direct path, but they are connected in a sense where every computer can communicate with every other computer without availing of any specialized service on another computer. In this sense, there is no computer in a peer-to-peer network that has power over any of the other computers. Each computer is independent. Each computer has the same power. Each computer can have the same functionality as the other computers, if it so chooses. Each computer can communicate with every other computer, and they provide services to each other without any discrimination. If any one computer in a peer-to-peer network decides to leave the network (they are free to do that!), there is no loss of functionality for the entire peer-to-peer network. It can continue to function without any degradation.

A peer-to-peer network is a more egalitarian and democratic architecture than a traditional computer network architecture. While nothing prevents one party from owning multiple nodes, it is highly unlikely (even impossible) for one party to own all the nodes in a peer-to-peer network. The most egalitarian peer-to-peer networks have nodes that are powered by open source software that are available to everyone and have no restrictions on who can join the peer-to-peer network. In the past, peer-to-peer networks have been set up for exchanging files, music, data, software, and games. Special-purpose peer-to-peer networks where all nodes (peers) are not equal have also been set up for voice and video calls using the internet.

In general, we can surmise that those in power tend not to like peer-to-peer networking architectures, perhaps because they are not able to control them or profit from them. Blockchain is a peer-to-peer network of computer nodes for the purpose of exchanging value. Perhaps those in power might feel threatened by it!

Let's not get ahead of ourselves though. In the next section, we will discuss how cryptology, distributed systems, and peer-to-peer network architectures come together for a successful blockchain implementation.

Blockchain Technology Integration

A blockchain is a clever implementation of cryptology, distributed systems, and peer-to-peer networks to create a decentralized[5] system chain. In this section, we review at a high level how these technologies are integrated and what functionality each technology provides to a blockchain implementation. We start in the reverse order in which these technologies were discussed in this section.

---

[5] We usually consider a centralized system as an antonym of a distributed system where one physical computer is capable of providing all the functionality needed to meet the requirements of the business. We also use the term "centralized" to characterize the ownership of a system. If all the computers in a distributed system are owned by a single party, then we refer to such a distributed system as having centralized ownership. When the computers in a distributed system are owned by multiple parties, then we refer to such a distributed system as having decentralized ownership. In this sense, blockchain is a distributed and decentralized system. For systems with decentralized ownership, mechanisms to govern all the parties become an important characteristic. Governance mechanisms are needed to maintain and update the distributed system.

All blockchain implementations consist of computers (or nodes) connected in a peer-to-peer network. This means that every computer in a blockchain implementation is capable of having the same functionality as any other computer. Blockchain software is freely available, and in its most robust decentralized[6] implementation, nodes can join the network anytime they want, and they can leave the network anytime they want without appealing to any permission granting authority. In their purest implementation, no one computer has power over any other computer in a blockchain, and no one computer has the power to dictate anything about what another computer can do.

Since blockchain consists of computers connected in a peer-to-peer network, it is a distributed system. It solves real-world problems related to complexity (scalability), failures (fault tolerance), and consistency. Scalability is handled by distributing the data and computation required for a value exchange system across several independent computers that are executing the same version of the software. Fault tolerance is handled by replicating the blockchain data across all the nodes in the blockchain and redundantly executing all computations on each blockchain node. Consistency is handled through the implementation of consensus protocols (or algorithms) that provide Byzantine Fault Tolerance. These are the algorithms that become the so-called mining component of a blockchain system. A computationally expensive consensus protocol usually results in a more reliable blockchain system because this protocol makes it difficult for nodes in the network to collude and thus compromise the blockchain. As we saw in the "Distributed Systems" section, the more computers that are part of a blockchain system, the less likely it will be for computers to collude and compromise the blockchain. In general, when we compare two blockchain implementations, the blockchain

---

[6] At least according to the authors of this book.

implementation that has a more computationally expensive consensus protocol and the blockchain implementation that has more nodes in its network will be more reliable, secure, and trusted.

The CAP theorem–related design trade-offs are reflected in the careful selection of the size of a block and the frequency with which new blocks are created. The size of a block determines the number of transactions a block can hold. The larger the size of the block, the greater the information that needs to be communicated among the nodes, increasing the chance that data in the nodes can get out of sync. Similarly, if blocks are created more frequently, then more data will need to be communicated among the nodes, again increasing the chance that data in the nodes can get out of sync. At the same time, smaller blocks and a lower frequency of creating blocks limit the throughput of the blockchain in terms of transactions per second.

Finally, cryptography ensures the security and anonymity of the transactions within a blockchain. For all transactions between parties, the parties are identified with their public key. Since parties can have multiple public keys, it is difficult to infer the identity of parties for all their transactions based on their public keys alone. Recipients of value in a blockchain transaction need to have their private key to access the value that they have received. Private keys belonging to a party are stored in secure wallets they control and only they can access. This makes it difficult for the value received by a party to be stolen or fraudulently taken away. Hashing functions are used extensively in the transactions in blockchain. They are used for compressing data, for security, and for implementing the consensus protocol. Information in blockchain transactions can go through multiple cycles of encryption and hashing, making it difficult for transaction information in a blockchain to be broken (as in "breaking the code"). It has been asserted by some that the multiple encryption-hashing in blockchain can even offer protection from quantum computers.

The hashing concept is also used for one of the widely used consensus protocols called Proof of Work, which will be described in Chapter 5. The consensus protocol requires the generation of a hash that adheres to a specific pattern. As we discussed in the section on Cryptology and Digital Signatures, algorithms for generating a hash are very efficient and do not require extensive computation resources. However, creating a hash with a specific pattern is computationally expensive because finding the hash with a specific pattern is a brute-force search process.

This section has provided a very high-level description of how cryptography, distributed systems, and peer-to-peer networks are essential for understanding not only the immense potential that value exchange using blockchain provides but also the design limitations of blockchain. It is this understanding of potential as well as limitations that is critical to the successful implementation of blockchain applications so that the economic inefficiencies that were described in the first chapter can be mitigated.

Chapter Summary/Key Takeaways

Key takeaways from this chapter are as follows:

- A business-level understanding of the technology concepts related to cryptography, distributed systems, and peer-to-peer networks is important to understand blockchain.

- Cryptography requirements for data at rest can be met by symmetric key encryption mechanisms.

- Cryptography requirements for data in transit can be met with asymmetric or public/private key encryption mechanisms and digital signatures.

- Hashing is an important function used in conjunction with asymmetric key encryption to optimize the amount of information that is communicated for digital signatures.

- Distributed systems purport to address real-world issues of complexity, failures, and consistency with goals of scalability, fault tolerance, and meaningful consistency semantics, respectively. Distributed systems use data partitioning, replication, and consensus mechanisms to achieve these goals.

- The CAP theorem postulates that distributed systems can only achieve two of the three following characteristics: strong consistency of data, high availability of data, and network partition tolerance.

- Peer-to-peer networks are egalitarian compute networks where all peer computers or nodes have equal power and similar functionality.

- A blockchain is a peer-to-peer network of computers with design trade-offs across the dimensions of scalability, availability, fault tolerance, and consistency.

In the first two chapters, we have completed reviewing the economic potential of blockchain and the core technologies (cryptography, distributed systems, and peer-to-peer networks) that underlie blockchain implementations. In the next chapter, we will start the process of describing how transactions are conducted within a blockchain and provide a business-level description of the capabilities within a blockchain, the notion of a distributed ledger, the categorization of various blockchain implementations, and a summary of blockchain limitations that should be taken into account when implementing blockchain applications.

Quiz Questions

1. Take the plain text "PIZZA BY THE BEACH", and use the Offset the Alphabet by 4 letters algorithm as our encryption technique to generate the ciphertext. What is the resulting ciphertext?

2. Please review a clip from the movie *The Imitation Game* at www.youtube.com/watch?v=mwFWMM9APLs and answer the following questions:

   a. What is the cipher that the Germans use? Was it a hardware cipher or a software cipher?

   b. How often were the Germans changing the key used with this cipher?

   c. How did Alan Turing and his team crack the key for the cipher?

   d. Why was the computer "Christopher" able to find the key for the cipher?

3. What are the advantages and limitations of symmetric key cryptography?

4. _____ technique is used to address the limitations of digital signatures.

5. What does "data at rest," "data in transit," and "data in use" mean?

6. What encryption technique is most suitable for data at rest?

7. What encryption technique is most suitable for data in transit?

8. How do distributed systems achieve the goal of fault tolerance?

9. What are the two types of uncertainty that need to be overcome in a fault-tolerant distributed system?

10. How much accuracy is needed for proper functioning of computers in a distributed system?

    a. 25%

    b. 50%

    c. 51%

    d. 75%

11. What do the acronyms ACID and BASE stand for? What do they mean?

12. What is the CAP theorem? What is its implication?

13. What do the client computer and server computer do in a peer-to-peer network?

14. What does centralized and decentralized ownership of a compute infrastructure mean?

15. When we compare two blockchain implementations, the blockchain implementation that has a more computationally expensive consensus protocol and the blockchain implementation that has more nodes in its network will be _____ reliable, secure, and trusted.

    a. more

    b. less

    c. not at all

Sidebar – Key Distributed Systems Terms and Definitions

- **Node:** Any participant in a distributed system.

- **Network:** Connectivity among nodes in a distributed system.

- **Partition:** Any disruption in the network between nodes.

- **Partition tolerance:** System is resilient/robust to partitions.

- **Fault (or failure):** Any error in the system, including device failures, software failures (including software defects), and communication protocol failures.

- **Byzantine fault:** When components fail, there is imperfect information on whether a component has failed or not.

- **Byzantine Fault Tolerance (BFT):** Any mechanism to be robust/resilient to Byzantine Faults. Examples include consensus protocols and error detection/correction mechanisms.

- **Availability:** Data (also known as state) always observable (or measurable) and can be updated.

- **Scaling/scalability:** Operations perform without any degradation regardless of the number of nodes (or users) in the network.

- **Replicas:** Replication of data and/or state is an essential component of distributed systems. The mechanism of sharing data and/or state defines the distributed system.

- **Atomicity:** An atomic transaction is an indivisible and irreducible series of operations such that either all occur or nothing occurs.

- **Consistency:** After each operation, all replicas reach the same state.

- **Strict consistency:** Immediate consistency after each operation.

- **Eventual consistency:** Consistent over time, but can take an arbitrary amount of time.

- **Liveness:** People actually use the distributed system regularly; that is, the state of the distributed system or the data in the distributed system are regularly changing. Liveness means active use.

References

Lamport, L., Shostak, R., Pease, M. The Byzantine generals problem. From Concurrency: The works of Leslie Lamport. Editor Malkhi, D. October 2019. Pages 203–226 https://doi.org/10.1145/3335772.3335936

Brewer, E. CAP twelve years later: How the "rules" have changed," in Computer, vol. 45, no. 2, pp. 23–29, Feb. 2012, doi: 10.1109/MC.2012.37

CHAPTER 3

Blockchain Components and Architecture

The four components of blockchain that working together create its enormous potential to alleviate economic inefficiencies in our current system are distributed ledgers, privacy preservation, algorithms for distributed systems consensus, and smart contracts.

Introduction

The core capabilities of blockchain that have the potential to drive enormous business benefits are a distributed ledger of cumulative transactions, computers with identical copies of the distributed ledger communicating with one another and staying in sync, privacy-preserving transactions that limit sharing of identity with only those who need to know, and the encoding of the terms and conditions underlying value exchange transactions in software that can be automatically executed to ensure the valid consummation of a transaction. These core capabilities are enabled by technology concepts from cryptography, digital signatures, distributed systems, and peer-to-peer networking.

© Weijia Zhang and Tej Anand 2022
W. Zhang and T. Anand, *Blockchain and Ethereum Smart Contract Solution Development*,
https://doi.org/10.1007/978-1-4842-8164-2_3

The foundational concept in blockchain is that of a transaction. A transaction is initiated by one party to transfer value to one or more parties based on mutually agreed terms and conditions. Computers connected to one another through a peer-to-peer network leveraging the internet communicate a transaction to all computers once they have been initiated. The software on each computer is able to autonomously and independently verify the validity of the transaction by executing a software-encoded version of terms and conditions that govern the transaction, accumulating a subset of transactions into a block, and communicating this block to peer computers that can all connect this block to previously created blocks, creating a blockchain. All the computers in the network are incentivized to work based on mutually agreed-upon rules, and any computer that is not following the rules can be easily detected and ignored.

Our goal in this chapter is to provide a conceptual and technical elucidation of the four components of a blockchain: distributed ledgers, privacy, consensus, and smart contracts.

We start by describing the conceptual and technical details of the logical mechanics of transactions, the rules for the creation of blocks, and their chaining to previously created blocks. The blockchain thus created represents the ledger within a blockchain. The rules represent the consensus mechanism that has been adopted by the blockchain network to keep all the peer computers in sync – veritably making the ledger a distributed ledger. This description is first illustrated by a narrative of human peers conducting a series of transactions and then translating this narrative into a technical explanation.

We also describe how the structure within a transaction encrypts information so as to preserve the privacy of the parties in a transaction. Finally, we explain how the terms and conditions that govern a transaction are encoded within a smart contract.

We also describe a categorization of blockchains that puts blockchain implementation on a continuum of how centralized or distributed they are. We end the chapter with a discussion about the limitations of blockchain.

Conceptual Overview of Blockchain Components

In this section, we will conceptually describe the various components of a blockchain system by examining a set of illustrative[1] or notional transactions as if they were happening on a blockchain.

Let's start with Candice. Candice has decided to sell many of her Marvel comics. These comics are prized by children, and she expects many of her friends to want to buy one of her comics. In this illustration, in order to simplify the conceptual components of blockchain, we will assume that Candice and her friends are aware of each other's identity. When Candice offers the first comic for sale, her friend Marco purchases it. We are going to assume that all of Candice's friends know Marco, and they all know that Marco has purchased the comic and the price that Marco paid for the comic.

Mechanically, how might that have worked?

For this example, we will assume that Candice and her friends are in communication with each other throughout the sale of the comics. They have individual sheets of a special paper on which they will record each sales transaction of the comics Candice has for sale. They have also invented and agreed upon a mechanism for confirming that each transaction is valid and that they are all recording the transaction on their

---

[1] An earlier version of this illustration appeared in Gupta (2017). The illustration here has been significantly expanded to include different types of blockchain implementations.

individual sheet of paper correctly. One mechanism by which they could do this is by Candice providing photographic evidence of the comics in her possession and her right to sell the comics; Marco providing evidence that he has authorization to spend the money that he is using to buy the comic; Candice sends a text message to all her friends involved in this transaction that Marco is purchasing the comic for $12; and all the friends provide photographic evidence that they have recorded the transaction accurately on their individual sheets of paper. This mechanism ensures that all the sheets of paper held by Candice's friends have the same exact information written using the same exact format that everybody involved understands. This is the beginning of our **distributed ledger**.

Let us take this process forward. Candice continues selling her comics. She sells to Ebony, Reena, Rodney, Tariq, and Tasha. Every time any of her friends purchase one of the comics, it is recorded exactly the same way – on the individual sheets of paper held by Candice and all of her friends, including the individual who is purchasing the comic. They continue to do this until ten sales transactions have been recorded.[2] Then they try to come to **consensus**.

What does that mean?

Even though Candice and her friends invented and agreed to a mechanism that ensured they all had the same data on their individual sheet of paper, it is not impossible that one of the friends might decide to cheat and have a sheet of paper that has different data. The process of consensus that we describe here will ensure that even if one or more parties are not following all the agreed-upon rules, the system overall has the ability to maintain the accuracy and integrity of all its rules and data.

Remember, when we started this illustration, we said that Candice and her friends all had "special" sheets of paper? These sheets of paper were special because they included a hidden puzzle to be solved. Once

---

[2] We will see later, when we discuss Bitcoin, why we decided on 10 transactions in this illustration.

this puzzle was solved, the paper automatically would have a watermark embossed on it that cannot be altered.[3] For the process of consensus to work, the majority of Candice's friends furiously work to solve this hidden puzzle on their sheet of paper. Whoever solves the puzzle first, declares that they have solved the puzzle, and then they send a copy of their sheet of paper with the watermark to everyone involved (Candice and all her friends) with the sale of comics. Here, it will also be helpful to point out that while the puzzle was not easy to solve, verifying that the puzzle has been solved correctly is extremely easy. When people receive the sheet of paper with the solved puzzle (represented by the watermark), they verify that the puzzle has been solved and and then stop solving the puzzle themselves, destroy their sheet of paper (without the watermark), and replace it with the sheet of paper with the watermark.

Let's say Maurice solves the puzzle first and this copy of Maurice's paper is sent to everybody. Everyone can verify that Maurice solved the puzzle correctly. As soon as they verify that, they stop working on solving the puzzle themselves. They throw their sheets of paper away. Maurice's sheet now becomes the official record of the last ten transactions. Maurice's sheet of paper has the watermark, and if any one tries to alter anything on that sheet of paper, the watermark will disappear.[4] This sheet of paper is the official record of the ten transactions. This is our first **block** in our distributed ledger. Because this sheet of paper cannot be altered, we say that it is **immutable**.

The process whereby all the parties involved in a transaction come to a consensus and create blocks in the distributed ledger is known as the **consensus protocol**.

Let us now develop this illustration further. Fatima, another of the friends involved in the sales of comics, wants to sell her Archie comics. We will now repeat the same process. Fatima will sell her comics, her

---

[3] This is a special paper indeed. Yes, I understand that we might be taking the illustration too far ... but please bear with me.

[4] This is a special paper, indeed.

friends will purchase the comics, we will have proof that Fatima indeed has the right to sell her comics, all the individuals who are purchasing the comics are authorized to spend the money to buy the comics, each sales transaction is recorded individually on a sheet of paper by all the individuals involved, and it is verified and validated that everyone is recording all the sales transactions correctly. Once ten sales transactions have been recorded, all the parties involved will once again try to come to consensus by solving a puzzle.

This time, there is a twist though. The watermark that results after this puzzle is solved will have information in it from the first watermark. This time, let's assume that Chen, another of Candice's and Fatima's friends, is the first to solve the puzzle. Chen will declare that they have solved the puzzle, make copies of their sheet of paper, and send these copies to everyone involved in the comic books sale. When people receive Chen's sheet of paper, they will be able to quickly verify that Chen solved the puzzle correctly; they will also notice information from the watermark in the first sheet of paper from Marco in the watermark on the sheet of paper sent by Chen. This will be their clue that the sheet of paper sent by Chen needs to be attached to the sheet of paper from Marco.

Chen's sheet of paper is our second block, and it is attached to, or chained to, the previous block from Marco. We now have the first two blocks of our blockchain! Please note that if someone were to alter the sheet of paper from Marco, resulting in the watermark on that sheet of paper changing, they will also need to change the sheet of paper from Chen because this sheet of paper has information from the previous watermark. So now changing the first block is even more difficult.

We can now imagine the earlier process repeating itself several times. After every ten sales transactions, a new sheet of paper with a watermark having information from the previous sheet of paper gets attached. In other words, more blocks are added to our blockchain. As more blocks are chained together, it becomes progressively harder to change the previous blocks. We can say with much confidence that each block in the blockchain is immutable, and all the transactions in any block cannot be altered. We can also see that there is an audit trail for all the sales transactions. We call this audit trail **provenance**.

You might ask, what would happen to the sheets of paper where the parties were cheating? Well, if someone solves a puzzle on such a sheet of paper and sends it to everyone, two possible things could happen: (1) people might reject this sheet of paper because they will not be able to verify the watermark or the transactions on this sheet of paper, or (2) they will not be able to attach this sheet of paper to another sheet of paper because they do not have a sheet with a watermark that matches the information for the previous sheet's watermark on this sheet of paper. This is how a blockchain maintains the accuracy and integrity of all its rules and data even though we cannot guarantee that all the participants in the blockchain are trustworthy. This is a very important point, and you must already be making the connection to Byzantine Fault Tolerance from Chapter 2 and inefficiencies in our economy because our systems do not ensure trust among the parties involved in a value exchange from Chapter 1.

In this section, we have used a hypothetical example, with some fancy storytelling, to explain conceptually how two of the important components of blockchain, the distributed ledger and the consensus mechanism, work and what they do. We have also understood how a blockchain gets the important characteristics of immutability and provenance. In order to make the concepts easy to understand how these components work, we made the identity of all the parties known, thus overlooking another important component of blockchain, namely, privacy.

In the next section, we will review the difference between centralized and distributed ledgers and technically describe how transactions are formed and communicated to participants in the blockchain network. This will help us reclaim the notion of privacy and explain how that works within a blockchain.

Distributed Ledgers and Technical Overview of Blockchains

In this section, we will review the differences between centralized and distributed ledgers. We will then build on that understanding to discuss the mechanics of how value exchange transactions are created and communicated among the participants (also known as nodes) of a blockchain network. These mechanics will help us understand how the privacy of all participants can be preserved in a blockchain.

To understand the concept of centralized ledger, let us look at an example of a bank and a company that serves as a custodian of your investment assets such as stocks.

When clients of a bank conduct transactions with their bank, the bank keeps a record of these transactions for them. The bank also sends you a copy of your transactions with them that you can choose to keep in some format. You could get this copy through a monthly statement that the bank sends you, or you can log into your account if the bank offers a website (almost all banks do) to review your transactions, search for transactions that meet certain criteria, and even download an electronic copy of the transactions for yourself. You are guaranteed that at the time you downloaded the transactions, they exactly matched the information that the bank had. In the situation as we have described here, only the bank has a record of all the transactions with all their clients. Each client refers to this record as the authoritative source of all the transactions – it can be said that the bank has the golden record! We can say that the bank has a **centralized ledger** of all bank transactions.

No one else other than the bank has a copy of or can access the record of all the transactions for all the clients. I am almost certain that you are going to ask "isn't that a good thing?" Well, it depends. If the bank were to get hacked and lose all the data, then we would have a problem. If a bank for malicious reasons decided to delete all your deposit transactions (of course, they would never do that, right?), then we would have a problem. A bank could also suffer data loss due to incompetence or negligence on their part. If a bank suffers a security breach, then all its clients would have an impact on their privacy. A bank can unilaterally decide the amount of history of your transactions they will make available to you. If you need anything older than the amount of history that the bank unilaterally keeps, then we would have a problem. If for some reason you disagreed with a transaction that the bank has recorded, then the bank will be correct, and you would be wrong 100% of the time. Of course, we trust the bank. How can they ever be wrong? If for some reason the bank was having technical difficulties and their centralized ledger was not available, then this would mean that not only could we not review our transactions, we would also not be able to conduct any transactions; that is, we would not be able to either deposit or withdraw any money. With centralized ledgers, the party that owns the centralized ledger has disproportionate power.

We can offer a similar narrative for firms that serve as custodians of our investment assets such as stocks. When we say we own stock, very rarely do we have anything physical stipulating that ownership,[5] and stock ownership is merely a record in a database at a company such as Fidelity Investments or Charles Schwab that serves as a custodian for your stock. The challenges outlined in the previous paragraph all apply: if these companies get hacked and suffer data loss, there will be an issue; if these companies maliciously alter their database, there will be an issue; and so on.

Centralized ledgers have advantages though. They can deliver on the ACID semantics we discussed in Chapter 2 much more easily and cheaply than distributed ledgers. Let us now turn our attention to distributed ledgers.

---

[5] In the olden days, stock ownership was stipulated by the possession of physical stock ownership certificates.

If a bank operated using a distributed ledger, then all of the bank's clients could, if they chose to, have a complete copy of all the transactions of the bank with all its clients. Each client would also be guaranteed that the ledger that they have authentically matches the copy that the bank has as well as the copy that every other client has. In addition, a bank would not be able to make any unilateral changes to the rules regarding the maintenance of the ledger without an agreement from at least a majority of the clients. These rules could include, for example, the amount of history that is kept in the ledger, the format of a transaction, and the data that should be included in each transaction. The bank or any client would also not be able to alter any transactions that has been committed to the ledger. The client would also know the rules for committing transactions to a ledger, and they would all follow these rules. The distributed ledger, as we have described it here, would mitigate many of the challenges associated with the centralized ledger described earlier in terms of the bank acting unilaterally, the bank acting maliciously, the bank experiencing data loss, or the bank having issues with their ledger being available for access.

You might, however, ask, why is it a good idea for a client to have access to transactions of other clients – wouldn't this impinge on the privacy of clients? In a blockchain distributed ledger, the privacy of involved parties is maintained by ensuring that a transaction does not include readily available identifying information about parties. Only parties who are involved in the transaction know the identity of the other parties. Even though all clients have a copy of the distributed ledger and they have access to all the transactions in the distributed ledger, they are not able to ascertain the identity of the parties involved in the transaction. Cryptographic keys (public keys) belonging to a party are used in the transaction to identify the party. The mapping of this public key to the identity of the party is not readily available. In this manner, the distributed ledgers used in blockchain are **privacy preserving**. A privacy-preserving distributed ledger will mitigate the impact of a security breach that a bank with a centralized ledger can suffer.

So how does all this work from a technical standpoint?

Let us now assume that the bank and all its clients have computers that are executing the same software. These computers are also known as nodes. The nodes are connected to one another in a peer-to-peer network. Let us assume a client wants to make a deposit. The following actions get executed across all the peer nodes:

1. The software on the client's node initiating the transaction creates the deposit transaction using a pre-defined format. This format has been agreed to as a consequence of all the nodes running the same software. The transaction will include the public key of the bank (a bank will have one public key for each client, thus obfuscating its identity as well as segregating deposits from each client into different accounts), the public key of the client (the client may also choose a different public key for each party it transacts with, thus obfuscating its identity), the amount of money being deposited, and an authentication indicating two facts. First, that the client indeed has ownership of the money they intend to deposit. Second, the node initiating the transaction has access to the client's corresponding private key for signing the transaction.

2. The software on the client's node will have the network addresses of one or more peer nodes that are executing the same software, and it will transmit the transaction to these nodes.

3. The nodes that receive the transaction will validate
    the format of the transaction and verify that the
    transaction is authenticated based on the rules in
    the software. Each node then does two things. First,
    it transmits this transaction to other peer nodes
    whose network address it has. Second, it includes
    this transaction into a list of valid transactions it has
    previously received. This process continues until all
    peer nodes have received the transaction. If a node
    receives a transaction that it has previously received,
    then it will not transmit it any further. Please note
    that all the nodes do not receive the transaction
    at the same time, unlike our conceptual narrative
    earlier in the chapter.

4. Concurrently, with the process of receiving,
    validating, and transmitting transactions, each
    node also selects a subset of valid transactions and
    starts the process of creating a block. The process
    of creating a block, the consensus protocol, is
    also called mining. This new block will include
    information about the previous block in the chain
    that this block needs to be connected to. Once
    a node successfully creates a block, it transmits
    the block to the peer nodes whose network
    address it has.

5. Once a node receives a block, it validates whether
    the block has been created following the agreed-
    upon protocol and if all the transactions in the
    block are valid. If that is the case, then this node
    does four things: it transmits this block to the peer

nodes whose network address it has (this process will continue until all the nodes have received the block; again, notice that all the nodes do not receive the block at the same time); it will append this block to the appropriate block in the blockchain on this node; it stops its current process of creating a block; and it starts the process of creating a new block with a subset of the remaining valid transactions (i.e., it will remove the valid transactions in the block that was just added to the blockchain from its list of pending valid transactions).

6. It is only after the deposit transaction has been added to a block and the block has been appended to the blockchain that we can say that the deposit transaction has been completed. In other words, the money from the client is deposited at the bank in the client's account.

Steps 1 through 6 explain how transactions are created, how transactions are validated, and how transactions are communicated to all the nodes in a blockchain; how privacy of the parties involved in a transaction is maintained; how a subset of transactions are "packaged" into a block through mining or the execution of the consensus protocol; and how blocks are communicated to all the nodes in the blockchain.

These steps explain how the narrative at the beginning of the chapter of creating a distributed ledger and making sure that all parties have the same copy of the distributed ledger is technically implemented.

Steps 1 through 6 are also followed for other types of transactions such as withdrawals. Please also note that these steps can also be executed to transfer money between any nodes; that is, parties are not limited to transactions between banks, nor are they required to include the bank when they want to transfer money among themselves. The bank is just another peer node. It does not have any extraordinary power.[6]

Jimmy Song, who is one of the proponents of Bitcoin and a leading authority and investor, summarizes the difference between databases and blockchain as follows:

> "The main thing distinguishing a blockchain from a normal database is that there are specific rules about how to put data into the database. That is, it cannot conflict with some other data that's already in the database (consistent), it's append-only (immutable), and the data itself is locked to an owner (ownable), it's replicable and available. Finally, everyone agrees on what the state of the things in the database are (canonical) without a central party (decentralized)." (Song, 2018)

All the peer nodes in the network agree on the state of the data in the blockchain database. We call that a canonical state, and the peer nodes come to that agreement without having a central party so this is decentralized and the database is a distributed ledger.

While privacy-preserving distributed ledgers mitigate the issues we outlined with centralized ledgers, they are always more difficult to implement than centralized ledgers. As we saw, distributed ledgers on different nodes will all not get to the canonical state at the same time, making it almost impossible to implement ACID semantics with blockchain. The nodes in the blockchain also conduct redundant computation, ostensibly "wasting" resources. We will discuss the limitations with blockchain in more detail later in this chapter. Due to the difficulty in implementing distributed ledger (or blockchain)–based applications, they

---

[6] In the next chapter, we will review a class of blockchain applications for Decentralized Finance or DeFi.

should only be considered when necessitated by the underlying business problem. In Chapter 4, we will discuss how system designers can determine if the business problem necessitates the use of blockchain.

In the chapter so far, we have reviewed three of the four conceptual components of blockchain: distributed ledgers, consensus, and privacy. The fourth component of blockchain is smart contracts, and we will discuss this component later in the chapter when we provide a summary of all the blockchain components. Next, we will discuss a classification approach for different types of blockchain implementations.

Blockchain Implementation Categorization

So far in this book, we have discussed blockchains as aiming for being as distributed and decentralized as practically possible. In this section, we will review a classification of blockchains that are in the continuum of being distributed and decentralized. This continuum helps us evaluate the type of blockchain that will best fit the business problem we are grappling with.

We classify blockchain along two dimensions: access and privacy. The access dimension determines who is allowed to participate in the blockchain network. Participation in the blockchain would imply getting access to the blockchain software, creating a node that executes this software, and being connected to one or more peer nodes. The privacy dimension determines whether transactions require information identifying the parties involved in the transaction or not.

For our classification, the access dimension can take on two possible values: public or private. The privacy dimension can also take on two possible values: permissioned and permissionless. Our classification then results in four possible types of blockchains: private permissioned, public permissioned, private permissionless, and public permissionless as shown in Figure 3-1.

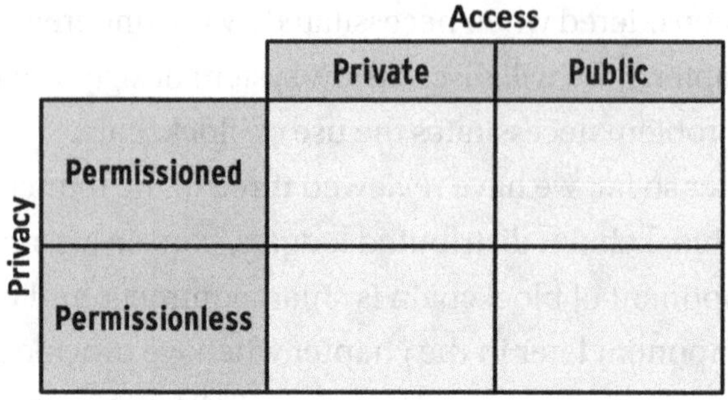

		Access	
		Private	**Public**
Privacy	**Permissioned**		
	Permissionless		

Figure 3-1. *Blockchain implementation categorization*

Public blockchains are those blockchains where anyone can be part of the blockchain network and choose to transact, participate in the consensus protocol, maintain a copy of the distributed ledger, and have visibility to all the transactions. There is no party that has the rights to grant or limit access to the blockchain. Private blockchains are those blockchains where one or more parties have the rights to approve participation of other parties to join the blockchain network. Consequently, these parties with approval granting rights can remove nodes from the blockchain network, with or without a valid rationale. Parties with approval granting rights can also grant or limit the actions that participants in a blockchain network are entitled to execute. For example, in a private blockchain, all parties might not be granted rights to participate in the consensus protocol or maintain a copy of the distributed ledger. In public blockchains, all nodes have the same power, while in private blockchains, nodes representing parties with approval granting rights have more power than the other nodes (or they have power over the other nodes). A private blockchain with an unequal distribution of power among the nodes leads away from decentralization and toward centralization.

Permissioned blockchains are those blockchains where before a party transacts on the blockchain, their identity has to be established, verified, and known. Those parties who play the role of establishing and verifying the identity of the other parties wield power over the participants in the blockchain. These parties also act as centralizing forces. Please keep in mind the distributed ledger in a permissioned blockchain is still privacy preserving. Easily accessible identity is not visible in the transaction. However, there are some parties who can map all parties in every transaction to their identity. Permissionless blockchains are those blockchains where transactions on the blockchain can be conducted anonymously. No easily available identity of any transacting party is available to any of the nodes in the blockchain.

In our conceptual and technical descriptions so far, we have described blockchains that are public and permissionless. The benefit of blockchain in terms of the lack of non-value-adding intermediary third parties is most prevalent in public permissionless blockchains. The benefit of blockchain in terms of all parties having access to the distributed ledger with the distributed ledger being the authentic state for all transactions is available across all types of blockchains. It can be argued that in private permissioned blockchain, there is a potential for reduced latency and quicker synchronization of the distributed ledgers across all the nodes. In some sense, this is the classic trade-off, getting a bit more consistency by sacrificing some availability and partition tolerance. The first blockchain implementation, Bitcoin, is a public permissionless blockchain. When the sole purpose of a blockchain is the creation of money and value exchange, in almost all instances, public permissionless blockchains are the most appropriate blockchain. In blockchains where the primary purpose is the sharing of consistent data among nontrusting parties, a private permissioned blockchain may suffice. Hyperledger and its Fabric blockchain is the most widely used private permissioned blockchain platform. Several successful enterprise business applications have been developed using Hyperledger Fabric. In Chapter 4, we will systematically review how system designers can determine what type of blockchain implementation is most suitable for their business problem.

Figure 3-2 shows examples of different types of blockchain implementations that have achieved success.

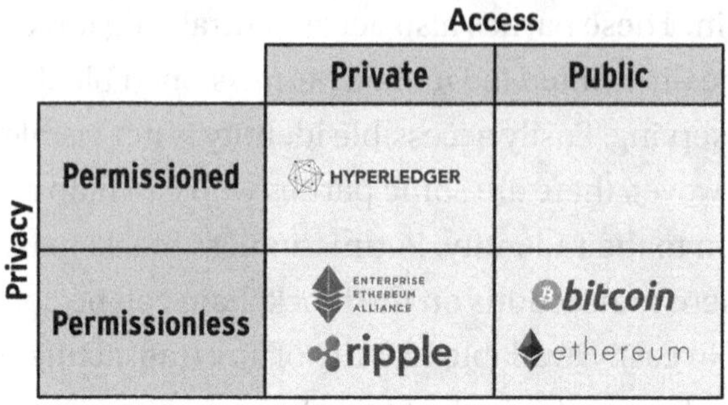

Figure 3-2. *Example of blockchain implementations by type*

In addition to Bitcoin, Ethereum is an example of a public permissionless blockchain. We will learn a little bit more about Ethereum in Chapter 5, and then Part 2 of this book will be focused exclusively on Ethereum.

As we mentioned earlier, the Hyperledger ecosystem that consists of several tools and frameworks is the most well-known and successful private permissioned blockchain implementation. We will provide a very high-level overview of Hyperledger in Chapter 5.

Enterprise Ethereum and Ripple are examples of private permissionless blockchains. In private permissionless blockchains, participants need permission before they join the network and are granted access to specific functions such as creating and validating blocks (participating in consensus). With Ripple, for example, a network of validators was formed for the purpose of creating and validating blocks.[7] In private permissionless blockchains, parties can transact anonymously. Enterprise Ethereum was created as a version of Ethereum that could be used by enterprise businesses to develop blockchain-based applications.

---

[7] Ripple Labs, the company behind Ripple, is the subject of an enforcement action by the Securities and Exchange Commission, claiming that Ripple's token or currency, the XRP, is a security (www.sec.gov/news/press-release/2020-338).

From a blockchain purist perspective, public permissionless blockchains such as Bitcoin and Ethereum are the most distributed and decentralized with the most equal distribution of power among the participating nodes. Bitcoin and Ethereum differ from each other in the governance mechanism they use to change or evolve the blockchain platform and the functionality for specifying transaction terms. We will discuss this in some more detail in Chapter 5. Similarly, on the distributed-decentralized continuum, applications developed using Hyperledger and other private permissioned blockchain platforms would be the most centralized.

In the next section, we will summarize the components of blockchain and review the fourth component, smart contracts.

Smart Contracts and Blockchain Components Summary

In this section, we provide a business-level summary of the four key components of blockchain. These four components are distributed ledger, consensus, privacy, and smart contracts as shown in Figure 3-3.

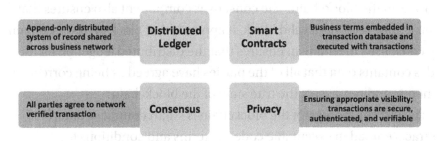

Figure 3-3. *Blockchain components summary*

So far in the chapter, we have already reviewed the distributed ledger, privacy, and consensus components of blockchain.

The distributed ledger is the system or record of all the transactions conducted in the blockchain network. All the nodes in the blockchain have an exact authentic replica of the distributed ledger – subject of course to the eventual consistency property of BASE semantics. The distributed ledger is an append-only system of record; that is, blocks with transactions can be added to the ledger, but blocks and transactions cannot be altered or deleted.

The privacy component of blockchain makes the distributed ledger a privacy-preserving distributed ledger ensuring that the identity of parties in a transaction is only accessible to those who should have access. The privacy component also ensures that all transactions are signed, thus making each transaction owned and authenticated. Finally, the privacy component verifies all transactions to ensure that the parties involved in the transaction have the rights to conduct that transaction.

The consensus component of blockchain is responsible for the creation of blocks and ensuring that all transactions in the block are verified and validated. It also makes sure that the block follows all the rules required for a block to be valid, and finally, it ensures that the node creating the block shows evidence of their right to create a block. One way they demonstrate this evidence is by showing that they have found the components that will produce a hash with a pattern prescribed by the rules in the blockchain. The consensus component also ensures that when a node receives a valid block, it appends that block to its blockchain. The consensus mechanism ensures that the distributed ledger on all the nodes contains data that all of the parties have agreed as being correct and authentic and represents the true state of the blockchain.

The last component of the blockchain is smart contracts. Smart contracts embed in executable code the terms and conditions for consummating the transaction. For example, when Candice sold her comic to Marco, the terms by which Candice can spend the money that Marco has given her are codified, and only when those terms are met will Candice be able to spend the money. These terms could be as simple as Candice having access to her private key, or these terms could be more complex and include a confirmation that Candice sent the comic to Marco. A smart contract example for a bank could include the provision that a deposit earns interest; the smart contract will ensure that an automated transaction deposits the amount of interest into the client's account at the agreed-upon rate at the agreed-upon frequency (monthly, quarterly, annual). Different blockchain implementations have varying amounts of versatility with respect to the type of logic that can be represented in a smart contract. A smart contract is built into the transaction; all the terms are executable by a computer and hence cannot be ambiguous or require human interpretation. In this sense, smart contracts have the potential of creating transparency for the transactions on the blockchain. Smart contracts carry costs and risks as well. A smart contract is executed by all the nodes on the blockchain for every transaction, creating computational costs that have to be borne by the owner of the transaction. Once a smart contract has been committed to a blockchain, it cannot be changed, creating unforeseen risks in terms of software defects.

In summary, the four key conceptual components of a blockchain are the distributed ledger, privacy, consensus, and smart contracts. These four components ensure the privacy of every transaction in every block of the distributed ledger, the authentic state of the data on every node in the blockchain, and the fulfillment of all the contractual terms before a transaction is settled. All of this is achieved without the involvement of any centralized third party. This is what makes blockchain powerful; these four components working together provide a blockchain with the functionality that has the potential for creating benefits for individuals, industry, the overall economy, and the society as a whole.

In the next section, we will discuss the limitations of blockchain.

Blockchain Limitations

So far in this book, we have described in detail the potential benefits of blockchain, the core technologies that are the basis of any blockchain implementation, and how four key conceptual components come together to deliver the potential benefits of blockchain. Throughout this chapter and Chapter 2, we have alluded to potential limitations of blockchain with some of the limitations being related to challenges with distributed system design. In this section, we will discuss the limitations of blockchain and classify them into five categories: energy consumption, scalability, risk of nefarious activities, change management, and confidentiality risk. These limitations create constraints, and they will drive design trade-offs that we should understand when we conceive, design, and implement blockchain applications.[8]

Let's start with the first limitation – energy consumption. There are three drivers of excessive energy consumption in blockchain that are necessary to have a system that is Byzantine fault tolerant. These drivers are redundant computation, consensus mechanism, and the need for a large number of nodes. In order for each node to be independent for Byzantine Fault Tolerance, each node repeats the computation that has been completed by other nodes. Each node verifies and validates the transaction when they receive the transaction, it also executes the code in the smart contract, and it validates the block when it receives it as well as reverifies the transactions contained in the block. These computations are necessary so that each node is self-contained, and this improves the overall trustworthiness of the blockchain network. The consensus mechanism is designed to be computationally expensive because this

---

[8] These limitations are specific limitations associated with blockchain. We should also keep in mind, as we have mentioned earlier, that blockchain applications in particular and distributed systems in general are more difficult to design and implement than centralized systems. They should only be considered if necessitated by the underlying business problem.

increases the confidence of immutability of the blocks (and thus of the transactions committed in the block). The consensus mechanism is also designed as a competition as this creates a more trustworthy blockchain network with no one node (or a group of nodes) having the opportunity to abuse the power of creating blocks. The need for a large number of blocks also serves the purpose of increasing the trustworthiness of the blockchain network. As we saw in Chapter 2, a large number of nodes makes it extremely difficult (if not impossible) for a majority of nodes to collude. While we accept that all the drivers for increased energy consumption are necessary, it does not negate the fact that we are consuming excessive energy. Energy comes with a cost, not only economic costs for the parties involved but also the impacts to the environment from this excessive energy consumption. Several countries, including China, have prohibited the execution of the consensus mechanism (mining) on computers within their borders. Many parties who operate nodes on the Bitcoin network are trying to migrate to renewable energy sources. With the risks to the planet from climate change, excessive energy consumption is a key limitation that has the potential to stymie the adoption of blockchain.

The second limitation of blockchain that we will discuss is scalability. We define scalability as the transactions per second committed to a blockchain network. The transactions per second metric is sometimes referred to as the throughput of the blockchain network. A transaction is committed to a blockchain (this is similar to saying that a transaction has settled), when a transaction has been included in a block and the block has been added to the blockchain by a majority of the nodes that are part of the blockchain network. The throughput supported by a blockchain should at least equal the transaction volume required by the business problem being addressed by the blockchain including the expected growth in the volume of these transactions. The transactions per second of a blockchain are determined by two factors: the number of transactions that can be supported in a block, which in turn depends on the underlying size of the block, and the frequency with which blocks are designed to be committed to the blockchain network. A blockchain can theoretically have a very high throughput if the block size it supports is large enough and it adds blocks with a high enough frequency. As we discussed at the end of Chapter 2, this high throughput will come at the cost of sacrificing eventual consistency, and hence, throughput will be reduced because we will not be able to unequivocally say if the majority of the nodes in the blockchain have added the block. The scalability limitation is thus driven by design trade-offs. The first design trade-off is how often a block is committed to the blockchain. If we commit a block too often, then we have a high chance that many of the nodes might be out of sync because they might have not yet received the latest block due to network latency. If we don't commit a block often enough, then we will reduce the transactions per second scalability of the blockchain. The second design trade-off we make is how large should a block be. If a block is large, then we can scale the blockchain much more than if a block is small. But if a block is large, then it will take longer to be transmitted through the network, creating issues related to network latency, and we have a high chance that many of the nodes might be out of sync because they might have not yet received the latest block. This design trade-off should be carefully considered by system designers when designing blockchain applications. The design trade-off itself is not a limitation. The design trade-off results in constraints on scalability and trustworthiness, resulting in scalability limitations. Several engineering solutions have been proposed to alleviate this limitation. We will discuss some of these solutions in Chapter 5.

The third limitation that we will describe is the risk of nefarious activities. This limitation is of concern for public permissionless blockchain networks. The question is, are people more inclined to conduct illicit transactions because they are less likely to be caught if they are conducting these transactions anonymously? The general belief is that the answer to this question is the affirmative, and there is anecdotal evidence reported in the media that this is indeed the case. There are two mitigating factors for this limitation. First is the property of provenance that creates an extensive audit trail of the lineage of the value exchanged in all transactions. This lineage can be used to trace the source of suspect transactions. Second, if any participants in the blockchain have obtained their wallet (or private/public keys) from a centralized exchange, these entities are required by "Know Your Customer" (KYC) regulations to disclose the mapping of the keys to the identity of the participant.[9]

The fourth and the fifth limitation, change management and confidentiality risk, respectively, are both related to smart contracts.

Once transactions are committed to a blockchain, they are immutable; that is, they cannot be changed. Smart contracts that represent the terms of a transaction within software are also committed to the blockchain either within the (data structure of the) transaction where they apply or independently, and then the address where they are committed is referenced by transactions that are governed by these smart contracts. Smart contracts once committed are immutable, creating the change management limitation. Smart contracts once committed cannot be changed either to address software defects or to make adjustments due to changing business requirements. The only recourse available to participants is to voluntarily cease using the problematic smart contract. There have been well-publicized instances where this limitation has led to a financial loss for participants and also the withdrawal of participants from a blockchain network.

Once smart contracts are committed to the blockchain network, for public blockchains, these smart contracts are visible to all participants. This creates a situation where business parties can potentially disclose their confidential business terms to competitors. While this helps with transparency, it could compromise confidentiality and competitiveness. In some instances, the visibility of smart contracts can also be used as a mechanism for collusion by market participants.

---

[9] For example, see the news story at www.facebook.com/FOX7austin/videos/four-texas-men-arrested-when-child-porn-website-is-shut-down/427236648217288/

In this section, we have described five limitations of blockchain: energy consumption, scalability, risk of nefarious activities, change management, and confidentiality risk. These limitations should be kept in mind when we design business applications using blockchain.

Chapter Summary/Key Takeaways

Key takeaways from this chapter are as follows:

- A transaction is the foundational concept in blockchain, and it is initiated by one party to transfer value to one or more parties based on mutually agreed terms and conditions. In a blockchain, parties transact with one another through peer-to-peer computer nodes. Each node can independently verify and validate each transaction that it receives.

- A block is a packaging of valid transactions – the process used by all the nodes in a blockchain to create blocks is known as the consensus protocol. Each new block is logically connected to a previous block, creating the blockchain. The consensus protocol makes it difficult to change the transactions in a block once it has been added to the blockchain. This is why blocks in a blockchain are considered immutable.

- A blockchain maintains an audit trail of the value being transferred between parties. This audit trail is known as the provenance of a transaction.

- The blockchain is a distributed ledger because conceptually all nodes have an exact replica of the chain of blocks. New blocks can be added to the blockchain, and previously added blocks cannot be altered, making blockchain an append-only distributed ledger.

- Privacy is preserved in the blockchain by including only the public keys of the parties involved in the transaction – each party controls who is able to map their public key to their identity.

- Smart contracts embed in executable code the terms and conditions for consummating the transaction.

- Conceptually, the four components of a blockchain are distributed ledgers, privacy preservation, consensus mechanisms, and smart contracts.

- There are four possible types of blockchains: private permissioned, public permissioned, private permissionless, and public permissionless.

- A blockchain has five limitations: energy consumption, scalability, risk of nefarious activity, smart contract change management, and smart contract confidentiality.

In the first three chapters, we have completed reviewing the economic potential of blockchain, the core technologies (cryptography, distributed systems, and peer-to-peer networks) that underlie blockchain implementations, and a conceptual description of the core components of blockchain. In the next chapter, we will describe criteria that can be used to decide if a business problem requires a blockchain solution, guidelines for making design decisions for blockchain applications, and illustrative applications of blockchain.

Sidebar – Blockchain Terminology

- **Block:** A data structure that holds a list of transactions and a header.

- **Blockchain:** A data structure that links blocks together.

- **Transaction:** A data structure that encodes information about the transfer of payments between parties, including the terms and conditions for that transfer.

- **Distributed ledger:** The data in a blockchain that is replicated across computers connected in a peer-to-peer network architecture.

- **Immutability:** The difficulty of changing any information in a transaction once it has been included in a block and that block has been added to the blockchain.

- **Provenance:** The audit trail of the money that is being spent in any transaction.

- **Privacy:** The ability to control the availability of identifying information of parties participating in a transaction.

- **Mining:** The process of solving a cryptographic puzzle for the purpose of creating a block to be added to the blockchain.

- **Smart contracts:** The software encoding of the terms and transactions for consummating a transaction.

Quiz Questions

1. Conceptually, what are the four components of a blockchain?

2. What is the process whereby all the parties involved in a transaction create a new block of transactions known as?

   a. Privacy preservation

   b. Consensus protocol

   c. Verification

   d. Validations

3. True or False: It is very difficult to alter a transaction in a block once it has been added to the blockchain.

4. What is the property whereby it is difficult to alter a transaction in a blockchain known as?

   a. Provenance

   b. Immutability

   c. Computational complexity

   d. Scalability

5. What is the audit trail for the value being exchanged in successive blockchain transactions known as?

   a. Provenance

   b. Value chain

   c. Linked list

   d. Smart contracts

6. Briefly describe how a blockchain is different from a database.

7. Explain what is meant by "a blockchain is a privacy-preserving ledger of transactions."

8. Which of the following is NOT a limitation of blockchain?

   a. Scalability

   b. Energy consumption

   c. Illegal activities

   d. Data loss

9. The two limitations of blockchain related to smart contracts are _____ and _____.

10. Which of these is NOT a driver of excessive energy consumption in blockchain.

    a. Redundant computation

    b. Consensus mechanism

    c. Network communication

11. Briefly explain the difference between private and public blockchains.

12. Briefly explain the difference between permissioned and permissionless blockchains.

References

Song, J. Why blockchain is hard. May, 2018. `https://jimmysong.medium.com/why-blockchain-is-hard-60416ea4c5c`

Gupta, M. Blockchain for dummies. 2017. John Wiley & Sons, Hoboken, NJ

CHAPTER 4

Blockchain Business Applications

Applications developed using blockchain technology have the potential to create a step increase in productivity. However, all business problems do not require a blockchain solution. Blockchain applications are more complex to build than traditional applications and should only be built when dictated by the business problem.

Introduction

Applications developed using blockchain for all their business and societal promises are at the end of the day technology deployments. Starting with the adoption of relational database management systems in the late 1970s, to the adoption of enterprise resource planning applications in the 1990s, to the digital transformations that are currently underway, we have learned several lessons about technology deployments. These lessons include the importance of the following critical success factors:

1. Clear understanding, articulation, and management of the business results, or business outcomes

2. Senior-level executive sponsorship and continued focus on change management to build and maintain support and enthusiasm for the technology

© Weijia Zhang and Tej Anand 2022
W. Zhang and T. Anand, *Blockchain and Ethereum Smart Contract Solution Development*,
https://doi.org/10.1007/978-1-4842-8164-2_4

      deployment across all levels of management and
individuals who will be impacted

3. Adaptable management of the technology
   deployment effort to control budget, scope,
   timeline, and quality

These factors continue to be critical success factors for blockchain
applications. If anything, they are now even more important and even
more difficult to achieve. With blockchain applications, the unit of analysis
shifts from a firm (or company, or enterprise) to the entire value chain
ecosystem that a firm operates in, including its competitors, suppliers,
partners, and customers. Instead of business outcomes such as inventory
turns, labor productivity, customer retention, and customer share that
are important for one firm, we would need business outcomes that are
relevant for the entire value chain, such as overall industry productivity
and profitability. Also, low-hanging (i.e., relatively easily measurable
and achievable) financial outcomes such as elapsed time for month-end
financial processing, elapsed time to collect payments from customers,
and amount of working capital are no longer relevant for a blockchain
network.

To manage the three critical success factors, it used to also be
important to select business problems for technology solutions after a
careful analysis of differentiation impact and feasibility. For blockchain
applications, this continues to be the case. Figure 4-1 shows the factors that
we recommend be considered for differentiation impact and feasibility
with each factor measured for an industry or a value chain ecosystem as
a whole.

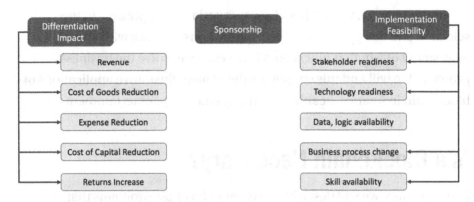

Figure 4-1. *Factors to evaluate the differentiation impact and feasibility of a technology deployment*

For a preliminary analysis, we recommend a high, medium, or low characterization for each differentiation impact factor. All the factors have a direct relationship with differentiation impact; that is, a high revenue impact implies a high differentiation impact. The overall differentiation impact for a technology initiative, aggregated across all factors, will be the highest characterization across all the factors. For the implementation feasibility analysis, we recommend a similar high, medium, or low characterization for each factor. All factors except business process change have a direct relationship with implementation feasibility. Business process change has an inverse relationship with implementation feasibility; that is, when business process change is assessed to be high, the implementation feasibility will be low. The overall implementation feasibility for a technology initiative, aggregated across factors, will be the lowest characterization across all factors. With this analysis, we recommend selecting those initiatives that have a high differentiation impact and a high implementation feasibility. If none of the initiatives have such a characterization, then our recommendation is to adjust the scope of the initiative to arrive at such a characterization.

In this chapter, we will first discuss criteria that apply only to the selection and design of blockchain applications, starting with an assessment of whether blockchain is necessary to solve the business problem. We will end this chapter by describing illustrative applications of blockchain in finance, healthcare, supply chain, and entertainment.

Is a Blockchain Necessary?

In this section, we will describe the types of business problems that are likely to require blockchain technology to address.

We start by examining if the business problem is related to the economic inefficiencies that were described in Chapter 1 that blockchain has the potential to address. Is the business problem dealing with one or more of the following seven opportunities?

1. Time to settle transactions

2. Fees paid to third parties for nonvalue activities

3. Data-related redundant work, rework, and reconciliation work

4. Constraints imposed by government regulations and other nongovernmental rules

5. High incidence of fraud

6. Privacy leaks during value exchange

7. Data security risks

A system designer can analyze a business problem and determine if there are opportunities related to more than one of the seven economic inefficiencies; then they could proceed with further analysis of the suitability of blockchain. Alternatively, a system designer can study a particular industry and determine if more than one of these seven economic inefficiencies exist and identify business use cases for the application of blockchain.[1]

The next step in determining if you need a blockchain would be to take the analysis of the business use cases with the seven economic inefficiencies and evaluate if the solution designs could be characterized into one of the three application themes that align with the capabilities of a blockchain network. These three application themes are as follows:

1. **Payments** – The first application theme is associated with digitizing payments between multiple parties perhaps across geographic boundaries. These payments could involve the transfer of fungible or nonfungible physical or digital assets. Fungible assets are where all the assets are equivalent, and nonfungible assets are where each asset is unique.

2. **Transparency** – The second application theme is associated with creating transparency and visibility among multiple parties involved in value exchange perhaps across geographical boundaries with varying regulatory jurisdictions. The transparency and visibility could be associated with the status of business process progress, product and service attributes, financial forecasts, or the provenance of data that are being shared between the parties.

3. **Data sovereignty** – The third application theme is associated with protecting the ownership and control of data that morally and legally belongs to a sovereign individual. Control is defined across

---

[1] In this chapter, we will take this alternate approach in describing use cases.

two dimensions: the ascertainment of accuracy
and the granting of access rights. Access rights
can be granted for read only; for read and update;
or for custody for a limited period of time or in
perpetuity; and for all of the data or only for selected
components of the data.

Similar to how a business case can address several of the seven
economic inefficiencies, it can also require a solution design with one or
more application themes. As long as the application functionality can be
teased apart and the design patterns associated with the three themes
applied, system design can be made manageable.

However, we should not decide on the suitability of using blockchain
just based on the economic inefficiencies being addressed and the
application themes that are apparent. As we have discussed in the previous
chapter, any blockchain application is a distributed systems solution
and will involve careful design trade-offs. This makes the development
of blockchain applications a complex endeavor. Building an application
with a centralized database or even a distributed database is going to end
up being relatively simpler than building a blockchain application. The
last piece of analysis that we recommend is an analysis of the underlying
transactions that the blockchain application will support. This analysis is
depicted as a flowchart and shown in Figure 4-2. This flowchart has been
adapted from Wust and Gervais (2018).

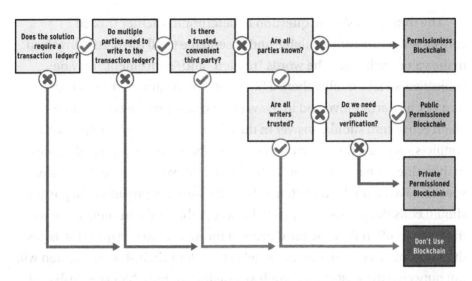

Figure 4-2. *Transaction-based analysis to determine the suitability of blockchain to address a business problem*

The first test in the flowchart asks the question if the systems solution we are considering for the business problem requires a transaction ledger; that is, will the system create a record of transactions representing the exchange of value in terms of how value was defined in Chapter 1 (currency, goods, services, data)? If the answer to this question is no, then we can be certain that the business problem does not require a blockchain-based systems solution.

If a transaction ledger is required, then we move on to the next test in the flowchart. This test asks the question to determine if multiple parties will need to write to the transaction ledger. If only one party needs to write to the transaction ledger, then the answer to that question will be no, and then we can be certain that the benefits of a blockchain-based solution will not outweigh the costs and complexity of developing a blockchain-based solution. If multiple parties will indeed be required to write to the transaction ledger, then the answer to that question is yes, and we will need to move to the third test in the flowchart.

The third test asks the question to determine whether trusted convenient parties are available and acceptable to all the parties involved in the value exchange. The words "trusted" and "convenient" may be subjective, so let's qualify them a bit more. For the answer to this test to be a yes, all parties involved in the value exchange in the entire value chain ecosystem should answer in the affirmative. This will help resolve conflicts such as a third party being trusted by the more powerful parties in the value exchange but not by the others. Convenience can be further specified based on the fees charged and the services provided. All parties should consider the fee charged to be acceptable and commensurate with the services offered by the third party. If the answer to this question is yes, then we can be certain that the benefits of a blockchain-based solution will not outweigh the costs and complexity of developing a blockchain-based solution. If the answer to the question for the third test is no, then we move to the fourth test in the flowchart.

The fourth test asks the question to determine if our business problem will result in a system design where all the parties who will need to write to the transaction ledger are known in advance. If all the parties are not known in advance, then we will most definitely benefit by having a blockchain-based solution. Furthermore, we will need a permissionless blockchain to implement the system solution. If all the parties who will need to write to the transaction ledger are known in advance, then we move to the fifth test in the flowchart.

The fifth test asks the question to determine if all the known parties who are expected to write to the transaction ledger are trusted. Similar to the question in the third test, this question is subjective as well. We will qualify this question similar to how we qualified the third question. For the answer to this test to be a yes, all parties involved in the value exchange in the entire value chain ecosystem should answer in the affirmative. If all parties trust all the other parties who will need to write to the transaction ledger, then the answer to this question is yes, and we can be certain that the benefits of a blockchain-based solution will not outweigh the costs and complexity of developing a blockchain-based solution. If all the parties who are expected to write to the transaction ledger cannot be trusted, then we will most definitely benefit by having a blockchain-based solution. Furthermore, we will need a permissioned blockchain to implement the system solution. We move to the sixth test in the flowchart to determine the type of permissioned blockchain that will be most appropriate.

The sixth test asks the question to determine if transactions that are written to the transaction ledger will need public verification. Public verification implies that all parties in a transaction need to be able to view the transactions and have knowledge that these transactions have been committed to the blockchain network. If public verification is required, then we need to ensure that the privacy of the transacting parties is preserved by making it possible for them to transact anonymously on the blockchain. We should therefore select a public permissioned blockchain. If we do not require public verification of transactions, then a private permissioned blockchain will be sufficient to meet our needs.

We recommend diligently going through this flowchart with its relatively simple tests to determine if the business problem requires blockchain or not. In addition, if the use of blockchain is likely to be beneficial, the flowchart helps identify the type of blockchain that is most suitable to address the business problem. Doing this upfront is important because the design trade-offs we have to make vary with the type of blockchain that we believe is most appropriate.

In the next section, we will review the design decisions that we will need to make to implement an application using blockchain.

Blockchain Application Design Decisions

Developing a blockchain-based application is a complex undertaking involving alignment and coordination across stakeholders with approaches rooted in equity and democracy, as well as seemingly simple technical decisions that can nevertheless have broad consequences. In this section, we will go through the design decisions that we believe are critical for all blockchain-based applications. This section discusses seven design decisions: transactions, tokens, smart contracts, data, consensus mechanism, stakeholder organization, and development stack. These seven design criteria are not independent – a design decision for one criterion can constrain or inform the design decisions in the other criteria. Many of the design decisions will also be informed by the economic inefficiencies being addressed, the theme(s) of the blockchain application, and the type of blockchain being implemented – topics that were covered earlier in the chapter. Finally, the seven design criteria outlined here are not comprehensive, and each blockchain application will require additional design decisions that will be specific to the application being created and the business problem being addressed.

- **Transactions** – This design decision addresses the question "What is the transaction semantics that the blockchain is going to be facilitating?"

  In the examples in the book so far, we have described transactions such as payment for the sale of a comic book, the deposit of money in a bank account, and the deposit of interest in a bank account. The transaction thus is the building block of value exchange. We all intuitively understand payment transactions, where some form of money is transferred between parties. We can also think of transactions that represent the transfer of other types of digital assets between parties, or some digital representation of a physical asset among parties. We can also think of the transfer of a digital representation of some type of rights as a transaction. For example, a transaction could represent the granting of access to a set of data. We can also think of the act of providing answers to a survey as a transaction, where our answers represent the transfer of value (in terms of our knowledge or opinion) to another party.

Transactions therefore raise questions such as follows: "Where in the transaction is the value?" "How is that value apparent?" "How will the value be digitally represented?" In the next design decision, we will discuss the concept of tokens, which can be helpful in answering these questions. The answers to these questions will determine the underlying economics of the blockchain.

Finally, we have described a transaction as the transfer of value from one party to another – a one-way transfer of value. From Chapter 1, we know that the transfer of value is a two-way process. When we make payment for a good or service, we expect to receive the said good or service per an expectation that was created when we agreed to the amount of the payment. Similarly, when we make a deposit into a bank account, we expect to receive interest payments into our account, per the terms agreed upon when we opened the bank account (another transaction!) or when we made the deposit into the account. We can thus see that there are various types of transactions and the relationships between the transactions are important for us to understand the business meaning and value of the transactions as a whole. This will then require us to design embedded links between related transactions so that the business meaning of the transactions can be reconstructed.

In its simplest form, a transaction is an exchange of value, but as you can see, to create applications that resolve the economic inefficiencies in our current systems, transaction semantics can indeed become more complex.

- **Tokens** – At a very high level, a token is the digital representation of a unit of value that will be exchanged. For any blockchain application, we should understand the role of tokens in the application, the types of tokens that will be required (one type or multiple types), the volume of tokens that will be generated, the process for generating tokens (including the frequency of generating tokens), and how parties will perceive and determine the value of tokens.[2] It is also important to understand the costs and incentives for generating tokens.

Some of the most well-known (though not always well understood) tokens are the cryptocurrencies such as Bitcoin and Ether, corresponding to two different blockchain implementations, Bitcoin and Ethereum. We will review Bitcoin in detail in the next chapter and provide a brief overview of Ethereum. Ethereum will be described in complete detail in Part 2 of this book. The Bitcoin and Ether

---

[2] The ultimate determination of the value of a token can be sentiment related and based on various tangible and intangible as well as endogenous and exogenous factors.

tokens are also referred to as native tokens because they are created on the blockchain through the execution of software that makes up the blockchain implementation.

In a taxonomy of tokens provided by Tapscott and Tapscott (2018), they describe Ethereum as a protocol token because it can be used to create other types of derived tokens via smart contracts for distributed applications (dApps). These derived tokens can be security tokens that represent stocks, bonds, and other financial assets. Derived tokens can also be natural asset tokens and represent carbon, air, water, land, as well as other natural resource assets that can be traded. Freni, Ferro, and Moncada (2020) provide a literature review of token categorization taxonomies and then provide their own taxonomy. Ankenbrand, Bieri, Cortivo, Hoehener, and Hardjono (2020) describe 14 attributes to classify tokens representing crypto and noncrypto assets. Tapscott (2020) has published a review of the Token Taxonomy Framework (TTF), a set of standards that define the various artifacts that make up a token, created by the InterWork Alliance (IWA),[3] a nonprofit membership-based organization.

In this book, we will describe two classifications of tokens that we believe are relevant for the development of applications.

---

[3] https://interwork.org/frameworks/token-taxonomy-framework/. The IWA was merged with the Global Blockchain Business Council in 2021 – https://gbbcouncil.org/membership/

The first classification categorizes tokens into native or nonnative tokens. Native tokens are generated by the consensus mechanism of the blockchain network, and they are a representation of a digital asset on their own. Their value is market driven and based on perception and sentiment that is not necessarily tied to any other physical or digital asset. Methodologies borrowed from valuing companies are being proposed to value native tokens. In general, there are two types of valuation methodologies: technical and fundamental. At a simplistic level, technical methods rely on trends, historical valuation, and historical reaction to events to value companies (or the stocks of companies). Fundamental methodologies rely on metrics such as earnings per share, revenue, profit margin, growth rate, and revenue per employee to value companies. Please note that these methods are not an exact science and different people can arrive at different valuations using the same underlying metrics and trends. Using the fundamental methodology, valuation of native tokens (cryptocurrencies) is based on metrics such as the number of transactions, the number of users, and the concentration/distribution of the nodes executing the consensus mechanism. According to us, these metrics are similar to the metrics used to value internet companies in the early days before the dot-com crash. We believe that it is prudent to view such valuation methods with a certain level of skepticism. Given the anonymity of transactions, many of the metrics that these methods rely upon can be easily gamed. Valuing crypto assets or cryptocurrencies is still in a very nascent stage.

Nonnative tokens are derived from native tokens. Nonnative tokens are mapped to either physical assets or other digital assets and derive their value from the assets they are mapped to. When we develop enterprise business blockchain applications, we are interested in nonnative tokens that we will map to the assets or payment currencies that we will be exchanging. An example of a specific nonnative payment currency token is a stable coin. The value of a stable coin is mapped to one or more national currencies.

The second classification categorizes tokens as fungible tokens or nonfungible tokens (NFTs). Fungible tokens can be exchanged one for another, and two tokens of the same denomination have the same value. A dollar is a fungible token – the ten-dollar bill in my pocket can be interchanged for the ten-dollar bill in your pocket since both have the same value. NFTs are one-of-a-kind assets; that is, each NFT is unique. One NFT cannot be interchanged with another NFT. An NFT on a blockchain is nothing but a "block of data" that cannot be changed, and its ownership can be authenticated. Ownership of an NFT can be exchanged, presumably for some payment, and that payment then signifies that value that has been ascribed to an NFT. We can think of NFTs as a mechanism to prevent counterfeiting of art, memorabilia, or anything that any individual determines to be art.[4]

We end the discussion on tokens by pointing out that the regulation of tokens depends on how a token is interpreted. If a token is considered a security, then in the United States, it falls under the jurisdiction of the Securities and Exchange Commission (SEC). If a token is considered a commodity, then in the United States, it falls under the jurisdiction of the Commodity Futures Trading Commission (CFTC). Similarly, depending on the use and interpretation of tokens, several other regulatory agencies could be involved.[5] Regulation for tokens is an area blockchain system designers should pay attention to while designing their applications and keep in mind that the regulation is nascent and evolving.

---

[4] Please see step-by-step instructions to create an NFT using Ethereum: www.wsj.com/articles/i-gave-my-mom-a-crypto-wallet-a-simple-guide-to-nfts-blockchain-and-more-11639404001?st=sweoi7bt6baes4o&reflink=desktopwebshare_permalink

[5] www.globallegalinsights.com/practice-areas/blockchain-laws-and-regulations/usa and www.lw.com/thoughtLeadership/gli2021-blockchain-crypto-not-in-kansas-anymore- are two excellent resources to understand the regulatory landscape with tokens.

- **Smart contracts** – So far, we have seen that a transaction represents the semantics of the value exchange and tokens represent the units of value exchange. Smart contracts are the executable software representation of the terms of the exchange. Earlier, when we described that a deposit in a bank account would lead to interest being deposited into a bank account, it is the smart contract associated with the deposit that determines the rate of interest and the frequency of interest payment deposits. The design question for blockchain application designers is determining the number of smart contracts that will be needed, the logic of each smart contract, and the process for developing, validating, and testing the smart contract. Different blockchain implementations provide varying programming languages for their smart contracts and varying development tools. In the next chapter, we will provide a very brief overview of the Ethereum smart contract development tools. In Part 2 of this book, distributed application development using Ethereum will be discussed in depth.

  There are two complications with smart contracts. Both these complications have a bearing on the complexity of the business logic that is encoded in the smart contract. The first complication is related to the computational power required to execute the smart contract. In general, smart contracts with more complexity can include sophisticated loops and several nested levels of conditional logic. Since a smart contract is executed by every node in the blockchain, the party on whose behest a node is expending computational and electrical power will need to provide compensation. Smart contracts with complicated logic can be costly. For example, if the smart contract to compute the interest for a deposit was very complicated, then the owner of the bank account and/or the bank will have to pay for the execution of the smart contract, reducing their financial incentive.

The second complication arises from the fact that once a smart contract is committed to the blockchain, it cannot be changed. The more complicated the logic within a smart contract, the greater the probability that our test and validation processes have been unable to find all the software defects. Any remaining software defect can lead to financial or security vulnerabilities. Mehar et al. (2019) provide a critical analysis of a defect in an Ethereum smart contract that set out to implement a Decentralized Autonomous Organization (DAO) that resulted in several million dollars being withdrawn in a manner incongruous with the intent of the developers of the smart contract. Eventually, resolving this defect resulted in a schism in the Ethereum community.

A careful, deliberate, and parsimonious design of smart contracts followed by a diligent development, test, and validation process is extremely important for blockchain applications. The stakes are higher in public permissionless blockchain networks than they are in private permissioned blockchain networks.

- **Data** – It can be flippantly said that any blockchain is nothing but bits and bytes of data, most of it cryptographically protected. This comment is true, and it implies that most of the value from a blockchain comes from the meanings assigned to and the interpretations made of these data. Therefore, the design of the data structures (or data models) that support a blockchain is an important design consideration for blockchain system designers.

  In addition to designing a data model that has high fidelity to the business problem being addressed and ensuring clarity and comprehension of this model by all stakeholders, a design issue that all application designers need to confront, blockchain system designers also have to deal with three design challenges that are specific to blockchain.

  The first design challenge involves determining the data that will be stored on the blockchain (on-chain) and the data that will be stored off-chain. The on-chain data is the distributed ledger, and it is replicated on every node in the blockchain network. The size of the on-chain data is one of the factors that drives the scalability (transactions per second) and consistency of data on the nodes. It also drives that amount of computational cost that will be incurred by each node. For these reasons, we should only store data on the blockchain that is absolutely necessary. Please keep in mind that this design decision is available only to system designers who are developing their own blockchain implementations, or using a private permissioned blockchain such as Hyperledger. For applications built using Ethereum, the on-chain transaction data structure is predetermined (and built in). For Hyperledger-based blockchain applications, privacy-related regulations should be one of the considerations in determining if data will be stored on-chain. As we have seen, once data is committed to the chain, it is very difficult (almost impossible) to remove that data. If personally identifiable information (PII) or personal health information (PHI) is stored on a blockchain, then compliance with privacy laws that give customers the right to remove their data would not be possible.[6,7]

The second design challenge involves determining where and how the off-chain data will be stored and managed. If the off-chain data is centralized, then that has the potential of defeating the trust-related objectives of the application – How can we trust the data that is not on the blockchain? This has come to be known as the "oracle" problem (Caldarelli, 2020). A preferred approach for storing off-chain data is by using distributed file systems (Huang, Lin, Zheng, Zheng, and Bian, 2020) such as IPFS.[8]

The third design challenge is the mechanism for integrating, or linking, the off-chain data with the on-chain data. This integration is usually achieved

---

[6] This is not an issue for pubic permissionless blockchains since public keys are not (at least at this time) considered PII.

[7] The implication of encrypted PII or PHI on the blockchain with respect to privacy regulations is as of yet unclear.

[8] www.ipfs.io for more information.

through smart contracts. The "oracle" problem manifests itself through the requirements that smart contracts have for accessing real-world authoritative data. For example, in the smart contract we described earlier where a deposit in a bank account accrues interest, we would need to know the interest rate. If this interest rate was a variable interest rate based on the federal funds rate,[9] then we would need to integrate with an external data source that could provide this information.

- **Consensus** – The next design challenge for blockchain applications that use a private permissioned blockchain is to determine the consensus mechanism that will be most suitable for the business problem being addressed.

  In private permissioned blockchain application platforms such as Hyperledger, the consensus mechanism is pluggable. A common consensus mechanism that is used by system designers involves getting explicit validation of a block from a majority of the nodes that have rights to create blocks – there is no puzzle to be solved. Several variations on this theme can be used.

  If you are using public (permissioned or permissionless) blockchain platforms, then the consensus mechanism is already decided for you. In general, we need computationally robust consensus

---

[9] https://fred.stlouisfed.org/series/FEDFUNDS shows how federal funds rate has varied since before 1960.

mechanisms for public blockchains compared to consensus mechanisms for private blockchains (one is not likely to collude and compromise the blockchain network if your identity is known). If you plan to use a public blockchain for your application, then the consensus mechanism offered by the blockchain platform could be a factor in your decision-making process. In the next chapter when we discuss Bitcoin in detail, we will describe the consensus mechanism used by Bitcoin. We will also describe other consensus mechanisms that can be used. For public blockchains, it is important to balance requirements for computational robustness against sustainability concerns regarding power consumption.

Stakeholder organization: This is a design decision for permissioned blockchain applications only. We need to determine the governance and structure of the blockchain network that will be most appropriate to enable success and long-term sustenance of the blockchain network over time.

Figure 4-3 shows three possible blockchain networks.

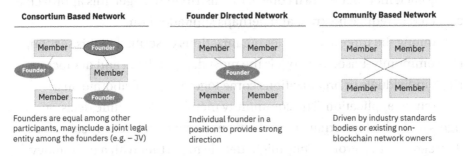

Figure 4-3. *Blockchain stakeholder organizational models*

The consortium-based network has multiple founders who collectively govern the blockchain network, recruit members and determine decision rights among themselves and for the members. The consortium usually provides the technology platform that members can use and assists them with implementation and training. There are several consortium-based networks that are either already in operation or being proposed for banking, insurance, and other industries. Consortium-based networks should be careful of violating antitrust regulations or being accused of collusion.

A founder-directed network usually starts with a company that is powerful within an industry or a specific value chain. This company usually partners with a technology company to propose a blockchain solution that it sponsors and recruits its suppliers and, in rare cases, customers and competitors to join as members. The founder is responsible for the governance of this blockchain network and for determining the decision rights for the founders. We can consider this type of blockchain to be centralized around the founder and concentrating power in the founder. In a lot of ways, it can be considered similar to the centralized data sharing systems that have, in retrospect, not impacted the three R's of inefficiency (redundant work, rework, and reconciliation work). By giving each member its own copy of the distributed ledger, this approach is expected to reduce mistrust and perhaps spur adoption.

Among the three stakeholder organizations described in this section, the community-based network is the most decentralized and democratic. Here, individuals or organizations come together to collaborate on a blockchain application. The community members determine decision rights and adopt governance mechanisms using democratic means that they agree to as a group. They might decide to partner with a technology company to help community members adopt, install, and get training on the blockchain technology. Examples of community-based networks could be artists collaborating to develop a blockchain network to protect and monetize intellectual property rights. Community-based blockchain networks need to think through how they plan to evolve their governance mechanisms based on feedback and input from new members who were perhaps not involved when the blockchain network was first formed.

In this section, we have discussed design decisions related to the management and the governance of the blockchain network tailored to permissioned blockchain networks. While governance is an issue for public blockchains as well, it is not something that system designers using the public blockchain for application development can influence.

In this section, we did not discuss stakeholder organization decisions related to sponsorship, roles, and responsibilities of the stakeholders in the project charged with creating the blockchain-based application. While these decisions are important and critical to ensuring the success of the project, and perhaps more complicated than similar decisions related to nonblockchain technology projects, we did not consider them design decisions related to the implementation of a blockchain-based solution.

Development stack: The last design decision that blockchain application system designers need to grapple with is understanding the architectural layers of a blockchain application, the development tools that they need to select to support the application development, and the application process that they will adopt to ensure a quality blockchain application.

Let's start by understanding the five architectural layers as described by Lesavre, Varin, and Yaga (2021) and depicted in Figure 4-4.

Application Layer	**User Interfaces**	
Integration Layer	**Middleware**	*Second Layer Execution* **Off-Chain Schemes**
Blockchain Layer	*Smart Contract Layer* **Custom Bytecodes (Compiled Smart Contracts)** *Base Protocol Layer* **Execution Environment** **Consensus Service Global State Storage**	
Network Layer	**Peer-to-Peer Communication**	
Physical Layer	**Node Hardware**	

Figure 4-4. *Blockchain application architectural layers*

The physical layer consists of the hardware used by any node computer in the blockchain network. In general, we would like our blockchain to be hardware agnostic and support diverse hardware-operating system configurations. In particular, it is a good design approach to not require any hardware that is specialized – as a best practice, we prefer our physical layer to be commodity hardware.

The network layer consists of software that manages the peer-to-peer communication between the peer nodes of a blockchain network.

The blockchain layer depicted in Figure 4-4 is sometimes referred to as Layer 1 of a blockchain implementation. It consists of the storage structures and mechanisms of the global data within a blockchain – the distributed ledger, the service that executes the consensus protocol, and the execution environment for the smart contract. Collectively, this capability is referred to as the base protocol layer. The smart contract layer consists of the compiled smart contract software that can be executed by the base protocol layer. The software in the smart contract layer is sometimes referred to as the chain code – since this is the software that will be executed on every node of the blockchain. Blockchain system designers do not need to be concerned with the implementation details associated with the base protocol layer other than understanding how it works to assess efficiency and power consumption requirements. Blockchain system designers will need to focus on the development of the chain code or the smart contracts that will be required for their business. In developing the software for smart contracts, they need to understand the programming constructs supported by the smart contract execution environment. In this layer, development tools will be required to support the application development process. These tools will include at least a development distributed ledger and an interactive development environment to support the creation and testing of the smart contracts.

The integration layer depicted in Figure 4-4 is sometimes referred to as Layer 2 of a blockchain implementation.[10] The integration layer needs to provide capabilities for the storage structures and mechanisms for all the off-chain data and any software that needs to be executed "off-chain" (referred to as off-chain code). The off-chain code at a high level has two functions: meet the data needs of the smart contracts in the blockchain layer and transform the data from the blockchain layer to meet the needs of the application layer. In the integration layer, the development tools that will be required would be an API (Application Programming Interface) to access the blockchain layer. The integration layer can also include middleware software that enables integration with other blockchains or other data and computational resources.

---

[10] You might from time to time read in the press about innovations being made within blockchain implementations. These innovations will sometimes be referred to as Layer 1 or Layer 2 innovations depending on where in the blockchain architecture these innovations are located. Making Layer 1 changes and having them adopted is usually a much more complex endeavor than making Layer 2 changes.

The application layer contains the interface for the blockchain application. This layer can be a web-based application or a mobile application. This is the layer that would house the wallet that stores the private keys for a user. Development tools in this layer can include wallet browser plug-ins.

Figure 4-5 depicts a high-level development cycle for a blockchain application.

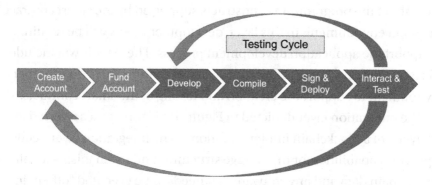

Figure 4-5. *Blockchain application development process*

The process consists of creating accounts representing the application or the users of the application on a development blockchain instance. These accounts are then funded, if the blockchain implementation being used has a native (or protocol) token. The rest of the effort involves developing the associated smart contracts; compiling these smart contracts to bytecode; signing and deploying the smart contract, first to the development blockchain instance and then to a test blockchain instance (sometimes referred to as a testnet); and then interacting and testing the application through the application interface. Once testing and validation are complete, the application can be deployed to the production blockchain (sometimes referred to as the mainnet) following a similar process of creating an account, funding the account (if necessary), and signing and deploying the smart contracts.

In this section, we have reviewed in detail the seven design decisions that blockchain system designers need to contend with. We will now describe illustrative blockchain applications in finance, healthcare, supply chain, and entertainment.

Blockchain Applications

Blockchain applications are being conceived and implemented in a variety of industries. Three excellent sources for understanding these case studies are the Hyperledger Foundation (`www.hyperledger.org/learn/case-studies`), the Blockchain Research Institute (`www.blockchainresearchinstitute.org/7914-2/`), and the Enterprise Ethereum Alliance (`https://entethalliance.org/use-cases/`). We will describe blockchain applications using a common structure. We will first start with a high-level description of the current state of the industry and understand the economic inefficiencies plaguing the industry. We will then enumerate business areas where the application of blockchain will alleviate the economic inefficiencies. In some instances, we will provide specific examples of blockchain applications that are already in production.

Blockchain Finance Applications

The financial services industry can be considered as comprising the following sectors: banking; credit cards; custody and trading of equities, bonds, commodities, and other financial instruments; loan underwriting; origination and servicing; and a range of advisory services from corporate mergers and acquisitions to investment advice. While we can lump all these sectors together under financial services because they all appear to have similar economic inefficiencies, these sectors are operationally quite different, and firms who operate in more than one sector have to contend with complex regulations to ensure that services in one sector are not used to manipulate services in another sector.

The financial services industry is the quintessential third party, though there are certain sectors where they add knowledge-based value, such as in the creation of derivative financial instruments and the provision of educational, advisory, and consultative services. Whenever we discuss reducing economic inefficiencies, it will involve tremendous displacement and disruption of the labor force. This makes it important to underscore the value-added sectors of an industry that have growth potential.

The capabilities of the financial services industry are buttressed by an immense and complex operations stack that includes clearinghouses for transfers, settlements, credit card processing networks, custodial management for asset ownership, and auditing, reconciliation, and reporting that is required for both transactional record-keeping and regulatory compliance. In our current systems environment, these operational services are essential and costly. The firms providing these services need to recover their costs and make a profit, leading to the fees that we bemoan, but acknowledge their necessity in the current environment. In several instances, these fees are exorbitant and do not necessarily represent just the cost plus profit but a pricing based on what the markets are willing to bear and the firms can get away with.

Economic inefficiencies associated with long settlement times (ranging from 24 hours for the settlement of equity trades to as many as 14 days for the settlement of international transfers) and third party fees are not the only economic inefficiencies that the financial industry needs to grapple with. Constraints imposed by government regulations and voluntary acceptance of rules/norms prescribed by professional organizations have also led to economic inefficiencies, though many of the regulations, rules, and norms start off with good intentions. Participation in the financial services industry requires consumers to make an immense privacy trade-off and establish their identity using mechanisms prescribed by the financial industry and/or government regulations. Consumers who, for one reason or another, are unable to conform to these requirements are cut out of the financial services industry. The Federal Deposit Insurance Corporation (FDIC) estimated that in 2019, 5.4% or 7.1 million households in the United States were "unbanked" (`www.fdic.gov/analysis/household-survey/index.html`) and did not consume financial services. Finally, the centralized databases held by financial services firms represent an attractive target for data breaches. According to the Verizon Data Breach Investigation Report (DBIR), the financial and insurance industries had 467 incidences of confirmed data disclosure in 2020.[11] These data breaches led to the unauthorized disclosure of personal data, internal bank data, and data about credentials.

The financial services industry has made a lot of progress in reducing the three R's – redundant work, rework, and reconciliation work – in all of its sectors except loan origination and underwriting. Except for loans, almost all data transfers in the financial services industry are electronic, and firms across the industry have standardized the syntax and semantics of data exchanges. Some of this standardization, though not all of it, was spurred on by compliance requirements mandated by various governmental jurisdictions. Due to these efforts, the reduction of inefficiencies associated with the three R's is not a major focus for blockchain applications in the financial services industry except for lending operations.

The themes addressed by blockchain applications in the financial services industry include payments with quicker settlement times and reduced fees, creation and management of digital assets, simplification and automation of operational processes, and the resulting increase in transparency. Collectively, these applications are being referred to as Decentralized Finance or DeFi.

---

[11] `www.verizon.com/business/resources/reports/2021/2021-data-breach-investigations-report.pdf`

- Ripple Labs (https://ripple.com/) has been successful working with banks on blockchain-based cross-border payments and transfers. Ripple's success has led to a partnership with SWIFT (Society for Worldwide Interbank Financial Telecommunications), the incumbent backbone for global currency transfers.

- Quorum is an open source blockchain platform based on Enterprise Ethereum (www.kaleido.io/blockchain-platform/quorum) founded by JPMorgan Chase. Quorum is used to build permissioned blockchain applications. According to Geroni (2021), Quorum is being used by financial firms such as the ING Group, Ant Group, HSBC, and JPMorgan Chase for commercial bank payments, exchanging information regarding sanctions, trade finance, institutional trading, capital market data, commodity posttrade processing, loan marketplaces and issuing debts, and interbank payments in association with central banks.

- Corda (www.corda.net) is a permissioned blockchain platform that has been used by institutions such as Nasdaq for capital markets solutions, Wells Fargo for banking, and Siam Commercial Bank for trade finance.

- Decentralized Autonomous Organizations (DAOs) are blockchain-based solutions that enable individuals around the world to organize and manage themselves without a controlling, centralized, management hierarchy. DAOs have been set up to raise and disburse private equity funds (see, e.g., https://dao.vc/), charitable contributions (e.g., Endaoment, https://endaoment.org/), social impact activism (e.g., Big

Green DAO, https://dao.biggreen.org/), and
microfinance lending (e.g., DLN – Distributed Loan
Network, https://dln.org/).

- Figure (www.figure.com/blockchain/) is a blockchain
solution to reduce economic inefficiencies associated
with the three R's in originating and underwriting of
mortgage loans.

These blockchain solutions provide access to financial services
without a centralized platform or party controlling the transactions or
extracting fees for facilitating the transactions. Transaction records, audit
trails, reporting, and reconciliation are automated by-products from these
trading platforms. While themselves not decentralized platforms, PayPal,
Venmo, and Square's Cash App[12] all support cryptocurrency transactions.
Trading records, spending records, and mortgage loan originations are
all activities that can be facilitated through a blockchain but without the
involvement of third parties as we do today. Similarly, several leading firms
such as AT&T, Amazon, Home Depot, Overstock, and Whole Foods accept
cryptocurrencies for ecommerce transactions.

Finally, let's comment on two other blockchain-related financial
applications: crypto exchanges and Central Bank Digital Currency (CBDC).

While crypto exchanges such as Binance, Gemini, Coinbase, and FTX
are used by people to trade cryptocurrencies, their trading platforms have
centralized ledgers with all the associated risks and pitfalls that we have
discussed earlier.[13] Crypto exchanges also need to comply with regulations
related to "Know Your Customer" or KYC.[14] Wallets obtained from these

---

[12] Square's point-of-sale application as of yet does not accept cryptocurrencies.

[13] We distinguish between Binance, the entity, which is decentralized with no
formal headquarters, and its trading platform. Binance also offers the Binance
Smart Chain ecosystem for building DeFi applications.

[14] Know Your Customer Quick Reference Guide – www.pwc.com/gx/en/financial-
services/publications/assets/pwc-anti-money-laundering-2016.pdf

crypto exchanges can be subpoenaed by law enforcement to obtain the mapping between one's identity and one's public key.

CBDCs are currencies that central banks of countries are introducing as the digital equivalent of fiat currencies. China launched a pilot for the digital yuan, e-CNY, in April 2020 and expanded the pilot in January 2022. The e-CNY works through a mobile app, and it is estimated that e-CNY app has over 260 million users.[15] India disclosed plans to launch the digital rupee by early 2023.[16] In the United States, the Federal Reserve published a white paper in January 2022 to "foster a broad and transparent public dialogue about CBDCs in general, and about the potential benefits and risks of a U.S. CBDC."[17] While the economic potential for CBDCs is impressive, it is not clear sovereign governments are implementing, or will implement, CBDCs using a distributed ledger or a blockchain. They can choose to implement CBDCs as a centralized ledger. This will enormously expand the power of the government to further centralize monetary and financial activities within a country. A CBDC will also further increase the surveillance powers of the state and do away with the anonymity of cash. Before advocating for or adopting CBDCs, we need to examine the underlying implementation and the regulatory regime under which CBDCs will operate.

This has been a very quick overview of blockchain finance applications, and we have only truly scratched the surface. According to CB Insights, venture capital funding for DeFi grew by 851% in 2021 compared to 2020 to reach $3.4B.[18] Funding was also strong for crypto

---

[15] https://techcrunch.com/2022/01/18/chinas-digital-yuan-wallet-now-has-260-million-individual-users/

[16] https://economictimes.indiatimes.com/news/economy/policy/indias-digital-currency-to-debut-by-early-2023/articleshow/89379626.cms

[17] www.federalreserve.gov/publications/files/money-and-payments-20220120.pdf

[18] www.cbinsights.com/reports/CB-Insights_Blockchain-Report-2021.pdf

exchanges and brokerages (remember, these might not be decentralized), custody and wallet providers, and NFTs.

Next, we examine blockchain applications for healthcare.

Blockchain Healthcare Applications

In this section, we will focus on the healthcare system in the United States, even though much of what we will describe in this section could apply to healthcare systems that rely on a combination of government and private health insurance to pay for healthcare. Some of the applications we describe could, theoretically, be beneficial to government-run single-payer healthcare systems as well, but because of our lack of experience with such systems, we do not feel comfortable making that claim.

In the healthcare system in the United States, consumers interact with clinical providers such as primary care physicians, specialty physicians, nurses, therapists, pharmacists, clinical technicians, home health aides, hospital health systems, diagnostic laboratories, pharmacies, nursing homes, and home healthcare providers. The value exchange in health care happens during the interactions between the healthcare consumer and the clinical provider. However, the remuneration for the clinical provider for the value provided during the exchange goes through a complex web of third-party administrators as shown in Figure 4-6. These third-party administrators include for the most part healthcare insurance companies and prescription benefit managers. There are other actors involved as well who work at the behest of the health insurance companies, providing data verification, data aggregation, clinical necessity verification, and other such services that are ostensibly set up to assist consumers and optimize healthcare spend, but in reality act as barriers to value exchange between the consumers and clinical provider and obfuscate the cost of healthcare services.

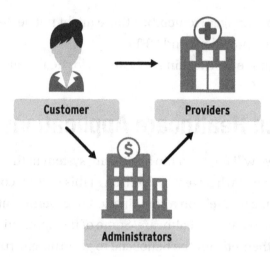

Figure 4-6. *Third-party administrators in the US healthcare system*

According to the Centers for Medicare and Medicaid Services (CMS), in 2020, the share of every dollar spent on healthcare was broken down as follows:[19]

- The federal government spends 36 cents.

- The consumer spends 26 cents.

- Private businesses spend 17 cents.

- State and local government since spend 14 cents.

- Other private entities spend about 7 cents.

Since federal, state, and local government spending is funded by citizen taxpayers, consumers are shouldering, in total, 76% of healthcare spend through direct and indirect outlays. These outlays are in part funding the for-profit third-party administrators who are providing the platform for payment calculation, collection, and reimbursement. It seems to us that we can do better!

---

[19] www.cms.gov/files/document/highlights.pdf

In addition to the third-party administrators and their delegated service providers, there are other stakeholders in the healthcare system. These stakeholders include pharmaceutical manufacturers, medical device manufacturers, and firms that provide information technology to clinical providers, consumers, and third-party administrators. The value exchange of these stakeholders with the consumer requires approval and authorization by clinical providers. However, third-party administrators are responsible for managing remuneration to these stakeholders as well and often further complicate this tri-party value exchange.

In addition to these stakeholders, the healthcare system in the United States includes research, public health, and regulatory agencies at the federal level such as CMS, the Food and Drug Administration (FDA), the Centers for Disease Control and Prevention (CDC), and the National Institutes of Health (NIH). Regulatory and public health organizations from state and local governments also play an important role in the delivery of healthcare in the United States. Finally, advocacy organizations that represent the health insurance companies, the prescription benefit managers, the hospital health systems, the pharmaceutical manufacturers, and the clinical providers (doctors, nurses, and pharmacists) work hard to tilt healthcare policy in their favor. It should be noted that there isn't an organized advocacy group for consumers in general, though there are advocacy groups for consumers who are dealing with specific health conditions (such as autism, scleroderma, and breast cancer).

We take the time to describe all these stakeholders so that it can be understood how the complexity of the healthcare system overshadows the value exchange between the consumer and the clinical provider. Power in the healthcare system has by and large devolved to the third-party administrators and the advocacy groups, even though they are superfluous in the value exchange.

Let us now look at the economic inefficiencies in the healthcare system by examining the seven main economic inefficiencies:

- Time to settle transactions in the healthcare system

  In general, about 80% of healthcare claims for payment calculation are finalized in less than two weeks; the remaining 20% of claims can take over six months to settle. CMS estimates that healthcare spending in 2020 was $4.1 trillion.[20] Twenty percent of this large number is more than $800 billion representing an immense improvement opportunity.

- Fees paid to third parties for non-value-added activities

  We can consider the profits at the health insurance companies and pharmaceutical benefit managers as well as the annual budgeted spend of the advocacy organizations as if they are fees paid to third parties for non-value-added activities.

- Data-related redundant work, rework, and reconciliation work

  We have data issues that lead to administrative waste, unnecessary care, and avoidable errors.

  Shrank, Rogstad, and Parekh (2019) report and confirm that 30% of the approximately $4 trillion spent on healthcare is considered waste or non-value-added. We believe this does not include the inefficiencies related to the third parties.

---

[20] www.cms.gov/files/document/highlights.pdf

In addition, the United States leads all countries in the amount of healthcare dollars that are spent on administrative tasks (Papanicolas, Woskie, and Jha, 2018).

- Fraud

  A 2011 estimate from LexisNexis estimated that 3% of spending in healthcare is lost to fraud.[21] Other estimates put the cost of fraud in healthcare to be closer to 5.5%. Three percent of 2020 healthcare spending would be the equivalent of approximately $120 billion.

- Regulations

  There is a patchwork of state and federal rules and regulations that are there to protect the consumers, but it's not clear that they end up doing that work.

- Privacy trade-off

  Consumers do not control their data. Their data is held for the benefit of the third-party providers.

- Data security

  According to the Verizon DBIR, the healthcare industry had 472 incidences of confirmed data disclosure in 2020.[22] These data breaches led to the unauthorized disclosure of personal data, medical data, and data about credentials.

---

[21] http://lexisnexis.com/risk/downloads/idm/bending-the-cost-curve-analytic-driven-enterprise-fraud-control.pdf
[22] www.verizon.com/business/resources/reports/2021/2021-data-breach-investigations-report.pdf

Target blockchain healthcare applications are focused on reducing economic inefficiencies related to the three R's, increasing operational transparency, and giving consumers control over their data. None of the applications are aiming to reduce or eliminate the role played by the third-party administrators since that would be a disruption that would most likely impede successful adoption. Many of the applications are actually being led by consortiums of third-party providers. Hashed Health (`https://hashedhealth.com/`) has emerged as an important catalyst for bringing healthcare stakeholders together to explore distributed ledger applications. Applications of blockchain in healthcare include the following:

- Claims processing

  Providing transparency of claims processing status and increasing the transparency of processing logic with smart contracts would be important in reducing economic inefficiencies for rework and reconciliation work as well as fraud. This could also reduce the settlement time for all claims, especially the 20% of claims that currently can take several months to settle. Claims processing represents a substantial legacy operations and technology footprint for health insurance companies. Any disruption in this area is fraught with risk.

- Provider credentialing

  Clinical providers have to present credentials to hospital systems before they are granted privileges to practice within a particular hospital system. Provider credentialing represents a significant amount of redundant work across the healthcare ecosystem. A blockchain application for provider credentialing will reduce economic inefficiencies with this redundant work as well as rework when provider credentials are not appropriately maintained. They also have the potential to reduce fraud. A provider credentialing blockchain application can also likely be integrated within the current legacy technology environment so there is a higher potential for successful adoption.

- Prior authorization processing

  Blockchain-based prior authorization processing is another use case that can be integrated into the healthcare legacy technology footprint. Automation through smart contracts can reduce economic inefficiencies as well as healthcare errors. A blockchain-based system will also protect privacy since patient data will not have to be shared beyond the provider and third-party administrator.

- Healthcare supply chain

  Supply chain issues in healthcare, specifically with medical devices and the tracking of prescription drugs, especially controlled substances such as opioids, where the provenance of the data is important, are an excellent use case for a blockchain application. The FDA in support of the US Drug Supply Chain Security Act (DSCSA) has begun a pilot program with KPMG, Merck, and Walmart to track and trace prescription medicines and vaccines.

- Clinical trials

  Clinical trials in the United States are rife with inefficiencies since it is difficult to recruit the appropriate patients and track the patients through the trial and ensuring appropriate provenance for reporting to the FDA is slow and manual. This use case is another good target for a blockchain-based application (Zhuang et al., 2020).

- Data sovereignty for the patient

  There are also blockchain use cases where if we can get the data to the patient with the patient having the control and being the sovereign, we can make sure that that data is available at the appropriate points in the healthcare system, which will also lead to efficiencies.

While there are a lot of potential blockchain applications in healthcare, the healthcare industry usually lags other industries in adopting technology. Successfully implementing technology projects in healthcare has historically been challenging, so our recommendation is to proceed with those use cases that can be integrated into the legacy technology and operations footprint. This is also an industry where incumbent power is respected by the consumers in spite of their overall frustrations. So our advice is to proceed with caution and deliberation.

Next, we will examine blockchain applications for improving the supply chain.

Blockchain Supply Chain Applications

Supply chains involve multiple parties, and between these multiple parties, we have product flows, information flows, and finance flows in multiple directions. This cross-border movement of goods and payments is heavily regulated, and it is very difficult to keep the product, information, and finance flows synchronized. Visibility in a supply chain is usually one level deep. You can only have visibility into the partner you are interacting with, not the partners of that partner. This creates inefficiencies in terms of availability of information as well as latency and volatility of information.

Each party in the supply chain tends to keep their own ledger with their own semantics. A breach anywhere in the supply chain affects the entire supply chain because of the interdependencies among all parties. Because of the complexity of the supply chain, there is potential for fraud and administrative waste.

In terms of supply chain inefficiencies, cross-border payments take an inordinate amount of time to settle. They involve uncertainty, not just in terms of exchange rates but also in terms of regulations and fees. There is quite a bit of reconciliation and redundant work that consumes a lot of labor for each party involved in the supply chain.

Fraud is rampant in the supply chain, not only in terms of fake goods and mislabeled goods but also because there is a patchwork of regulations across jurisdictions that is exploited by unscrupulous parties. The impact of any security breach is material to all parties involved.

Blockchain has a huge potential to improve the efficiency of a supply chain. Let's look at two examples.

- First is a project called Trade Lens. Trade Lens was developed by IBM and a company that spun out of Maersk called GTD Solution, Inc.. The goal here is global trade digitization. Trade Lens is an ecosystem of all of the parties involved in the transportation of goods within the supply chain. So we'll have all the third-party logistics providers and all the inland and intermodal providers such as trucks and railways. We also have ports and terminals as well as ocean carriers – the largest ocean carriers, including Maersk, the Mediterranean shipping company. All of these competitors join together to improve the efficiency of the overall system. Trade Lens has more than 175 participants right now. They process more than 2 million events per day on their Hyperledger-based blockchain.

- The second example we'll look at is the blockchain sponsored by Walmart for food safety. This is also implemented in Hyperledger. It includes Walmart and all of its food suppliers. The goal is to track each food item from the farm to the store to the consumers. This not only improves the transparency and visibility of goods in the supply chain but also helps rapidly track the source of any health issue. In the past, if there was an *E. coli* breakout, it would take Walmart weeks to track down the source of the issue. This leads to food waste and uncertainty among consumers. Now, with this blockchain-based system, Walmart can track a breakout in hours and alert the public. This allows Walmart to only recall the product that is affected rather than unnecessarily wasting a lot more product.

Blockchain Entertainment Applications

In this section, we will describe the potential of blockchain applications in the arts and entertainment industry, or broadly, in the creative intellectual property industry.

This industry as a whole, like healthcare, includes a lot of complexity where the relationship between the artist and the appreciator is mediated by several third parties ostensibly for the purpose of economies of scale, marketing, and branding. However, these third parties tend to take an enormous chunk of value out of the exchange between the artist and the appreciator, negatively impacting both the artist and the appreciator.

Let's take a look at the complexities:

- Each piece of art, whether it's music, audio, or any kind of intellectual property, can have multiple creators, and the remuneration among the multiple artists is usually quite complex.

- Art can be distributed via multiple media with complex different remuneration arrangements, so somebody can have the rights to a particular media for a particular amount of time and for a particular geography. The rights of art are sliced and diced in ways that add to the inherent complexity of the remuneration.

- There are usually two types of remuneration in the art industry: first, the acquisition of the original piece of art or intellectual property and second, the reuse remuneration, also known as royalties. Royalties can be paid when art is reused either in its entirety or when portions of it are reused.

- There are also scenarios where some of the art is commissioned on a work-for-hire basis, and the remuneration of this kind of art can be even more complex.

- Remuneration especially related to reuse, or royalties, can take months to be distributed.

While the complexity of the remuneration creates a need for platforms and third parties for the efficient and scalable distribution of art, the third parties who are the owners of these platforms have outsized power over the artists. The platform tells artists what their royalty-related remuneration should be, and they can either take it as is or they can request an audit. Most audits can take an enormously long time, and in the audit, the data is completely controlled by the platform or by the third party giving them enormous amounts of power.

The appreciator ends up being a passive consumer even though the value of art is directly created by its consumption by the appreciator. There is very little interaction happening between the appreciator and the artist, and the artist is really not controlling the relationship even though it might seem like they are.

With this background, let's look at the inefficiencies in the arts and entertainment industry.

- Transactions take, what seems like, forever to settle. It is not uncommon for royalty-related transactions to take over a year to settle.

- While third parties are needed for marketing and distribution scale, the balance of power is tilted disproportionately toward the third parties who control the platform.

- Data is centralized and not shared, audit rights are cumbersome, and in most cases, efficient ledgers simply do not exist.

- Fraud can consist of impersonation, unauthorized duplication, and creating fake works.

In addition to all these inefficiencies, the regulations in this industry favor the platforms and the third parties. This is an industry that is ripe for disruption with blockchain. While there is a lot of incumbent power as well as legacy technology and operations, this industry has been disrupted before and can be disrupted again. Previous disruptions in the industry ended up creating new centers of power and did not really alter the relationship between the artist and the appreciator.

The potential for blockchain is to have a disruption that does not result in another centralized source of power.

Chapter Summary/Key Takeaways

Key takeaways from this chapter are as follows:

- Applications developed using blockchain should be mindful of all the lessons learned and critical success factors associated with large-scale technology deployments.

- Blockchain-based solutions are suitable for business problems related to time to settle transactions; fees paid to third parties for non-value-added activities; data-related redundant work, rework, and reconciliation work; constraints imposed by government regulations and other nongovernmental rules; high incidence of fraud; privacy leaks during value exchange; and data security risks.

- Blockchain solutions are suitable for applications related to payments, transparency, and data sovereignty.

- Blockchain solutions should be preferred over traditional solutions only if multiple parties are expected to write to a transaction ledger, these parties do not trust one another, and no convenient and trusted third party is available.

- The implementation of blockchain-based solutions requires system designers to make design decisions related to transactions, tokens, smart contracts, data, consensus mechanism, stakeholder organization, and development stack.

- The themes addressed by blockchain applications in the financial services industry include payments with quicker settlement times and reduced fees, creation and management of digital assets, simplification and automation of operational processes, and the resulting increase in transparency.

- Target blockchain healthcare applications are focused on reducing economic inefficiencies related to the three R's, increasing operational transparency, and giving consumers control over their data.

- Blockchain applications in the supply chain are focused on improving transparency, reducing administrative waste, speeding cross-border payments, and tackling fraud.

- Entertainment applications with blockchain tackle transparency, reduction of settlement times and administrative waste, as well as balancing power between artists and centralized platforms.

In the next chapter, you will learn about the technical details of the Bitcoin blockchain implementation. We will also provide a quick overview of Ethereum and Hyperledger; a comparison of Bitcoin, Ethereum, and Hyperledger Fabric; and a quick rundown of emerging blockchain developments.

Quiz Questions

1. What is the application theme that does not align with the capabilities of a blockchain solution?

    a. Payments

    b. Business process reengineering

    c. Data sovereignty

    d. Transparency

2. True or False: A blockchain solution is not needed if multiple parties write to a transaction ledger in the presence of a trusted and convenient third party.

3. What type of blockchain should be used if all parties who write to a transaction ledger are known and public verification of transactions is not needed?

    a. Permissionless

    b. Private permissioned

    c. Public permissioned

    d. None of the above

4. Among the blockchain application layers listed in the following, which layer is considered "Layer 1" of a blockchain implementation?

   a. Physical layer

   b. Network layer

   c. Blockchain layer

   d. Integration layer

   e. Application layer

5. Among the blockchain application layers listed in the following, which layer is considered "Layer 2" of a blockchain implementation?

   a. Physical layer

   b. Network layer

   c. Blockchain layer

   d. Integration layer

   e. Application layer

6. Ethereum is a _____ type of token.

7. What are two types of classifications of tokens? What are their subclassifications?

8. Describe the three data design challenges, specifically related to the implementation of blockchain-based solutions.

9. Execution of every smart contract requires the same amount of computational power and in turn costs the same fee. True or False.

10. What are the three possible models for organizing blockchain networks? Please elaborate on their advantages and disadvantages.

References

Wust, K., Gervais, A. 2018. Do you need a blockchain? 2018 Crypto Valley Conference on Blockchain Technology (CVCBT), 2018, pp. 45–54, DOI: 10.1109/CVCBT.2018.00011. https://ieeexplore.ieee.org/document/8525392

Tapscott, D. Tapscott, A. 2018. Blockchain revolution: How the technology behind Bitcoin and other cryptocurrencies is changing the world. 2018. Portfolio/Penguin. New York, NY.

Freni, P., Ferro, E., Moncada, R. 2020. Tokenization and blockchain tokens classification: A morphological framework. 2020 IEEE Symposium on Computers and Communications (ISCC), 2020, pp. 1–6, doi: 10.1109/ISCC50000.2020.9219709

Ankenbrand, T., Bieri, D., Cortivo, R., Hoehener, J., Hardjono, T., 2020. Proposal for a comprehensive (crypto) asset taxonomy. https://arxiv.org/pdf/2007.11877.pdf

Tapscott, D. 2020. Token taxonomy: The need for open-source standards around digital assets," Blockchain Research Institute, 19 Feb. 2020, adapted 16 June 2020. https://interwork.org/wp-content/uploads/2020/07/Tapscott_Token-Taxonomy_Blockchain-Research-Institute_InterWorkAlliance.pdf

Mehar, M. I., Shier, C. L., Giambattista, A., Gong, E., Fletcher, G., Sanayhie, R., Kim, H. M., & Laskowski, M. (2019). Understanding a Revolutionary and Flawed Grand Experiment in Blockchain: The DAO Attack. Journal of Cases on Information Technology (JCIT), 21(1), 19–32. https://doi.org/10.4018/JCIT.2019010102

Caldarelli, G. 2020. Understanding the blockchain oracle problem: A call for action. Information 2020, 11, 509; doi:10.3390/info11110509 www.mdpi.com/journal/information

Huang, H., Lin, J., Zheng, B., Zheng, Z., Bian, J. 2020. When blockchain meets distributed file systems: An overview, challenges, and open issues. IEEE Access. Volume 8, 2020. DOI: 10.1109/ACCESS.2020.2979881 https://ieeexplore.ieee.org/stamp/stamp.jsp?arnumber=9031420

Lesavre, L., Varin, P., Yaga, D. 2021. Blockchain networks: Token design and management overview. National Institute of Standards and Technology. https://doi.org/10.6028/NIST.IR.8301

Geroni, D. 2021. Quorum blockchain and their use cases a comprehensive guide. June 2021. https://101blockchains.com/quorum-blockchain-use-cases/

Shrank WH, Rogstad TL, Parekh N. 2019. Waste in the US Health Care System: Estimated Costs and Potential for Savings. *JAMA*. 2019;322(15):1501–1509. doi:10.1001/jama.2019.13978

Papanicolas, I., Woskie, L., Jha, A. 2018. Health care spending in the United States and other high-income countries. JAMA. 2018;319(10):1024–1039. doi:10.1001/jama.2018.1150

Zhuang, Y., Sheets, L. R., Shae, Z., Chen, Y. W., Tsai, J., & Shyu, C. R. (2020). Applying Blockchain Technology to Enhance Clinical Trial Recruitment. AMIA ... Annual Symposium proceedings. AMIA Symposium, 2019, 1276–1285

CHAPTER 5

Blockchain Implementations Overview: Bitcoin, Ethereum, and Hyperledger

Bitcoin, introduced in 2008, is considered the first implementation of blockchain. Subsequent implementations of blockchain have made changes to Bitcoin to ease application development, improve scalability, and enhance versatility in terms of the types of applications that can be created.

Introduction

We started this book by grounding ourselves and understanding the seven economic inefficiencies – time to settle transactions; fees paid to third parties for non-value-added activities; data-related redundant work, rework, and reconciliation work (the three Rs); rules and regulations from

© Weijia Zhang and Tej Anand 2022
W. Zhang and T. Anand, *Blockchain and Ethereum Smart Contract Solution Development*,
https://doi.org/10.1007/978-1-4842-8164-2_5

governmental and nongovernmental organizations; fraud; privacy trade-off; and data security – that our current technologies have not been able to address. We attributed this to the inability of our systems to create trust among inherently untrusting transacting parties.

After reviewing the capabilities and design issues with technologies associated with cryptography, distributed systems, and peer-to-peer networking, we discussed how these technologies can be integrated to create a blockchain system that includes four major components: distributed ledger, privacy preservation, consensus, and smart contracts. After conceptually exploring how these four components of blockchain work together to address the seven economic inefficiencies, we took an in-depth look at when blockchain is a suitable technology for addressing business problems; we provided design guidelines for building blockchain-based applications and provided examples of use cases for blockchain applications in finance, healthcare, supply chain, and entertainment.

Armed with all this knowledge, we feel it is necessary and appropriate to understand at a sufficient technical depth the original cryptocurrency and blockchain implementation, Bitcoin.

Bitcoin was introduced to the world through a paper published under the pseudonym Nakamoto (2008), to coincide with the subprime financial crisis that had undermined confidence in the banking system. Though Bitcoin was not the first electronic cash system implemented, it was the first system to include a credible solution for mitigating the double spend problem (Lee, Choi & Rhee, 2003). Nakamoto created the first block, referred to as the genesis block, in the Bitcoin blockchain on Jan 3, 2009, mining 50 BTCs (Bitcoins) for himself, and then on Jan 12, 2009, sent ten BTCs to Hal Finney,[1] a cryptographer, as the first transaction on the

---

[1] Hal Finney's obituary when he passed away in 2014 – www.nytimes.com/2014/08/31/business/hal-finney-cryptographer-and-bitcoin-pioneer-dies-at-58.html

Bitcoin blockchain. After Nakamoto shared the original paper to an email list, there were a flurry of comments from other researchers, highlighting issues that Nakamoto responded to. The email thread is archived at https://satoshi.nakamotoinstitute.org/emails/cryptography/threads/1/#014810.

In this chapter, we will describe Bitcoin at a technical level.[2] We will also provide a very brief overview of Ethereum and Hyperledger and a comparison of these three blockchain implementations. We also provide a brief overview of several consensus protocols that are being considered and used instead of the consensus protocol used in Bitcoin. We will end this chapter with a very brief summary of recent emerging developments.

Bitcoin Transactions, Blocks, and Mining

Let us start by looking at the life cycle of a Bitcoin transaction by reviewing how the Bitcoin blockchain will instantiate a payment from Alex to Sonia as shown in Figure 5-1.

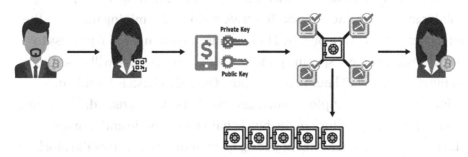

Figure 5-1. *Bitcoin transaction life cycle*

Alex starts by opening his digital Bitcoin wallet. In this wallet, Alex has all the money that he can theoretically spend. Alex now wants to spend

---

[2] Antonopoulos (2017) provides far more comprehensive technical description of Bitcoin.

some of his money by sending it to Sonia. To do that, he scans or copies
Sonia's address. This is Sonia's public key. He then fills the amount that
he would like to send, and he decides what fee he wants to give for this
transaction. He then hits the proverbial send button. So look at how Alex is
in control and determines the transaction fee that he wants to spend.

Once Alex has entered Sonia's address and entered the amount of
money he wants to send and the transaction fee that he is willing to pay,
Alex's wallet software signs this transaction with Alex's private key, formats
the transaction that will include the conditions that the receiver (Sonia)
will need to meet (custody of their private key) to spend the money, and
communicates this transaction to other nodes that are running the Bitcoin
software.

When a Bitcoin node receives Alex's transaction, it verifies that the
transaction is formatted correctly, the addresses in the transaction are
valid, and Alex met the conditions that were imposed on him before he
could spend the money that he is now sending to Sonia. The node[3] then
adds this transaction to a list of verified transactions that it maintains.

Some Bitcoin nodes serve as "miners" – these mining nodes package
valid transactions into a block. To create a block, the mining nodes do the
equivalent of solving a puzzle. They execute a computational process to
find a hash that has a specific pattern. This is a process we will describe
in much more detail later in the chapter. Once this hash is found, the
mining process is complete, and a new block has been created. The mining
node adds this new block to the blockchain on the node and transmits
the new block to other Bitcoin nodes. Each node that receives the block
verifies the block by ensuring that the block leads to a valid hash and all
the transactions contained in the block are valid. The verified block is then
added to the blockchain by each node.

---

[3] Whenever we say that a node has taken an action, what we are really saying is
that the Bitcoin software running on that node is programmed to take that action.

Once the block with Alex's transaction is added to the blockchain,
Alex has successfully sent the money to Sonia. Sonia now has this money
available in her wallet, and whenever she applies her private key, assuming
that was the condition that Sonia had to meet to spend the money, she will
be able to spend the money.

Let's now step back and look at the components of Bitcoin as shown in
Figure 5-2.

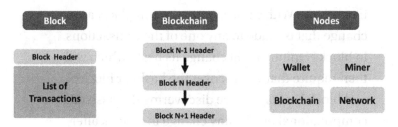

Figure 5-2. *Components of Bitcoin*

- First, let's examine a transaction.

  The transaction, as in the example we just saw, was
  from Alex to Sonia; it had Alex's public key, and it
  had Sonia's public key; the transaction was signed
  by Alex's private key, and the condition for Sonia to
  spend the money was that she needs to have access
  to her private key, and if she does, then she can
  spend the money.

- Next, let's look at a block.

  A block is a list of transactions with a block header
  that contains information about all the transactions
  in that block.

- A block chain is several blocks that are connected
  together.

  The key aspect of blockchain is that the block header
  for block N has the hash that was discovered for
  block N minus one, and the block header for block
  N plus 1 will have the hash that was discovered for
  block N. This is how blocks are connected in the
  blockchain. With these connections in place, any
  change that is made to any one of the transactions
  in block N minus 1 will change its hash, which will
  then require that we discover the hash for block N
  and block N plus 1. Since discovering the hash takes
  computational power, any change in a block after
  blocks have been chained to it is extremely difficult,
  if not impossible. This is what gives blockchains the
  property of immutability or tamper resistance (Yaga,
  Mell, Roby & Scarfone, 2018).[4]

- Any node in a Bitcoin implementation has four
  software components.

  These four components are the Wallet, the
  Distributed Ledger, the Miner, and the Network.

  The wallet software component is responsible for
  formatting the transaction, maintaining custody
  of the public and private keys of the owner, and
  interfacing with the distributed ledger to perform
  simple verification of transaction inputs.

---

[4] If a block was changed, it will be evident to all what the change was and when it
was made. This is the primary mechanism by which Bitcoin addressed the double
spend problem.

The distributed ledger software component manages the blockchain and provides other software components an interface with the blockchain and the data in the blockchain.

The miner software component interfaces with the blockchain and executes the computational processes to discover the hash for a block.

The network software component is responsible for the peer-to-peer communication of transactions and blocks with peer Bitcoin nodes.

A Bitcoin node can choose to execute all these four software components, or it can choose just to have the wallet, or the distributed ledger, or the miner software component. A Bitcoin node can also choose one or more combinations of these software components. All Bitcoin nodes, however, need to include the network software component.

This flexibility is in concert with the peer-to-peer networking ethos of Bitcoin. Needless to say, Bitcoin software is open source software that is free to download and relatively easy to install.[5] It does not require the purchase of any special purpose hardware. All one needs is a (any) computer and an internet connection.

Next, we look at the structure of the Bitcoin transaction in more detail. Table 5-1 shows the salient fields of the Bitcoin transaction data structure.

---

[5] You can get more information at `https://bitcoin.org/en/download`

Table 5-1. *Bitcoin transaction data structure*

Name of field	Description of the field
tx_in_count	The number of inputs into a transaction.
tx_in	The structure for each input that is part of this transaction
tx_out_count	The number of outputs from a transaction
tx_out	The structure for each output from this transaction

A Bitcoin transaction consists of a number of inputs and a number of outputs. The inputs into a Bitcoin transaction are the Bitcoins in our wallet that we intend to spend. The outputs describe how we intend to spend these Bitcoins. The outputs from one Bitcoin transaction become inputs for future Bitcoin transactions – cementing the notion of value exchange in our economy. Later we will describe a special kind of transaction that only has outputs, but no inputs.

To understand this structuring of inputs and outputs, let's take the analogy of cash money in our physical wallet. If in your physical wallet you had two five-dollar bills, one ten-dollar bill and one one-dollar bill. Let's say you needed to spend 17 dollars. Characterizing this transaction in the structure of a Bitcoin transaction, you will have three inputs: the ten-dollar bill and two five-dollar bills. With the denominations of money available to you, this is the only way you can spend 17 dollars. Your transaction will need at least one output, the 17 dollars that you want to spend (based on how Bitcoin transactions are structured, it does not matter that there is no 17-dollar bill), directed to the address of the person you want to send this money to. If you do not have any other output in the transaction, then the difference between your inputs and your outputs becomes the transaction fee for the miner node that will include your transaction in a block. In this case, the transaction fee will be 20 – 17 or three dollars. Let's say you only

want to pay a transaction fee of one dollar. You will then need two outputs:
the 17 dollars that you want to spend and a "change" of two dollars back to
you (see the following flowchart).

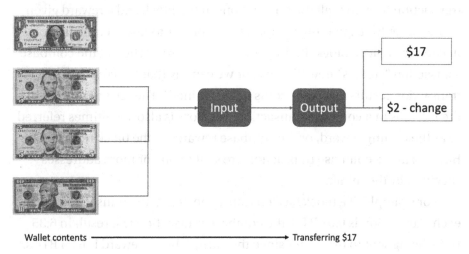

Wallet contents ──────────────────────→ Transferring $17

Any input into a transaction must be an output of some other
transaction. This is how Bitcoin keeps an audit trail or provenance of all
the money being spent. We will explain this further when we drill down
into the structure for the inputs into a transaction and the outputs from a
transaction – what we have shown in Table 5-2 is conceptual.

Table 5-2. *Summary of values in a notional transaction*

Name of field	Value
tx_in_count	3
tx_in	10
	5
	5
tx_out_count	2
tx_out	Receiver address 17
	Your address 2

Before we go any further, let's understand a specific type of transaction called the coinbase transaction. This is the transaction that only has outputs and no inputs. The coinbase transaction is the sum of the transaction fees from all the transactions in the block and a reward given to the miner for expending computational power to discover the hash needed to create a block. In this sense, the reward portion of the coinbase transaction "creates" new Bitcoins, or we can say that the coinbase transaction results in new Bitcoins being "mined." The reward portion of the Bitcoins in a coinbase transaction therefore is also sometimes referred to as the mining reward, or the coinbase reward, or the block reward. The Bitcoins in the coinbase transaction are sent to one or more addresses specified by the miner.

For example, if a block has ten transactions and the transaction fee in each transaction is 0.01 BTC, the coinbase transaction will result in 6.35 BTCs being sent to the miner since the current block reward is 6.25 BTCs. Later in our discussion on Bitcoin equilibrium economics, we will discuss the history of block rewards.

Except for the coinbase transaction, every input in a transaction has to be an output from a previous transaction. Figure 5-3 shows how the Bitcoin blockchain creates and maintains an audit trail of all the money being spent.

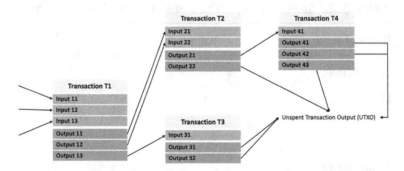

Figure 5-3. *Audit trail of money being spent in Bitcoin*

Transaction T1 has three inputs that were outputs from other transactions, not shown in Figure 5-3. Transaction T1 has three outputs; two of these are inputs for transaction T2, and the third output is an input for transaction T3. Transaction T2 has two outputs. The first output is an input for transaction T4. The second output from transaction T2 and the two outputs from transaction T3 are not yet inputs for any transaction; these outputs have not yet been spent and are referred to as an "unspent transaction output" or UTXO. Bitcoin keeps track of all the UTXOs in the blockchain and ensures that all the inputs in new transactions are UTXOs and thus include money that can be spent. This extensive "cradle-to-grave" audit trail in Bitcoin is sometimes referred to as triple-entry accounting[6] because we can trace money from its source to wherever it's being spent and wherever it's going to be spent. This is a nifty feature of the Bitcoin blockchain; we can actually trace our economy and all the value exchanges in one ledger, albeit the distributed ledger.

Next let's drill down further into the structure of inputs and outputs within a transaction to understand how Bitcoin maintains this audit trail and includes terms (or smart contracts) within a transaction. Table 5-3 shows the relevant fields for our purpose within the input data structure of a Bitcoin transaction.

---

[6] As opposed to the well-known single-entry and double-entry accounting.

Table 5-3. *Fields for an input in a Bitcoin transaction*

Name of field	Description of the field
txid	The identifier of the transaction where the output corresponding to this input is located
vout	The index number of the output in transaction txid to get the value for the input
scriptSig	The signature or signatures required to spend the unspent money represented in vout

The field "txid" is the identifier or the address of the output transaction where the corresponding output for this input is located. For transaction T3 in Figure 5-3, the txid for Input 31 is T1.[7] The field "vout" identifies the value in the corresponding output index for the input in transaction txid. For Transaction T3, the vout for Input 31 will correspond to the value in Output 13.

Table 5-4 shows the relevant fields for our purpose within the output data structure of a Bitcoin transaction.

Table 5-4. *Fields for an output in a Bitcoin transaction*

Name of field	Description of the field
value	The number of Bitcoins that are being made available for spending
scriptPubKey	The conditions that have to be met before the Bitcoins in the value field can be spent – sometimes referred to as the locking script

---

[7] Please note we are simplifying to help with understanding. All the identifiers are serialized hexadecimal numbers.

The field "value" represents the number of Bitcoins that are being made available for spending. This is the value that the vout field in the corresponding input will be an index to. The field "scriptPubKey" sets forth the terms or conditions under which the Bitcoins in the value field can be spent – in the language we have used in the book, this is the smart contract. Bitcoin supports very rudimentary smart contracts as we will see in a minute.

For an input to be able to spend the Bitcoins in the value field, the scriptSig field should contain what the scriptPubKey requires. In this sense, scriptPubKey is referred to as the locking script, and scriptSig is referred to as the unlocking script. Another common terminology refers to scriptPubKey as the challenge script, and scriptSig is referred to as the response script. Both these fields are specified in a language called Bitcoin Script, which is a simple Forth-like[8] stack-based programming language. The sidebar presents a simple example of how a stack-based programming language works. The Bitcoin Script language is limited because it does not support loops and conditional branching beyond the evaluation of simple conditional tests. Bitcoin takes the Bitcoin Script program specified in scriptSig and scriptPubKey, and if the output of executing all the commands in these two programs evaluates to a TRUE, then the money can be spent. In general, the programs contain references to public keys and digital signatures. These are hashed and encrypted using secure algorithms to preserve privacy.

Next, we drill down into the detailed structure of a block header.

As shown in Figure 5-2, a block in Bitcoin consists of a list of transactions and a block header. Bitcoin nodes maintain a list of all transactions that are valid but have not yet been added to a block. These transactions are referred to as unverified transactions, and the structure that holds these transactions is referred to as the mempool. Miner nodes select a subset of these transactions to include in the block by optimizing the transaction fee they will earn within the 1MB size of a Bitcoin block.

---

[8] https://forth-standard.org/

Table 5-5 shows the relevant fields for the block header in Bitcoin.

Table 5-5. *Fields for a block header in Bitcoin*

Name of field	Description of the field
nversion	This is version that communicates to other nodes what version of rules should be used to verify that the miner has discovered the hash
hashPrevBlock	The hash of the previous block header
hashMerkleRoot	This is the encoding of the information in all the transactions in the block
nTime	A timestamp identifying that the data and time the miner started the process of discovering the hash
nBits	The number of leading zeros that the discovered hash needs to have – the greater the number of leading zeros, the more difficult it will be for the miner to find the hash, that is, it will take more time and computational power; nBits signifies the difficulty threshold
nNonce	This is a number that miners can change in order to produce a hash that has the appropriate number of leading zeros – a hash that is less than or equal to the difficulty threshold

To start the process of creating a block, the miner node selects transactions from mempool to include in that block. It then goes to the last block that was added to the blockchain and extracts all the fields from its header and hashes[9] those fields to determine the value of the hashPrevBlock field for the block it is trying to create as shown in Figure 5-4.

---

[9] For ease of understanding, we are describing a slightly simpler version of the process.

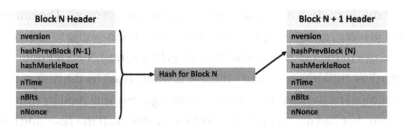

Figure 5-4. *Linking blocks during the block creation process*

It then creates the hashMerkleRoot field. The Merkle root is the hash of all the transactions in the block. The software takes two transactions at a time and hashes them, and it keeps repeating this process until it has one hash as shown in Figure 5-5. This hash is called the Merkle root hash, and it represents the information contained in all the transactions. So in a way the Merkle root process reduces the volume of all the transactions into this hash. A change in any transaction will result in the hash Merkle root changing the block header, making the hash of the block invalid.

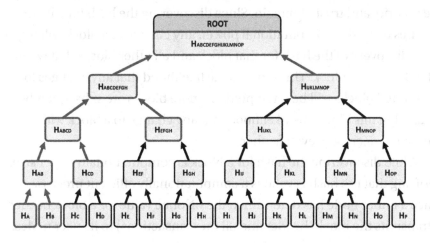

Figure 5-5. *The hash Merkle root of transactions in a block*

The fields nversion and nBits do not have to be computed by the miner node. They are global configuration variables available to the miner. The field nTime is system generated.

The miner node is now ready to start the mining process. The mining process involves generating a hash. The input to the hashing function is the values of the fields nversion, hashPrevBlock, hashMerkleRoot, nTime, nBits, and nNonce. The value for nNonce is set by the miner. If the computed hash has the number of leading zeros specified by nBits, then the miner has discovered the hash for the block. If the resulting hash does not have the appropriate leading number of zeros, then the miner can change the value of nNonce and recompute the process. nNonce is the only field in the block header that the miner can change to search for a valid hash. The iterative process of changing nNonce to recompute the hash until a valid hash is found is the mining process in Bitcoin. This mining algorithm in Bitcoin is referred to as proof of work (POW).[10]

We have learned previously in Chapter 2 that computing a hash is a very efficient computational process. However, searching through a large search space of the possible values for nNonce can take substantial computational power. This computational requirement is important for the security and trust of Bitcoin. Since discovering the hash for a block requires extensive computational power, any change to a block will require the rediscovery of the hash for that block and all other blocks that were added after this block. This reduces the likelihood that any changes to committed blocks will be attempted. As more blocks are subsequently chained to this block, the likelihood that any change to a block will be attempted decreases even further.

While discovering the hash for a block is computationally expensive, verifying that the hash is valid is a computationally efficient process. Once a miner node has determined the nNonce value for a block header, it transmits the block (header and all the transactions) to its peer nodes.

---

[10] Discovering the correct value of nNonce that will result in a valid hash required the miner to do work in terms of expending computational power. Presenting the discovered value of nNonce along with all the values of the other fields in the block header represents proof that the miner has done work.

When a node receives the block, it recomputes the hash (once) to ascertain its validity and confirms that all the transactions are also valid. Once the block has been validated, it chains it to the block with the matching hashPrevHeader.

When a node has received a valid block and has added it to its blockchain, then if it was involved in the mining process, it stops that process, resets its mempool, and selects a new subset of valid transactions to start the process of creating the next block.

At any given time, several Bitcoin miner nodes are working on creating a new block. Let's assume that two nodes are working on creating Block N. We shall call these new blocks as candidate blocks, Block N(A) and Block N(B). Let's assume that Block N(A) completes first and broadcasts its block. Another node – let's call this node Node Q – receives Block N(A) and adds it to its blockchain as shown in Figure 5-6 at time T = t. All nodes in the Bitcoin network do not receive Block N(A) at the same time due to network latency. In fact, the node that is working on creating Block N(B) does not receive Block N(A) and proceeds to finish creating Block N(B) and broadcasts this block to its peer nodes. When Node Q receives Block N(B), it will attach this block also to Block N as shown in Figure 5-6 at time T = t + 1. The blockchain now has a fork. This type of fork is called a natural fork because it is created as an artifact of the natural functioning of the blockchain network. At time T = t + 1, we cannot make a determination which of the two blocks, Block N(A) or Block N(B), will eventually end up as being part of the blockchain. At time T = t + 2, Node Q received Block N(A)+1. Block N(A)+1 is added to Block N by Node Q as shown in Figure 5-6.

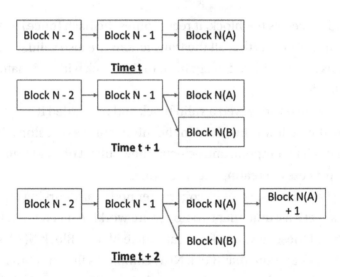

Figure 5-6. *Illustration of natural forks*

At time T = t + 2, the likelihood that Block N(A) will eventually be part of the blockchain is higher than the likelihood that Block N(B) will be part of the blockchain. At any given time, Bitcoin considers the longest chain of blocks to be the valid blockchain. Each node tries to extend the longest chain. This illustration is consistent with the BASE semantics of eventual consistency that were discussed in Chapter 2.

Similar to the description in the preceding text, we should also acknowledge that it is possible that there are nodes who might receive Block N(A)+1 before they receive Block N. If a node receives a block that it cannot add to the blockchain because the hashPrevBlock does not match the blocks it has in its chain, then it saves the block as an orphan block. If at a later time the node receives Block N(A), then at that time, both Block N(A) and Block N(A) + 1 will be added to the blockchain.

At any given time, there is a high probability that the leaf nodes of a blockchain will not be consistent. The notion of eventual consistency reassures us that eventually all the nodes will be consistent and the likelihood that nodes will be consistent away from the leaf nodes of the blockchain is high.

Based on the aforementioned, it is prudent for a transaction to not be considered settled until it is in a block to which a few more blocks have been chained. For transactions with large amounts, a rule of thumb is to wait for six blocks to be chained to a block before considering a block to be immutably added to the blockchain.

Let's translate this for a merchant who has decided to accept Bitcoin as a form of payment. The merchant will share their address (public key) that their prospective customers can use to direct payments to them. If a customer buys from this merchant at time t, they will initiate a transaction; at some point after time t, this transaction will get added into a candidate block; and at some point, after that, this candidate block will get added to the blockchain. Once a merchant has confirmation that the block with the transaction has been added to the blockchain, they can perhaps wait for a few more blocks to be added to this block, and then they can consider the transaction fully committed. At this point, the merchant can ship the goods to the customer.[11]

The Bitcoin software is designed to add a new block to the blockchain every ten minutes. This was a design decision and represented a trade-off to settle transactions as quickly as possible while also ensuring that the blockchain on individual nodes got out of sync for as little time as possible. How does the Bitcoin software ensure that this design goal is achieved?

After the creation of every 2016 blocks, the Bitcoin software calculates the average time it took for the miners to create a new block. If this time is greater than ten minutes, then it reduces the difficulty level represented by nBits so that miners can create blocks faster. To reduce the difficulty level, the Bitcoin software reduces the number of leading zeros required in the hash that the miners have to find. On the other hand, if the average time to create a block is less than ten minutes, then the Bitcoin software

---

[11] The smart contract for the transaction can have a condition that the merchant cannot spend this money until they can confirm that they have shipped the merchandise.

is programmed to automatically increase the difficulty level represented by nBits. The Bitcoin software increases the number of leading zeros that should be in a valid hash, making the hash harder to find.

This section has provided an in-depth description of how Bitcoin works. While the technical details were simplified, no important technical details were omitted. Next, we examine the economics of Bitcoin.

Bitcoin Economics

In the previous section, we have described the structure of transactions in Bitcoin, how transactions are validated, the mining process used to create blocks, and the process used to add blocks to the blockchain. We also discussed how when a miner creates a block, they are compensated through the coinbase transaction that includes transaction fees and a block reward. The block reward results in the "creation," "minting," or "mining" of new Bitcoins.

One of the design goals that Nakamoto had when the Bitcoin blockchain network was created was to limit the supply of Bitcoins. This was motivated by the point of view that the power governments have over the money supply is abused by expanding the supply of money. This was considered inflationary, and it was felt excess supply can lead to the debasement and devaluation of a currency. So not only did Nakamoto intend Bitcoin to be free from government intervention, but in order to protect the value of Bitcoin, Nakamoto limited the supply of Bitcoins.

The Bitcoin software is designed such that only 21 million Bitcoins will ever be minted.

The smooth and trustworthy operation of the Bitcoin network depends on mining nodes volunteering to expend their compute power, their electricity, and other resources to create new blocks. Because miners expend resources, they are compensated with the block reward through the coinbase transaction. When Bitcoin was launched in 2008, this block

reward was 50 Bitcoins. The Bitcoin software "halves" this reward after the
creation of 210,000 incremental blocks or approximately every four years
as shown in Figure 5-7.

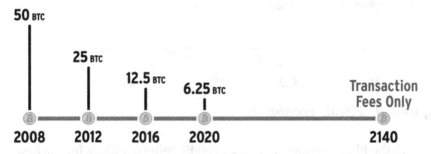

Figure 5-7. *Bitcoin block reward halving*

In 2012, the block reward was halved to 25 Bitcoins. In July of 2016,
it was reduced to 12.5 Bitcoins, and on May 11, 2020, at around 3 p.m.
Eastern time, the reward was reduced to 6.25 Bitcoins. By 2140, we will
reach the 21 million Bitcoin limit in the Bitcoin software. From that
point onward, there will be no more block reward for miners. The only
compensation that will be available to miners for the resources they
expend on mining will have to come from transaction fees.

When there is no more block reward, we say that Bitcoin has reached
equilibrium economics.

Let us do some simple mathematics to understand how much the
mining process might be costing the economy. We already know that we
create a block every ten minutes. That means we create six blocks an hour;
that means we create 144 blocks a day; and that translates to 52,560 blocks
being created each year as shown in Figure 5-8.

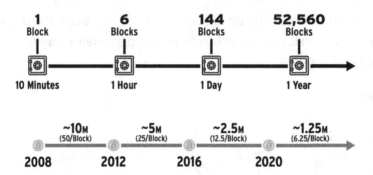

Figure 5-8. *Bitcoin economics*

With the block reward per block of 50 Bitcoins per block for the first 210,000 blocks, we can calculate that approximately 10 million Bitcoins were mined for the first four years. Approximately 5 million Bitcoins were mined for the next four years and so on. At the current US dollar-to-Bitcoin conversion rate, this is equivalent to tens to hundreds of billions of dollars in wealth being created for miners.

That's a lot of money. That's how big this Bitcoin economy can be, and it kind of makes you pause and think whether this is sustainable. Is this something that can go on? Will volunteer miners continue to create blocks if the only compensation they receive is transaction fees? Will the transaction fees be low enough to support value exchange? Will I ever buy coffee and donuts using Bitcoin? What will happen to the US dollar–Bitcoin exchange rate once we are at equilibrium economics?

Well, these are things that we still have to figure out, but having an understanding of this economics as to how much Bitcoins we create and what the value of the Bitcoins is makes this a very interesting topic.

Consensus Protocols

In the previous section, we learned about the proof-of-work consensus mechanism used by Bitcoin. We noted that proof of work was an extremely computationally expensive consensus mechanism. The proof

of work guarantees immutability at the cost of scalability and perhaps
sustainability. In this section, we will review other consensus mechanisms
such as proof of stake, delegated proof of stake, and proof of authority.

In proof of stake, nodes stake a certain amount of their currency or
wealth to serve as validators (nodes that have the functionality to create
new blocks).[12] These nodes take a certain amount of their wealth (the units
of the wealth vary depending on the blockchain) and set it aside, or reserve
it, for the privilege of serving as validators. This stake creates an incentive
for these nodes to make sure that the blockchain is not compromised
and stays immutable. The theory is that if the blockchain were to be
compromised, these nodes would lose the stake that they have reserved.

Of all the nodes that stake a certain amount of currency, a validator is
selected using a deterministic algorithm. This deterministic algorithm can
change depending on the blockchain implementation. An example of a
deterministic algorithm can be selecting validators in a round-robin fashion
starting with the node with the highest stake. Other deterministic algorithms
could select validators by weighting their stake, so nodes with a higher stake
will be selected more frequently than nodes with a lower stake. Whichever
node is selected then creates the block. There is no race for solving the
puzzle or finding a hash with a certain number of leading zeros like we had
in proof of work. In proof of stake, validators do not receive a mining or block
reward; they merely take the transaction fees in all the transactions.

The advantages of a proof of stake are that it is more energy efficient,
it consumes less electricity, and it doesn't require expensive specialized
hardware, and we are already at equilibrium economics where everything
is working based solely on transaction fees rather than on a block reward
and a transaction fee.

The risks with proof of stake are that selecting validators can be
problematic. Some consensus protocols try to insert some kind of
randomness in the selection of validators, but this can be gamed and that

---

[12] Validators and miners can be considered to be similar.

creates risks that the blockchain may be compromised. Staking cannot also be uniquely guaranteed. What this means is we are staking based on public keys. We might have the same individual with many multiple keys doing the staking. So they are creating a lot of centralized control on the blockchain, and that can be a problem. Finally, staking doesn't always guarantee higher performance in terms of transaction throughput. We save electricity; we save computational power, but that in some cases does not necessarily translate into better performance in terms of transactions per second.

As an improvement over proof of stake, another consensus mechanism called delegated proof of stake has been invented.

In delegated proof of stake, we take all of the nodes that have a stake or have staked something for validation, and they make a proposal to the community of what they want in return for doing the validation or doing the mining and what they're willing to guarantee in terms of their performance for doing the validation.

The network then votes on which of these proposals should be selected as nodes who can do validation, and then among those selected, the algorithm selects a panel of validators, and then among those in the panel, some deterministic way is used for selecting the validator.

Now the delegate or whoever does the validation can get a reward if they said that they wanted a reward in the proposal and they were voted into the panel by the community. The delegated proof of stake creates a certain level of democracy in the voting process. We have some improvement over proof of stake, but some of the disadvantages still stay.

In general, both proof of stake and delegated proof of stake move us closer to centralization, but they give us some advantages in terms of energy consumption and sustainability.

Another type of consensus mechanism is proof of authority. In proof of authority, what is done is the validators who want to be selected establish their identity. They decide that they no longer will be anonymous; and once they have established that identity and now we know uniquely that this address refers to this identity, we can follow either the proof-of-stake

method or the delegated proof-of-stake method. But what we've done is
by confirming their identity, they have created disincentives for them for
colluding or compromising the blockchain.

This is an exciting area of research within the blockchain and
distributed computing community. There are many more consensus
mechanisms, such as proof of elapsed time and proof of history,
being proposed than the three we have briefly described in this
section. Oyinloye, Teh, Jamil, & Alawida, M. (2021) provide an overview of
alternate consensus protocols.

Ethereum

Part 2 of this book takes a deep dive into Ethereum and Enterprise
Ethereum, explaining how blockchain business applications can be
developed using Ethereum. In this section, we provide a brief overview of
Ethereum and the implementation differences with Bitcoin. Ethereum is
an alternate implementation of blockchain, different from Bitcoin in some
very important ways.

In the previous section, we saw that in Bitcoin, the terms and
conditions underlying transactions had to be very simple. Bitcoin wanted
to keep the smart contract very simple because complicated smart
contracts had risks of high computation costs and a higher likelihood of
software defects.

The founder of Ethereum, Vitalik Buterin,[13] who was involved early on
in the Bitcoin community, felt that while Bitcoin was great digital money,
the scripting language, Bitcoin Script, that was used to specify smart
contracts was too weak. In addition to value exchange payments facilitated
by Bitcoin, Buterin envisioned a class of decentralized applications
that would be enabled by the features of distributed ledgers, privacy
preservation, consensus, and smart contracts. Buterin outlined a vision

---

[13] https://en.wikipedia.org/wiki/Vitalik_Buterin

of a smart contract language that would be a lot more robust and enable
the creation of sophisticated decentralized applications on top of the
blockchain. He wanted to create a Turing complete language for smart
contracts that supported loops and complicated conditional branching.
Ethereum includes a very easy JavaScript like language, called Solidity, to
enable the development of smart contracts that could represent real-world
business logic associated with transaction terms and conditions.

The availability of Solidity has led to Ethereum being referred to
by some as programmable money or programmable currency. The
blockchain applications developed with Ethereum are sometimes referred
to as dApps or distributed applications.

In addition to the introduction of Solidity, a Turing complete
programming language, Ethereum has also simplified and strengthened
the tracking of transactions and spending. The Bitcoin software tracks
every transaction, its inputs, its outputs, and the unspent transaction
output (UTXO) from all transactions even if we have to go all the way back
to the original genesis block.

In Bitcoin, if one transaction produced an output of one Bitcoin and
another transaction produced another output of half a Bitcoin and a third
transaction produced an output of another half of a Bitcoin, we couldn't
combine these three to create two Bitcoins in our wallet without creating a
transaction and paying transaction fees for that transaction. Bitcoin tracks
the UTXOs for these three transactions separately as shown in Figure 5-9.

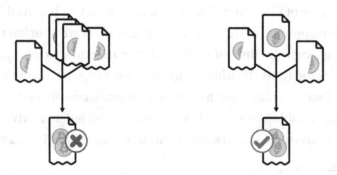

Figure 5-9. *Bitcoin UTXOs vs. Ethereum accounts*

Instead of only tracking transactions, Ethereum created a structure for accounts where transactions owned by an account could be brought together and aggregated. This created other advantages where we could theoretically segregate and hold different kinds of assets or tokens in our account that are all based on the Ethereum native token or the Ethereum currency (Ether).

Of course, there are risks associated with the extensive functionality provided by Solidity to make Ether a very highly programmable money.

- The flexibility of Solidity makes it more likely that smart contracts will have defects when deployed. It is an inevitable fact of life – the more software there is, the more errors there are likely to be; when it is easy to create software, it is also easy to make mistakes, and so on. In blockchain, once a smart contract is deployed and committed to the blockchain, then it's immutable. The software defect cannot be fixed. The only recourse available is to hope that people don't use the defective smart contract anymore – this is unlikely if the smart contract defect creates a financial advantage for users. So this creates a lot of risk.

- Ethereum also has a larger state than Bitcoin; that is, Ethereum stores more data on the chain than Bitcoin. This can introduce latency and computational issues.

- Transactions that execute smart contracts are responsible for compensating the blockchain network for the computational costs of executing the smart contract. This cost is called Gas, and it depends on the complexity and size of the smart contract.

- Before a Solidity smart contract is deployed to the
  blockchain, it is compiled into bytecode. However,
  there is an option whereby in addition to the bytecode,
  a readable version of the smart contract can also be
  deployed. While this improves transparency, it can also
  create privacy and confidentiality risks.

The currency behind Ethereum is Ether. The lower denominations of
Ether are Finney, Szabo, and Wei as shown in Figure 5-10. Finney, Szabo,
and Wei are all luminaries in the cryptocurrency world. They were all
involved early on in the Bitcoin community.

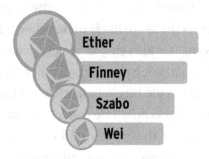

Figure 5-10. *Ether denominations*

Ethereum has two types of accounts: accounts that are externally
owned and contract accounts. Externally owned accounts are the most
common. They have a balance, and they're held in wallets. Contract
accounts store and execute smart contract code. Contract accounts
also have an associated balance representing the balance held by the
associated smart contract for the programmable money.

A transaction in blockchain requests a change in the state of the
blockchain. Unlike Bitcoin where all transactions were of the same
type – payment transactions to send Bitcoins from one address to
another – Ethereum has three types of transactions; transactions are not
restricted to sending payments.

1. Payment transactions send Ether from one account to another account.

2. Smart contract creation transactions that instantiate the smart contract on the blockchain.

3. Smart contract execution transactions that move money between accounts based on the business logic in the smart contract.

One of the key achievements of Ethereum was the creation of the Ethereum Virtual Machine (EVM) or the World Computer. The Ethereum Virtual Machine sits on top of the blockchain and functions as a compiler that takes smart contract software written in Solidity and compiles it for the EVM into what is called EVM bytecode as shown in Figure 5-11. It is this bytecode that is executed on the blockchain. The blockchain network is going to expend computational power to run the smart contract, and all the nodes are going to have to execute the smart contract; the owner of the transaction executing the smart contract pays Gas in Ether for the execution of the smart contract.

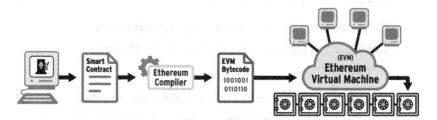

Figure 5-11. *The Ethereum Virtual Machine*

The vision with Ethereum was the creation of distributed applications or dApps. This vision has been realized, and there are currently thousands of Ethereum dApps in production driving the excitement around blockchain. The creation of a dApp involves the development, testing,

and deployment of smart contracts and a front end that interacts with the
blockchain. Figure 5-12 shows the architecture of a dApp and examples of
development tools that are available to dApp developers.

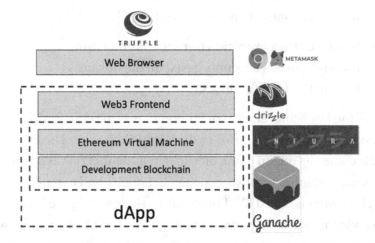

Figure 5-12. *Ethereum dApp architecture and development tools*

- Truffle is an interactive development environment for
  the creation of Solidity software.

- Ganache provides a development blockchain for
  the testing of the smart contract software during
  development.

- Drizzle is a set of libraries that provide functionality
  for account and contract instantiation from the front
  end of a dApp. We call the dApp architecture a Web
  3.0 architecture to differentiate it from the Web 2.0
  architecture and the front end of the dApp as the Web3
  front end.

- The dApp front end interacts with the EVM and the blockchain through a set of remote procedure calls (RPCs). Infura encapsulates these RPCs into an API (Application Programming Interface) that eases the development of the dApp.

- MetaMask is a Chrome plug-in and a software wallet. These tools simplify the development of distributed applications or dApps.

Hyperledger

Hyperledger is the blockchain implementation that is used to develop enterprise business applications between transacting parties such as those in a supply chain.

The Hyperledger blockchain solution is provided and managed by the Linux Foundation. This is a collaborative effort created to advance cross-industry blockchain technologies for enterprise business applications. Founded in February 2016, there are now more than 200 member organizations in the Hyperledger collaborative.

Hyperledger has an open source, open standards, open and transparent governance mechanism. This is a governance model that many in the software world are familiar and comfortable with because it is the governance used by Linux and Apache, two well-known operating systems and web development platforms, respectively, for a long time.

Hyperledger comes with frameworks and tools that are highly modular technologies that can be integrated together.

Let's look at some of the tools and frameworks that are available with Hyperledger (please also see Figure 5-13):

- Hyperledger Aries, Indy, and URSA are tools and frameworks used to manage cryptographic identity and communicate these identities across the blockchain network.

- Hyperledger Fabric is the core distributed ledger within the Hyperledger ecosystem, and for Hyperledger Fabric you can write smart contracts using the Go programming language. You can also plug in different consensus mechanisms.

- Hyperledger Besu is an Ethereum client built for the Hyperledger ecosystem. Here, you can write smart contracts using the Solidity programming language and create private or public permissioned blockchains.

- Hyperledger Sawtooth is a framework and tool set to help you build blockchain applications using the proof of elapsed time or the practical Byzantine fault-tolerant consensus mechanisms.

- Iroha is specifically designed for IoT-based blockchain applications, and it uses the C++ programming language.

- Hyperledger Cactus is a blockchain integration tool where applications running on different blockchains can communicate and operate together.

- Cello is an operational dashboard that can be used to track multiple blockchain applications.

- Hyperledger Explorer provides a very simple web-based interface to query the data in the blockchain.

- Hyperledger Quilt is a Java implementation for an interledger payment mechanism. Here, you can work with crypto payments as well as fiat payments. Fiat payments or fiat currencies are currencies that are issued by sovereign governments.

Figure 5-13. *Hyperledger ecosystem*

Hyperledger provides a very rich developmental tool set that can be used to build enterprise business applications. All applications so far built using Hyperledger use a permissioned blockchain. Many of these applications are private permissioned, but they can also be public permissioned.

Bitcoin, Ethereum, and Hyperledger Comparison

In this section, we will compare Bitcoin, Ethereum, and Hyperledger and then take a quick tour to cover exciting developments that have been happening in blockchain over the past few years.

Bitcoin is the original implementation for blockchain, and we will compare Bitcoin, Ethereum, and Hyperledger using the following criteria:

- What is their purpose?

- What is the governance mechanism they use?

- What is their currency?

- What is their mining reward?

- What is their underlying data structure and consensus mechanism?

Bitcoin was made for payments. It's native for transferring value from one party to another. Ethereum was built as a general-purpose development platform where you could facilitate payments but also build distributed applications. Hyperledger was also designed as a general-purpose enterprise application development tool.

Bitcoin is governed by Bitcoin Improvement Proposals (BIP), where an attempt is made to get consensus across all the Bitcoin nodes, and once a certain percentage of Bitcoin node agrees to a proposed change, consensus is deemed, and the community agrees to move to the next version. Those who don't want to agree can go their own way by creating a hard fork.

The Ethereum blockchain also uses an Ethereum Improvement Proposal (EIP), and there is a core group under the leadership of Vitalik Buterin that drives that process.

The Hyperledger governance is based on the Linux foundation where people and companies come together as a collaborative and offer up their services as projects, frameworks, and tools.

The native currency for Bitcoin is BTC, and lower denominations are in Satoshis. The native currency of Ethereum is Ether, and lower denominations are Finney, Wei, and Szabo. Hyperledger doesn't have a native currency. Its purpose is less payment based and more data sharing and trust enabling.

The mining reward for Bitcoin is currently 6.25 BTCs. We've seen that this was halved from 12.5 BTCs in May 2020. Ethereum has a mining reward of 2 Ethers. Hyperledger does not have the notion of a mining reward.

The core data structure within Bitcoin is a transaction. In Ethereum, the core data structure is an account where outputs of transactions are consolidated. The underlying data structure within Hyperledger is an attribute-value database.

Bitcoin uses a proof-of-work consensus mechanism. Ethereum uses a proof-of-work consensus mechanism as well, and they are planning a move to a proof-of-stake mechanism. As we saw when we talked about Hyperledger, the consensus mechanism within Hyperledger is pluggable.

Bitcoin is a permissionless public blockchain. Ethereum implementations are available as permissionless or permissioned. In the more well-known setting, where we build distributed applications, we use the permissionless public implementation of Ethereum. If you want to build enterprise applications, you can use an implementation of Ethereum called Enterprise Ethereum, and this can be permissioned public or permissioned private.

Hyperledger is permissioned and provides scalability. We have many nodes in Bitcoin; however, the performance is low. In Ethereum, again, we have many nodes, and the performance is also low. Usually for each Hyperledger blockchain application implementation, you do not have many nodes, but you have very high performance and high throughput.

The smart contracts in Bitcoin with the Bitcoin Script programming language are very limited. In Ethereum, you have Solidity, which is a Turing complete programming language. The native Hyperledger Fabric gives you a Turing complete smart contract language with the Go programming language. Other frameworks in Hyperledger support smart contracts in other programming languages.

The following table summarizes the differences between Bitcoin,
Ethereum, and Hyperledger.

	Bitcoin	**Ethereum**	**Hyperledger**
Purpose	Payments	Payments Distributed applications	Enterprise distributed applications
Governance	Bitcoin Improvement Proposal	Ethereum Improvement Proposals	Linux Foundation
Currency	BTC	ETH	None
Mining reward	6.25 BTCs	2 ETH	None
Data structure	Transaction	Account	Flexible (attribute-value database)
Consensus	Proof of work	Proof of work (proof of stake is planned)	Pluggable
Smart contracts	Bitcoin Script	Solidity	Go

Emerging Blockchain Implementations

Let's now look at some of the exciting new work that is happening within
blockchain. Both Bitcoin and Ethereum are currently suffering from
network congestion, high transaction fees, as well as scalability issues.
Bitcoin has released over the past 36 months two Layer 1 improvements.
Layer 1 changes are to the core blockchain layer of a blockchain
implementation, whereas Layer 2 changes are to the integration layer
of a blockchain implementation as described in Chapter 4. Bitcoin has
made data structure improvements to how data in transactions are stored,

how scripts or smart contracts within a transaction are stored, and how scripts are hashed and communicated over the Bitcoin network. Layer 2 innovations have included developments such as the Lightning Network. The Lightning Network allows parties to transact offline but then commit to the main blockchain network an aggregation of their offline transaction value. This improves scalability.

Ethereum also has many Layer 1 improvements in progress, and these are primarily for scalability and security. These include the following:

- Sharding, where the main Ethereum chain will be broken up into 64 chains to improve performance.

- Staking, which is the implementation of the proof-of-stake consensus mechanism. A development called the Beacon Chain with proof of stake has been released, and the plan is to slowly merge this chain into the main Ethereum network.

Ethereum also has Layer 2 innovations such as Arbitrum, which were done outside the Ethereum core group. Arbitrum lets you roll up transactions out of Ethereum and write the aggregate result back into the Ethereum mainnet, improving scalability and reducing transaction fees.

Polygon was originally a side chain from Ethereum, but now it is used to develop multichain Ethereum systems. This also helps with scalability.

Cardano is what some people call a next-generation blockchain. It has a currency called Ada and a consensus mechanism called Ouroboros, which is an innovation on proof of stake. It has the smart contract development platform, Plutus, which is similar to the Ethereum Virtual Machine, based on the Haskell programming language.

Solana is another next-generation blockchain where a consensus mechanism called proof of history is used. This consensus mechanism enables very high transaction throughput.

Finally, Polkadot like Polygon is an up-and-coming multichain system.

Blockchain research and development continues at a torrid pace, and many exciting developments are in process.

Chapter Summary/Key Takeaways

Key takeaways from this chapter are as follows:

- Bitcoin was released in 2008 to enable transactions between parties without an intermediary. Each Bitcoin transaction contain inputs and outputs. Inputs in a Bitcoin transaction correspond to outputs from other transactions, providing an audit trail (provenance) for all payments in Bitcoins.

- Bitcoin outputs create challenge scripts that, when used as an input, require response scripts to unlock spending of the output. These scripts are implemented using Bitcoin Script, which is a highly limited language for implementing smart contracts.

- In Bitcoin, transactions are packaged into blocks using the proof-of-work consensus mechanism. On average, a new block is created every ten minutes. A Bitcoin node that creates a block is called a miner, and a miner receives a reward that is the sum of the block reward and the transaction fees for all the transactions in the block. As of 2020, the block reward is 6.25 BTCs. The block reward is halved every four years, and by 2140, the block reward will be zero.

- Bitcoin software includes four components: wallet, distributed ledger, miner, and network communications.

- Ethereum is a blockchain that includes a Turing complete programming language, Solidity, for developing smart contracts. Ethereum has enabled the creation of innovative distributed applications or dApps.

- Ethereum also uses the proof-of-work consensus mechanism though it is planning to migrate to the proof-of-stake consensus mechanism.

- Hyperledger is a blockchain that is suitable for developing enterprise applications.

- Blockchain development is still nascent, and several second-generation blockchains such as Cardano, Solana, Polkadot, and Polygon are now getting increased adoption.

Sidebar – Stack-Based Programming Language

Figure 5-14 demonstrates the workings of a stack-based programming language for a simple program: 4 5 OP_ADD 12 OP_SUB 3 EQUAL.

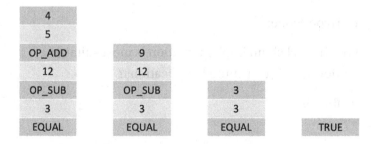

Figure 5-14. *Illustration of a stack-based programing language*

Each element in this program is pushed onto a stack as shown in the figure. Elements are popped off the stack until we get to an operator. The operator is applied to the popped elements, and the result is pushed back on to the stack. For our program, first, 4 is popped off the stack; then 5 is popped off the stack; when OP_ADD is popped off the stack, it is applied to 4 and 5, that is, they are added together since the OP_ADD operator performs addition, and the result 9 is pushed back on to the stack. Next, we pop 9 and then 12, and when the operator OP_SUB is popped, 9 is subtracted from 12, and the result 3 is popped back on to the stack. Next, we pop 3 and then 3; when EQUAL is popped, we check if 3 equals to 3; the result TRUE is pushed back on to the stack. When TRUE is popped, it becomes the final output for our simple program.

Operators such as OP_ADD, OP_SUB, and EQUAL are referred to as opcodes in Bitcoin Script.[14]

Quiz Questions

1. Which blockchain implementation is most suitable for developing enterprise blockchain applications?

    a. Bitcoin

    b. Ethereum

    c. Hyperledger

2. Which blockchain implementation is most suitable for developing distributed applications?

    a. Bitcoin

---

[14] You can see all the opcodes available in Bitcoin Script at https://wiki.bitcoinsv.io/index.php/Opcodes_used_in_Bitcoin_Script

   b. Ethereum

   c. Hyperledger

3. What is the consensus mechanism used by Bitcoin?

   a. Proof of work

   b. Proof of stake

   c. Distributed proof of stake

   d. Proof of authority

4. Which of the following is NOT a denomination
    of Ether?

   a. Finney

   b. Szabo

   c. Wei

   d. Satoshi

5. What is the consensus mechanism used by
    Hyperledger?

   a. Proof of work

   b. Proof of stake

   c. Distributed proof of stake

   d. None of the above

6. In a blockchain block with ten transactions, the
    difference between the input and output for each
    transaction was 0.05 BTC. What would be the total
    amount in BTC received by the miner for mining
    this block?

7. In a blockchain block with ten transactions, the difference between the input and output for each transaction was 0.03 BTC. What would be the total amount in BTC received by the miner for mining this block?

8. In a blockchain block with ten transactions, the difference between the input and output for each transaction was 0.06 BTC. What would be the total amount in BTC received by the miner for mining this block?

9. A Bitcoin transaction has inputs that add up to 5.25 BTCs and outputs that add up to 5.15 BTCs. What is the transaction fee for this transaction?

10. Please explain briefly how Bitcoin maintain an audit trail of all spending.

11. What kind of transaction in Bitcoin does not have an input?

    a. Genesis transaction

    b. Coinbase transaction

    c. Orphan transaction

    d. Simple transaction

12. Describe the three types of transactions supported by Ethereum.

13. Explain how Bitcoin ensures that it creates, on average, one block every ten minutes.

14. When there is no more block reward, we say that Bitcoin has reached _____ economics.

15. What is the smart contract programming language used in Ethereum?

    a. Script

    b. JavaScript

    c. Solidity

    d. Go

16. The structure that holds all the unverified transactions in Bitcoin is referred to as the

    _____.

17. These outputs of Bitcoin that have not yet been spent are referred to as _____ _____

    _____ or _____.

18. What is an interactive development environment for the creation of Solidity software?

    a. Ganache

    b. Truffle

    c. MetaMask

    d. Infura

References

Nakamoto, S. (2008) Bitcoin: A peer-to-peer electronic cash system. https://bitcoin.org/bitcoin.pdf

Lee, H., Choi, M., Rhee, C., (2003) Traceability of double spending in secure electronic cash system, 2003 International Conference on Computer Networks and Mobile Computing, 2003. ICCNMC 2003. 2003, pp. 330–333, doi: 10.1109/ICCNMC.2003.1243063

Antonopoulos, A. (2017). Mastering Bitcoin: Programming the open blockchain. (2nd. ed.). O'Reilly Media, Inc.

Yaga, D., Mell, P., Roby, N., Scarfone, K. (2018) Blockchain technology overview. National Institutes of Standards and Technology. October 2018. https://doi.org/10.6028/NIST.IR.8202

Oyinloye, D. P., Teh, J. S., Jamil, N., & Alawida, M. (2021). Blockchain Consensus: An Overview of Alternative Protocols. Symmetry, 13(8), 1363. MDPI AG. Retrieved from https://doi.org/10.3390/sym13081363

PART 2

Ethereum Smart Contract Development

In Part 1 of this book, the context of blockchain has been mentioned. In Part 2, you will learn about the Ethereum blockchain and how to write smart contracts with Solidity and then build decentralized applications. Students in our smart contract development courses have built over 30 applications, and we believe that you can learn to do so as well once you follow this book.

In Chapter 6, we go over the Ethereum architecture and decentralized applications. The architectural components at the network layer, core blockchain layer, enterprise component layer, tooling layer, and application layers are explained. Once readers have a good understanding of the Ethereum overview and architecture, the ecosystem and decentralized applications are introduced. To provide readers a better hands-on experience, this chapter also includes setup and development tools, such as geth client, MetaMask, Remix, Truffle, and Web3, to interact with.

Chapter 7 is composed of six modules that cover hands-on development tutorials for the Solidity programming language.

- Module 1 starts with basic concepts and syntax for Solidity programs. A "HelloWorld" example is presented to explain how to declare a Solidity program, import another Solidity file, and write constructors and functions.

- Module 2 describes Solidity data types with emphasis on mapping and structs that are unique to Solidity programming.

- Module 3 is focused on events as a messaging mechanism for the Ethereum blockchain and Web3 communications. Readers will learn how to write smart contracts to define and emit events.

- Module 4 is about smart contract security and covers various vulnerabilities in functions, data types, access scopes, randomness, signature, etc.

- Module 5 describes how to use the security scan, testing tools, and the debugger to improve Solidity code.

- Module 6 covers client applications that use Web3 to interact with smart contracts that are deployed to blockchains.

Once readers go through Chapter 7, they should develop a good skill set for writing an end-to-end Solidity program.

Chapter 8 is dedicated to security, with emphasis on various vulnerabilities and best practices to ensure the security of the decentralized applications.

Chapter 9 covers scalability to improve performance and reduce gas fees for the Ethereum blockchain. Layer 2 solutions such as state channel, plasma, rollups, and sharding are introduced and compared.

Chapter 10 describes processes and guides for funding decentralized applications. Token design and distributions are discussed. Transaction gas fee is also explained in this chapter.

Chapter 11 is a real-world example to build a smart contract application from specification to design, followed by the implementation with smart contracts and Web3. This provides an end-to-end experience for readers to develop a smart contract program.

CHAPTER 6

Ethereum Architecture and Overview

Introduction

The Ethereum blockchain is a fascinating platform that uses innovative smart contract capability to empower decentralized applications in almost all major business sectors. Pioneered by Vitalik Buterin and several cofounders, Ethereum has gone through the milestones of initial launch, stable coins, ICO (Initial Coin Offering), DeFi (Decentralized Finance), DAO (Decentralized Autonomous Organization), NFT (nonfungible tokens), and L2 (Layer 2) for scalability. The Ethereum blockchain and infrastructure are transitioning to POS (proof of stake) with sharding and are on the way to impose big impacts on CBDC (Central Bank Digital Currency) and enterprise blockchains with promising potential. After years of astronomical growth, Ethereum has reached a market cap of $400 billion, just trailing behind Bitcoin. Compared with bitcoin, the Ethereum blockchain has advantages such as supporting the Ethereum Virtual Machine (EVM) and smart contracts, supporting more diverse use cases, and being more nimble by changing consensus from POW to POS to save energy costs.

© Weijia Zhang and Tej Anand 2022
W. Zhang and T. Anand, *Blockchain and Ethereum Smart Contract Solution Development*,
https://doi.org/10.1007/978-1-4842-8164-2_6

Ethereum is a complex and dynamic platform that has been consistently expanding. Learning the Ethereum blockchain is not easy. It takes tremendous effort to truly understand Ethereum architecture and master the skill set for carrying out smart contract and decentralized application development. To lower the barrier of learning of the Ethereum blockchain platform, we separate the content of this part of the book into three tracks as shown in Figure 6-1. The first track is business oriented with focus on an overview of Ethereum, its ecosystems, decentralization, and token economy design. The second track is for technical programming to develop a smart contract project and covers Ethereum architecture, Solidity programming, debugging, testing, security checking, and deployment. The third track is a project track to build and deliver a hands-on decentralized application from user requirement to token design, to blockchain smart contract and client implementations.

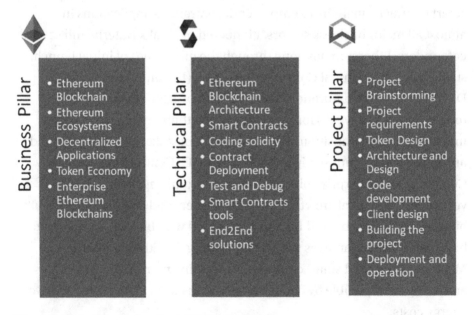

Figure 6-1. *Three tracks/pillars for Ethereum smart contract development*

Both business and technical track contents will be covered in subsequent chapters. This chapter is focused on the following three main topics: (1) Ethereum architecture and its components; (2) Ethereum ecosystem projects; and (3) Ethereum tools required for smart contract development.

Ethereum Architecture

There are different ways to present the Ethereum blockchain architecture. One of the architectural representations is developed by the Enterprise Ethereum Alliance (EEA) and shown in Figure 6-2. Similar to the Open Systems Interconnection (OSI) that models internet network representation into seven layers, the EEA divides Ethereum architecture into five layers containing network, core blockchain, enterprise components, tooling, and applications layers.

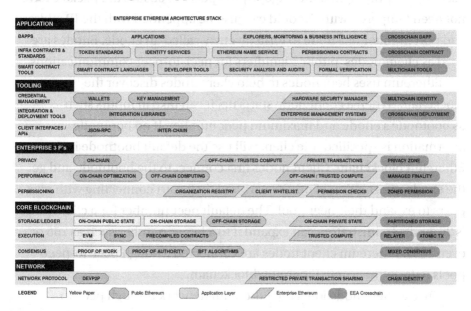

Figure 6-2. *Ethereum blockchain components architecture and overview*

Network Layer

The network layer located at the bottom of the architectural diagram is exactly the same as the TCP/IP/P2P internet network. Although sometimes people view blockchain as a new generation of internet, the Ethereum blockchain itself does not change anything on the network level. The network layer provides three key capabilities for the Ethereum blockchain: discovering blockchain, communicating with network nodes, and managing peer nodes.

Ethereum is a permissionless public blockchain, which means that any client node can join the Ethereum blockchain without a centralized authority. Each client node can be identified through a public and private key pair through secp256k1 elliptic curve cryptography. The client node's private key is also called nodeKey, and the public key is called nodeId. The nodeKey is used to sign the communication packets, and the public key is used to verify the signed messages by the peers to ensure the packets have not been tampered with. NodeId can also be appended with the IP address and port number of a node to form an entry called an enode. Enodes are used as client nodes' public identifiers for peer-to-peer communications.

Ethereum uses boot nodes to help client nodes discover the blockchain. When a client node starts up, it can take in inputs such as bootnode's enode and maximum peer number. If no bootnode information is specified, the client will use the default bootnode in the Ethereum blockchain. Client nodes first connect to the bootnode and get the enode information of other peers and then start connecting with new peers to expand their peer pool. The default peer number for a client node is 25, and administrators can expand it to a larger number such as 256 or even 1024. Ethereum client nodes are connected through peer-to-peer pools to form the whole Ethereum blockchain.

Once a client node joins the Ethereum network through peer-to-peer connection, it can start syncing up blocks, receiving and sending transactions, proposing new blocks, etc. Ethereum client nodes are constantly downloading new blocks to their local data storage, so a fast network and a large disk space are needed for node operation. It is very important to safeguard nodeKey, as client nodes need to sign peer-to-peer communication packets with their nodeKey.

Sometimes, peer pools are not connected properly due to lack of peers, slow network of peers, or even malfunctioning peers. In that case, client node administrators can manually add or delete peers in their own peer pool. The number of peers connected and the peers' information can be retrieved using Web3 APIs.

Core Blockchain Layer

One of the key technical innovations of blockchain lies in its core blockchain layer. There are three important components at this layer: consensus, EVM, and storage.

One unique novelty of blockchain is its capability to reach computational consensus among participating nodes. The first blockchain consensus is POW, that is, proof of work, invented in the Bitcoin blockchain. POW consumes a lot of energy in computing cryptographic hashes through arrays after arrays of heavy computation machines in mining farms. Currently, the computing power of Bitcoin has consumed more energy than the electricity usage of a medium-sized country.

Ethereum also uses proof of work for the current mainnet, but it is transitioning to proof of stake (POS) in Ethereum 2. The difference between proof of stake and proof of work is that proof of stake actually takes into consideration the amount of Ether staked in the Ethereum system, so that the more Ether staked, the higher chance to be selected to propose blocks.

Besides POW and POS, there are other blockchain consensus such as POA and BFT. POA, proof of authority, is used more for enterprise blockchains or Ethereum testnets. Only authorized nodes whose nodeId is recorded in a whitelist configuration file can join the blockchain to propose blocks. For enterprise blockchains, there is BFT (Byzantine fault tolerant) consensus. This is a very well-adopted consortium blockchain consensus. With BFT, any node can propose a block, and the proposal will be accepted with a certain number of verification votes. For example, you can have ten nodes for a BFT consensus blockchain, and they will accept a block when three votes verify the block. You can also adjust the percentage of verification votes for BFT consensus. One advantage of BFT is its single block finality, meaning that once a block is proposed and verified, it is final and will not roll back.

Besides the four consensus mentioned with Ethereum-compatible blockchains, there are other consensus being adopted by other blockchains or under development. Basically, all public blockchains are permissionless networks, and all enterprise blockchains are permissioned networks. POW and POS consensus are permissionless for public blockchains, and POA and BFT are permissioned for enterprise blockchains.

The EVM, Ethereum Virtual Machine, is another innovation for the Ethereum blockchain. The EVM is a critical component of Ethereum nodes, as it executes the bytecode of smart contracts. The EVM and smart contracts' capability empowers thousands of decentralized applications, dubbing the Ethereum blockchain the second generation of blockchain after Bitcoin. More details on the EVM will be discussed in the smart contract programming of Chapter 7.

Storage is another important component in the core blockchain layer. When the EVM runs smart contracts, it needs to store a lot of data, and it needs to store the states. When you look at the EVM, there are thousands of machines working on the same program, and the same state has to be saved on every machine. You cannot just throw everything on Ethereum storage. Some people ask if it is feasible to store videos on Ethereum blockchain, and the answer is "no," because their videos will need to be stored in thousands of machines, which would be too expensive. Maybe you can only store like 32-byte hash of the media, but you cannot store the whole video.

There are also gas fees for each storage that you need to pay attention to when you write a smart contract program. Gas fees can be expensive. Today, an Ethereum gas fee is almost $100 for a normal sized smart contract transaction, so there's no way for a smart contract to be operational if it consumes a lot of CPU time or consumes a lot of storage. This is a challenge for Ethereum public blockchain – right now, it just costs too much. When gas fees are high, a single transaction can cost $60 to $100. So when you write and run your smart contract program, you need to take gas consumption into consideration.

Enterprise Components Layer

There are some limitations with Ethereum public blockchains; therefore, the EEA (Enterprise Ethereum Alliance) added the Enterprise blockchain components to its architecture. There are three things that are important for the enterprises: first is privacy, second is performance, and third is permission for enterprises.

In the original architecture, the Ethereum public blockchain did not consider these enterprise features by design. The Ethereum public blockchain does not support privacy. All the transactions on the public blockchain are open. The sender's and receiver's addresses and the transaction amounts are known to the outsiders scanning the blockchain states and logs.

The second thing is that performance for the Ethereum blockchain is not good because the gas mechanism, transaction and storage structure, and EVM are not fast and optimized. This gives the opportunity for alternative blockchains such as Polkadot to compete. Galvin Wood, a cofounder of Ethereum blockchain, proposed another blockchain called Polkadot that they claim runs faster and better. Polkadot also replaced EVM with WASM to make smart contract development more similar to web development.

There is another drawback for Ethereum public blockchain, which is related to permissions. Ethereum's public blockchain is permissionless, and everyone can join the blockchain and mine the blocks. This increases the challenges for the security and stability of the Ethereum public blockchains.

Tooling Layer

The Ethereum blockchain has the most comprehensive tools to help developers and users build and use decentralized applications. First, there are compilation tools such as Truffle and Remix that compile and deploy smart contracts written in Solidity. There are other tools that can compile other programming languages as well. On top of compiling tools, there are integration libraries such as the OpenZeppelin source library that can be imported into smart contract Solidity code to speed up development and modulizations.

Ethereum also has a rich variety of wallet tools to access assets and use dApps. There are hardware wallets such as Ledger and Trezor that store private keys in a hardware device. For a hardware wallet, all transactions are signed in the hardware device, and the private key will never leave the device. A hardware wallet is the most secure wallet to use for cryptocurrency users.

There are also desktop wallets that need to be installed onto laptop or desktop systems to interact with blockchain accounts. Additionally, there are mobile wallets that run as stand-alone apps on handheld devices. For users using a web interface to run dApps, MetaMask is the most popular one. It is a web plug-in or extension to a web browser such as Chrome or Firefox. It can be integrated with a hardware wallet as well to combine convenience of the web with the security of hardware devices. When you install MetaMask, it will generate a 12-word mnemonic phrase and create an account associated with that mnemonic phrase. Users need to write down the phrase to recover the MetaMask account in case the extension or plug-in is accidentally uninstalled.

For wallets or clients to connect to the Ethereum blockchain, JSON RPC protocol is used to connect with the Ethereum blockchain and smart contract. A JSON RPC is a communication protocol between a blockchain node and a Web3 client. A blockchain node runs in the Ethereum blockchain and can open up an RPC service through a dedicated port. The Web3 clients then connect to this RPC port and exchange information between the client and the blockchain. The RPC server can be a stand-alone blockchain node provided by the dApp application or can be a proxy node provided by a third party such as Infura. Projects such as Infura provide a large set of Ethereum nodes to be used by clients. Client applications can use an API key to connect to Infura nodes.

In summary, compilation tools such as Remix and Truffle, smart contract libraries such as OpenZeppelin, wallets such as hardware, mobile and MetaMask wallets, and JSON RPC provide major tooling capabilities to develop and build decentralized applications in the Ethereum blockchain.

Application Layer

The application layer contains software applications, tokens, and smart contract languages.

First, the software application has three elements as shown below:

A web interface	A web GUI is needed for a decentralized application
A dApp connector	A connector uses Web3 to connect web pages with blockchain smart contracts
Smart contracts on blockchain	Smart contracts provide business and transaction logic for your applications

The second important component in the application layer is the token. This is unique with blockchain, and the token economy is essential to sustain a blockchain and decentralized applications. Token designs include the kinds of tokens to issue, the amount of tokens supplied, who governs the administration of token supply, and whether a new token should be generated or an existing token can be reused.

Smart contract languages are also a major factor to consider. Besides Solidity, there are other languages such as Vyper, Yul, FE, and Serpent that can be leveraged to write smart contracts.

In summary, the Ethereum blockchain architecture contains the following layers: Network Layer, Core Blockchain Layer, Enterprise Blockchain Layer, Tooling Layer, and Applications Layer. Each layer serves essential functions for the Ethereum blockchain. We will describe in more detail the Tooling and Applications Layers for developers in the subsequent chapters.

Ethereum Blockchain Ecosystem and DeFi Projects

Before building a project using the smart contract development technology, it is essential to learn about the current Ethereum ecosystems. There are thousands of smart contracts and dApps deployed to the Ethereum blockchain already. We will walk through some of these projects so that you are aware of what kinds of projects are available already. It is better to brainstorm new ideas rather than reinvent the wheel.

Wallet to Manage Assets

The first class of blockchain applications are wallets that are used to manage assets.

In traditional finance, if you want to manage your asset, you most likely will go to a bank to open an account and let the bank manage the asset for you. But in the Ethereum blockchain, the assets are stored in a distributed ledger, and therefore, there are multiple ways to manage it.

Hosted Service

You can open an account with Coinbase and let Coinbase host the management of your crypto asset. When Coinbase is hosting your asset, you do not manage the private key for the asset; rather, you create a login account with the Coinbase service and let Coinbase do the transactions on your behalf. These kinds of services are centralized. There are asset management services around the world that offer services similar to Coinbase.

For users who prefer managing assets without a central portal, they can have full control of their assets by using Coinbase wallets that store their private keys locally. Coinbase wallets allow users to create accounts by themselves and do the asset management directly with the blockchain without going through a custodian.

MetaMask

MetaMask is one of the most popular web browser extension wallets and most versatile to use. Figure 6-3 shows how MetaMask interacts with blockchain to manage assets.

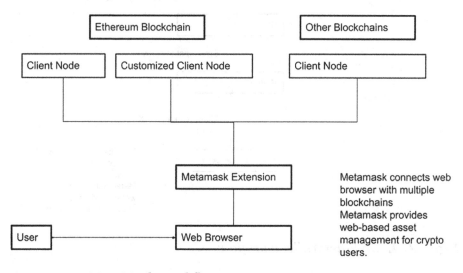

Figure 6-3. *MetaMask workflow*

MetaMask can be installed on the Chrome or Firefox browser. For Chrome installation, you simply download it from Chrome web store and install it to your browser. When MetaMask is first launched, it will create crypto accounts for you. Instead of generating private keys directly, MetaMask uses BIP39 specifications to generate mnemonic words, i.e. seed phrases, that are 12 common and easy-to-remember English words. The seed phrase can be used to generate multiple private keys and addresses. You need to write down the seed phrases in order to recover MetaMask accounts if the extension is uninstalled.

MyEtherWallet

MyEtherWallet (MEW) is an open source, client-side interface that allows users to interact directly with the Ethereum blockchain without having to join a centralized exchange. Figure 6-4 shows the workflow of transactions from user action to the blockchain.

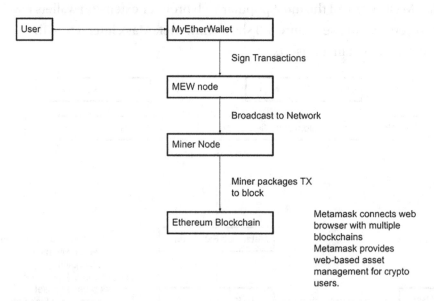

Figure 6-4. MyEtherWallet workflow

Although MyEtherWallet only works on the client side with no blockchain information sent back to the web server for processing and storage, there are still possibilities for phishing attacks. Using a hardware or mobile wallet of MyEtherWallet is recommended. The web-based MyEtherWallet is not recommended and should be used in offline settings only.

Fortmatic

Fortmatic is another kind of wallet that allows users to create accounts with their social identities. This is similar to a PayPal service where you can create an account with an email address. Fortmatic provides APIs to connect with various web-based decentralized applications and is very convenient for users who do not mind using a custodian wallet for crypto transactions and applications.

In this section, we mention asset management tools such as the web wallet, web extension wallet, mobile wallet, and custodian wallet. When choosing or developing a wallet, there are many factors to be considered:

- **Private keys** – Who generates, stores, and manages private keys?

- **Decentralization** – Is the wallet managed by a central service or custodia?

- **Security** – Have there been any security breaches or vulnerabilities reported in this wallet?

- **Ease of use** – Are the GUI and UX of the wallet user-friendly?

- **Open source** – Is wallet open source or proprietary?

- **Central control** – Is the wallet a client-side or server-side application?

- **Recovery** – Is there a trusted way to recover the account if the wallet gets lost or damaged?

Since the crypto wallet is needed to manage assets in blockchain, it is worth some time to research and choose the most trusted one.

Smart Contract–Enabled Banking dApp

In a conventional bank, customers can open accounts, deposit, and borrow money. The bank has to maintain huge databases and IT systems to keep track of all transactions and compute the interest on the savings accounts and loans. The Ethereum blockchain is a public distributed ledger, and crypto banking functions such as lending can be easily implemented with smart contracts.

One popular DeFi project in this category is Compound. Compound is a decentralized DeFi protocol (open API) to enable lending and borrowing of cryptocurrency through smart contracts. A lender is an actor who deposits supported cryptocurrencies such as ETH, USDT, USDC, and DAI to the Compound platform to earn interest. When a lender deposits cryptocurrency X to Compound, the smart contract will lock the asset and issue the same amount of cX token to the depositor. The lender can use the cX token to trade or redeem the X token back later. The smart contract will also calculate the interest earned by the lender for each deposit period. A borrower can borrow the cryptocurrency deposited by the lender to the Compound repository. Borrowers need to deposit a collateral asset in order to borrow the cryptocurrency they want. Borrowers pay interest for the cryptocurrency they borrow and can repay the borrowed cryptocurrency to get the collateral back.

If a borrower's collateral value factor falls below the balance of the loan, the borrowing account becomes insolvent and triggers a liquidation event. A third party can pay a portion of the loan and get the corresponding collateral originally deposited to this account. To incentivize third parties to participate in liquidation, an incentive determined by Compound's governing system is provided.

In a smart contract-enabled banking function, there is no central agency to manage the asset; the community needs to look at the smart contract and check for security risk. There is always a risk that the smart contracts are breached and customers' funds are lost. To minimize the risks, smart contracts are always open source, and the project team normally has a third-party security audit before releasing them to the mainnet of the public blockchain.

Decentralized Exchange in Ethereum

Crypto exchanges are used to transfer asset ownership between two different users. There have been some centralized exchanges such as Coinbase and Binance. Decentralized exchanges are fully built on smart contracts, and there is no need to build a centrally managed database for the exchanges. Popular decentralized exchanges include DDEX, Loopring, Uniswap, etc.

The Decentralized Exchange (DEX) using the Automated Market Maker (AMM) has some innovations over centralized or conventional exchanges. The AMM uses smart contracts and algorithms to adjust prices of assets in the liquidity pool and enables transactions without the need of maintaining an order book. For example, Uniswap is a popular AMM DEX that uses the following mechanism through smart contracts:

> **Automatic Liquidity Protocol** - Uniswap allows users to set up liquid pools by depositing an equal value of trading pairs to a smart contract. Traders can then trade their tokens with assets in the liquidity pool.

Automatic Price Adjustment – With the Uniswap liquidity pool, the amount of both tokens in a token pair (X,Y) needs to be balanced. If the amount of token X increases, then the amount for token Y decreases, and the price of token Y increases. This triggers negative feedback to balance the pool.

Arbitration: Arbitration is a process for traders to balance the price fluctuation in a liquidity pool. When the amount of token X in token pair (X, Y) increases, the amount of token Y decreases, and the price of token Y increases. The arbitrator then sees that token Y's price is higher than in other exchanges and will sell token Y from other exchanges to Uniswap to increase the supply of token Y to balance the liquidity pool. When the liquidity pool is balanced, the token prices should be similar to the token prices in other exchanges.

Using the Automated Market Maker mechanism, Uniswap was able to grow the TLV (total locked value) to 5 billion dollars within three years of development with an impressive 5% day-over-day growth.

NFT Applications

The NFT is a kind of token that has a unique identification and cannot be replaced or swapped with another. The specification of the NFT is in ERC721 and in a later version of ERC1440. One key feature of ERC721 is a field called id that contains a unique value for each token. ERC721 is most frequently used to represent creative artwork. Projects in NFT include 0xcert, OpenSea, Decentraland, CryptoPunk, etc.

0xcert is an SDK tool set that allows you to develop NFTs. Most of the tokens issued in Ethereum for ERC20 are fungible, meaning that there is no difference between token items. Fungible tokens are value based and like dollar bills are swappable. For NFTs, each token is different, and they are not replaceable. For example, a certificate or diploma can be represented as a nonfungible token because it is uniquely issued by an institute to a particular person. In the future, there will be more and more dApps developed to work with nonfungible tokens. For example, original art works, court documents, and college certificates all belonged to this category.

OpenSea allows users to submit NFT works for sale or buy NFT collections with cryptocurrencies. They also support auctions so that the highest bidders are granted the right to purchase an NFT artwork by smart contract. All transactions are controlled by smart contracts automatically, and no manual intervention or third-party hosts are needed.

Oracle Service

An Oracle service is used to provide connection between blockchain and conventional IT systems. Blockchain is self-confined, and there is no direct way for a blockchain client to talk to web servers directly. This is most likely designed for security considerations. Neither Bitcoin or Ethereum blockchains have a web API integrated on chain to call web services hosted by conventional IT systems. In order for blockchains to interact with conventional IT systems, Oracle services need to be used.

Chainlink is one of the most popular Oracle services that allow linkage of traditional web services with Ethereum blockchain. If you have a decentralized application that needs to get outside data, you need to use an Oracle service. For example, if your smart contract needs to get weather information, you have to use an Oracle service, as the blockchain itself does not have any weather information. To get information about FIAT/CBDC values, currency exchange rate, or cryptocurrency values, you need to connect to Oracle services provided by banks or third parties services as well.

There are other Oracle services provided by Provable and Band projects. Provable project also provides some SDK and example code to work with Oracle services with dApps and is very convenient.

DAO Platforms

DAO (Decentralized Autonomous Organization) is a platform to use smart contracts to manage an organization or community. The DAO platforms provide registration services and assign identities to constituents. Each member of the community can propose proposals and can also vote on proposals. There are many DAO platforms in the blockchain space already. In fact, many projects such as Compound and Uniswap have their own DAO communities and governing tokens to vote for proposals in the community.

Decentralized Insurance Platform

The Decentralized Insurance Platform allows smart contracts to manage the signing up of insurance services, provide insurance service from various sources, and then manage claims for the insured accounts. For example, if you want to prevent a heavy loss from a Bitcoin price crash, you can actually send a transaction to a smart contract to pay a premium as insurance, and there are people on the provider side who will accept the insurance request. All the terms of insurance are recorded and enforced through smart contracts. If unexpected events happen and trigger the insurance actions, the smart contract will execute the corresponding function and compensate the insured person.

Decentralized KYC and Identity

KYC (Know Your Customers) and Identity are services and tools to identify a real person and gather needed personal information to be in compliance with regulations. There are projects such as Civic, Hydro, Sovrin, and uPort that provide decentralized identity service for decentralized applications. To build KYC features within a decentralized application is quite challenging. It is much easier just to use a third-party KYC service.

Stablecoin

One of the challenges of cryptocurrencies is its volatility. Bitcoin and Ether's values fluctuate a lot, and using them to represent values for products and services will cause fluctuations in prices. Stablecoin is an asset that has relatively stable values when pegged with fiat currencies. These stablecoins are normally ERC20 tokens in the Ethereum blockchain. Their values are maintained to be stable in several ways. For example, a stablecoin can be backed by US dollars with a one-to-one ratio. These stablecoins include Gemini Dollar, TrueUSD, USD Coin, etc, as reported in some publications.

There are other kinds such as MakerDAO's Dai that are an aggregation of various assets and controlled by automatic burning and minting of stablecoins to make the value stable.

In summary, there are many big decentralized applications built on Ethereum already in almost all major categories. There are some applications that are still emerging. Small smart contract projects such as rental sharing, on-demand music service, and decentralized voting platforms are all possible projects that can be built with smart contracts. Smart contract development is a fascinating area. Developers can find unlimited possibilities to develop revolutionary decentralized applications once they learn how to program smart contracts.

Tools to Set Up a Smart Contract Development Environment

There are multiple ways to set up environments to interact with the Ethereum blockchain. Figure 6-5 shows an overview of various tools and components.

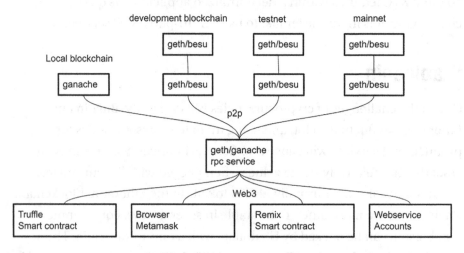

Figure 6-5. *Some basic tools for Ethereum blockchain*

The top layer shows various kinds of Ethereum blockchains. Ganache tool produces a local and single-node Ethereum blockchain and allows for development and quick testing of smart contracts and clients. Development blockchain allows developers to change the genesis file and start a fully controlled blockchain. Developers can issue Ether tokens in the development blockchain and can decide on a permissioned list for blockchain nodes. Testnets are public Ethereum blockchains that are built by the Ethereum community for testing purposes. Testnet Ether tokens can be obtained through some public faucets. There is no tradable crypto value for the testnet token. The public mainnet is the production blockchain of Ethereum, and the Ethers have value and can be traded in exchanges. In this section, we mention minimal viable tool sets including wallet, browser, node client, smart contract IDE, and Web3 to interact with Ethereum blockchains.

MetaMask: The Simplest Way to Interact with the Ethereum Blockchain

To get hands-on experience with the Ethereum blockchain, one of the easiest steps is to use a wallet to create an account and do some simple transactions of sending and receiving crypto tokens. This can be done in Ethereum by using MetaMask. MetaMask is a web extension that can be installed onto a web browser to create accounts to interact with Ethereum with the following steps:

Step 1: Install the MetaMask extension and create crypto accounts

Go to `https://metamask.io` and install MetaMask to your web browser such as Chrome or Firefox. After the installation, open MetaMask and write down the mnemonic passphrase of the wallet. The passphrase is 12 English words that are used to represent the private key of a wallet. This passphrase needs to be stored securely because it is needed to recover the wallet if the MetaMask is mistakenly uninstalled or the computer system stops working and the MetaMask needs to be reinstalled. Once you create a crypto account with MetaMask, there will be a public address for the account. This address is also called the account address and can be used to receive cryptocurrency for the account.

Step 2: Fund MetaMask account

Depending on the type of Ethereum blockchain you are connecting with, there might be different ways to get the wallet account funded.

For development blockchains that are created by developers or through ganache_cli, there will be some default accounts created and funded. Whoever starts the development blockchain will have some Ethers minted automatically in the accounts owned by the developer. Developers can import these funded accounts to their MetaMask wallet.

For testnets such as Rinkeby, Kovan, Ropsten, and Goerli, the test token can be obtained through a faucet. Developers can go to the faucet URL, paste a social media message with the wallet account's public address, and send it to the faucet web server. The faucet will then send a small amount of testnet Ether to the address specified in the message.

For mainnet Ethereum, the Ether needs to be purchased. This can be done by opening an exchange account from services such as Coinbase and paying with FIAT to get Ether.

Step 3: Send and receive tokens

Once the crypto account is created and funded, users can start sending and receiving tokens.

To send tokens, simply click Send and fill in Nonce, receiving amount, and receiver address and then click "Send" after verifying information.

To receive tokens, just give the account address to
the sender, and let the sender send cryptocurrency
to that address.

Etherscan: The Most Comprehensive Blockchain Browser

When transactions are transported to and executed in Ethereum, they
induce Ethereum state changes in account balances, blocks, transactions,
smart contracts, and event logs. The Ethereum blockchain only records
raw data in its storage. To browse the blockchain and make sense of it,
some of the data will need to be processed and stored in databases for
easy query and visualization. Etherscan is a web service that provides an
excellent Ethereum blockchain browsing experience. To use Etherscan,
simply open any web browser and point the URL to `http://etherscan.io`.

You can use the Etherscan browser to browse every account, smart
contract, block, and transaction in Ethereum blockchain. For developers
who need to use the blockchain data programmatically, Etherscan also
provide API functions and an API key to integrate dynamic Ethereum
blockchain data into your decentralized applications. Etherscan, as well
as other Ethereum blockchain browsers, only works with Ethereum public
blockchains, such as mainnet, Rinkeby, Kovan, Ropsten, and Goerli; it
does not work with development blockchains.

Geth: The Swiss Army Knife for the Ethereum Blockchain

Geth stands for Go Ethereum and is a stand-alone Ethereum client that
can run on an operating system as a miner node to earn Ether, or as an
RPC node to provide RPC services to client applications. We recommend
developers download a version of geth and use it as a sandbox with
following steps to interact with Ethereum blockchain.

Task 1: Prepare a geth standalone client

Geth client repository is located at `https://geth.ethereum.org/downloads/`.

You can also download it from GitHub at the following location: `https://github.com/ethereum/go-ethereum`.

Geth client is supported by major operating systems such as Linux, Windows, and MacOS. Since it is open source, it is recommended that developers run it in Linux systems such as Ubuntu.

To compile geth from its source code, the Go programming language compiler will need to be installed. Developers can use the Golang compiler for geth compilation.

Task 2: Run geth application

The geth application can run with various options. The full instruction is located in `https://geth.ethereum.org/docs/`. You can run it with the --miner option to do mining, but this is not recommended because Ethereum mining difficulty level is high, and it is almost impossible to compete with big mining pools in proof-of-work (POW) blockchains.

Geth can run as a sandbox for the following functions:

- Use geth to build a development blockchain.

- Use geth as a full blockchain client to download the whole Ethereum testnet or mainnet blockchain.

- Use geth as an RPC service to query blockchain information and broadcast transactions to all blockchain nodes.

- Use geth as a JavaScript console to interact with blockchains.

Task 3: Interact with geth RPC service

Once a geth node is set up with RPC service running, users can use wallets, applications, or the JavaScript console to connect to the RPC endpoint.

A. Through MetaMask custom RPC connection

To connect to an RPC service from MetaMask, simply open MetaMask, click to open the Network list, and choose Custom RPC to open up a new network widget. Specify a network name, and enter the RPC endpoint and the chainId of the network. The chainId is an identifier that is unique for all blockchains as specified by Ethereum standard EIP-155. If you are working on building a development network, you can specify a chainId in the genesis file. You can optionally specify the currency symbol for the blockchain and a URL for the block browser. Click Save to attach the new RPC node.

Once MetaMask is attached to the RPC node specified earlier, it will interact with the blockchain to which the node is connected. You can use MetaMask to send and receive transactions through the RPC node for a development blockchain.

B. Through JavaScript console

Geth can run not only as a blockchain node but also as a client to attach to an RPC endpoint and involve a command-line console to provide interactive scripting to the blockchain.

To attach to an RPC node and open up a JavaScript console, simply type

```
geth attach [rpc_url]
```

Here, rpc_url is the RPC endpoint for an Ethereum client node with RPC service enabled.

The JavaScript console will allow users to query block information, balances, transactions, blockchain syncing status, event logs, etc. For JavaScript console syntax, refer to the following document.

```
https://geth.ethereum.org/docs/interface/
javascript-console, Console syntax
https://web3js.readthedocs.io/en/v1.2.9/,
```
Ethereum JavaScript API

C.   Through a third-party application such as Truffle or Remix

Third-party applications will attach to an RPC endpoint to interact with Ethereum blockchains. Smart contract compiling tools such as Truffle and Remix all have features to connect to an RPC server. Once an RPC endpoint is connected, the smart contract bytecode files that are compiled will be sent to the attached RPC server and then broadcasted to the rest of the blockchain network.

Geth is the most popular Ethereum client adopted by the developer community. Besides geth, there are other clients such as Java-based Besu and quorum clients that can be used. Geth nodes can download the full blockchain to local storage, so having a system with hundreds of gigabyte storage is a requirement for running geth in full node mode.

Truffle: The Most Comprehensive Smart Contract Development Tool

Truffle is a smart contract development tool that allows users to compile, test, debug, and deploy Solidity code. It is easy to try out Truffle in a sandbox to get a good understanding about how to compile and deploy smart contracts.

Task 1: Install Truffle package

The Truffle package can be downloaded and installed through node package manager (npm):

```
npm install -g truffle
```

Here, the flag g means to install it globally so that the Truffle application can be launched from any directory.

Task 2: Prepare a project

Truffle has an init command that allows a developer to create a sandbox project for smart contracts. Simply go to a target directory and run the following command:

```
truffle init
```

A sample project will be created with sample smart contract and configuration files.

You can also replace the sample smart contract with your own smart contract and use a new configuration file.

Task 3: Compile and deploy a smart contract

Before compiling or deploying a smart contract, the Truffle configuration file will need to be configured. The Truffle tool uses the default file name of truffle-config.js file to look for the configuration. This configuration file has two major components to configure. The first is the network component, where you need to specify which blockchain network the compiled smart contract will be deployed onto. The configuration for the network will include network name, host address for the RPC endpoint, port number for the RPC endpoint, and network_id. The second configuration component is the compiler. For compiler configuration, the Solidity compiler version will need to be specified.

```
module.exports = {
  networks: {
    development: {
      host: "127.0.0.1",
      port: 8545,
      network_id: "*" // Match any network id
    }
  },
  compilers: {
    solc: {
      version: "^0.8.0"
    }
  }
};
```

Once the project is ready for compilation, simply run

```
truffle compile
```

The compiled result will be stored in the directory of build. This directory will contain the bytecode and ABI (Application Bytecode Interface) files. Smart contract bytecodes are the executable codes that will be deployed to the blockchain. The ABI code is used as a function lookup map for external applications to call the smart contract.

To deploy a compiled smart contract from Truffle, simply type

```
truffle deploy
```

This command will invoke deployment operation using the truffle-config.js file. It will deploy the smart contract to the network by using the RPC client service specified in the network section of the configuration file.

There is one more thing that needs to be emphasized. When deploying a smart contract, the developer needs to have a wallet to send the deployment transaction to the blockchain. For development blockchains, because this is internal and there are no security concerns, a user can simply add a wallet address in the configuration file. For production deployment, strict production security procedures will need to be followed, including using a hardware wallet or signing offline transactions.

Task 4: Use the Truffle console to interact with blockchains

Truffle provides a console command to interact with the attached blockchain node. There are two types of consoles available. One is a console that is connected to a testnet or mainnet blockchain. This console is launched through the following command:

```
truffle console
```

Another console is connected to a development blockchain. This console is launched through the following command:

```
truffle develop
```

The major difference between a regular console and a development console is that a regular console connects to an existing blockchain, while a development console creates an embedded blockchain, default accounts, and issued tokens for use by the developers.

Once a Truffle console is launched, developers can use it to query blockchain information, send and receive tokens, and call smart contract functions. To call a smart contract function, the following steps are followed:

- From the console, instantiate a smart contract object from its address and corresponding ABI.

- Get an account from the blockchain.

- Call the instance smart contract function with a sender account and other parameters.

The full example can be referenced at the following location:

```
www.trufflesuite.com/docs/truffle/getting-started/interacting-
with-your-contracts
```

Truffle is a very comprehensive and complex system. This section only mentions the features needed for compiling, deploying, and testing smart contracts. For details, refer to the Truffle office website:

```
www.trufflesuite.com/docs/truffle/quickstart
```

Remix: The Most Convenient Web-Based Smart Contract Development Tool

Remix is a web-based smart contract programming suite that is very easy to use. Remix can run as a browser web page or as a desktop application. To use Remix on a browser, simply open the Chrome or Firefox browser and point to the following location:

```
https://remix.ethereum.org
```

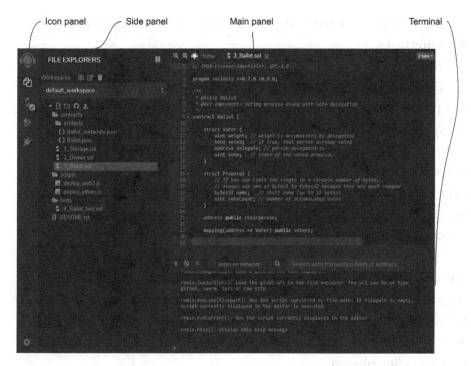

Figure 6-6. Remix compiler

There are four sections in the IDE: the icon panel on the left, the side panel in the middle, the main panel on the top right, and the terminal on the bottom left as shown in Figure 6-6.

Icon panel – Shows the file explorer, remix plug-ins, plug-in manager, and general setup icon.

Side panel – Shows source code files and GUI for each plug-in when selected.

Main panel – Shows the source file content for each smart contract. Source files can be edited in this panel.

Terminal – Shows the result of compilation, deployment, and interaction with the blockchain. Can also run scripts on this panel.

For the remix web console, you can easily experiment with the following tasks:

Task 1: Set up and install plug-ins

The Remix IDE (integrated development environment) uses component models to add basic features and third-party plug-ins to the system. The icon panel by default activates and shows three basic components: the file explorer, Solidity compilation, and deploy and run transactions. These three components should be sufficient for quick smart contract development. For other operations such as debugging, security scan, and visualization, developers can click the Plugin Manager icon and select the intended plug-in to activate.

Plug-ins can be activated or deactivated as needed by the developers. The icon panel also contains a settings button that can launch a settings page to configure the theme of the GUI, the source code editor, access to GitHub, etc. Once plug-ins are activated, developers can click each plug-in icon, and the side panel will show the interface and GUI details of the corresponding plug-in.

Task 2: Browse, edit, and compile a smart contract

The Remix packages some sample smart contracts in the web server. Click the File Explorer icon to open up the smart contract browsing panel. The source file of the smart contracts can be created as a new file or imported from repositories such as Gist, GitHub, Swarm, IPFS, or an HTTPS URL. One thing to note is that if a source file is imported from an external repository, the modified file will not be written back to the repository, and some manual operations are needed. For example, a workspace can be published as a gist in a GitHub repository. For other repositories such as IPFS, HTTPS, and Swarm, manual uploads outside Remix are needed.

To compile a smart contract, first, browse the source files and click the file you want to edit. The file content will be shown on the main panel. Developers can then simply modify the source code using the embedded editor. Once files are edited, click the Solidity Compiler button. This will launch a compiler GUI in the side panel. After selecting the Solidity compiler version and EVM to use, developers can click the Compile button to start compilation. Any compilation errors will be shown on the compiler panel, and developers will be prompted to modify the source code to fix the error. Once a smart contract compiles successfully, bytecodes and ABI files will be generated.

One thing to note is that the modified source code is stored in the browser only, and additional steps need to be taken to save it to permanent storage. This can be done by downloading the file to local storage, or publishing the file to a new gist in GitHub storage. Since the Remix browser does not have persistent storage, files that are edited but not downloaded or published will be erased if the browser data is cleared. To synchronize the Remix browser with persistent storage, the Remix web page will need to be connected to local storage. This is done by running a remixd in the background that provides shared persistent storage for Remix.

Task 3: Deploy a smart contract and execute functions

Once a smart contract is compiled successfully, developers can use the "*deploy and run transactions*" plug-in to deploy smart contracts and run transactions. After clicking the Deploy and Run transactions icon, a deployment GUI will prompt developers to choose a network connection environment, deployment account, smart contract to deploy, gas fee, etc., as shown in Figure 6-7.

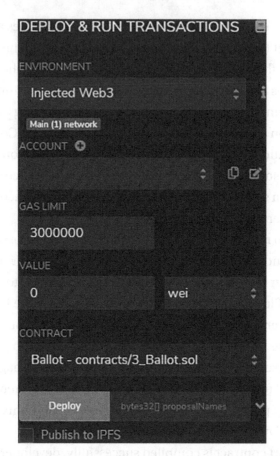

Figure 6-7. *Remix compiler widget*

There are three kinds of deployment environments: JavaScript VM, injected Web3, and Web3 provider. The JavaScript VM is an environment where the EVM is embedded within the Remix web page and is a simulated use case where no blockchain is actually connected. This is the easiest case for deploying and testing a smart contract. The injected Web3 environment uses the MetaMask extension to connect Remix with an external blockchain through MetaMask configurations. Instead of using

Remix, the MetaMask is used to connect to the blockchain and serves as a proxy to deploy the smart contract to the intended blockchain. The "Web3 provider" environment connects Remix with an RPC endpoint and deploys the smart contract to that RPC server and then broadcasts to the rest of the network.

Besides choosing a blockchain network environment, developers also need to specify an account for sending the deployment transactions. This account should have some Ether to pay for the gas fee for the deployment. This account will also become the owner of the smart contract. There are other miscellaneous parameters to configure. "Gas limit" specifies the maximum amount of gas that the transaction can consume. "Value" is the token to be sent to a target address. For smart contract deployment, the "Value" is irrelevant and should be set to zero. Once all parameters are set correctly, click the "Deploy" button to send out the deployment transaction. Some smart contracts might have constructors that take input parameters. In that case, the input parameters need to be specified in the input field beside the Deploy button.

Once a smart contract is deployed successfully, it will return an address that is called the smart contract address. Developers can browse the blockchain by clicking the address shown at the bottom of the deployment GUI. The deployment smart contract will then show variable names and values, functions, and other internal storage information. Developers can then input parameters into a function and execute the function. When calling a smart contract function, the developer is actually sending a transaction; therefore, there should be an account to pay for the transaction, and the transaction parameters should be specified as well. The execution results will be shown in the same panel, and some output will be shown in the terminal panel.

Summary

Three topics are mentioned in this chapter: overview of the Ethereum blockchain, ecosystem and dApps, and essential tools for smart contract developments. In the next chapter, the Solidity programming and deployment technology will be covered to teach how to build decentralized applications with smart contracts.

CHAPTER 7

Programming Smart Contract with Solidity

Introduction: What We Learned in the Last Chapter

In the previous chapter, we discussed Ethereum architecture, ecosystem, and decentralized applications. We also described development tools such as MetaMask, Remix, Truffle, and Geth. In this chapter, we are going to learn detailed Solidity programming skills for smart contract and decentralized application development.

What Is Smart Contract

Smart contract is an overloaded phrase. Although there are different interpretations for smart contract, we define it as follows:

"A smart contract is an executable computer program that runs on Ethereum Virtual Machine (EVM) on the blockchain to access and alter the states of blockchain blocks." Different from conventional computer programs that normally run on one single system, smart contracts run on every node of the blockchain.

© Weijia Zhang and Tej Anand 2022
W. Zhang and T. Anand, *Blockchain and Ethereum Smart Contract Solution Development*,
https://doi.org/10.1007/978-1-4842-8164-2_7

For Ethereum, smart contracts are compiled as executable bytecode and deployed to Ethereum blockchain. The bytecodes of a smart contract are sent through the data field of a transaction. Once the transaction is included in a block, a smart contract address is generated, and the bytecode is stored in that address. To call a function in a smart contract, a transaction is sent to the smart contract address, and the function name and input data are supplied through the data field of the transaction. When a transaction to call a smart contract is sent to a node, the Ethereum Virtual Machine loads the bytecode from the smart contract address and executes the function.

For a business person, a smart contract defines business attributes and processing logic to let multiple parties to execute and witness the processing of the business logic to ensure transparency, reliability, fault tolerance, immutability, and integrity for all parties (when the smart contract is well written).

Smart contracts differ from stand-alone computer programs because they are on all the machines and all parties have access to the smart contract to take advantage of transparency, reliability, and other benefits of blockchain.

But this is only the case where the smart contract is well written. If a smart contract is poorly written, then all these benefits go away.

For a technical person, a smart contract is a computer program that can be coded, compiled, tested, deployed, and executed on a blockchain.

From technical point of view, the phrase "smart contract" can mean several things.

Firstly, it can mean smart contract source code. Secondly, it can mean a compiled bytecode of a smart contract. Thirdly, it can mean a deployed smart contract residing on a blockchain.

When a smart contract is compiled, two files are generated: a bytecode file and an ABI (Application Bytecode Interface). The bytecode of a smart contract can be deployed to Ethereum blockchain and can be executed by the Ethereum Virtual Machine. The ABI code is a definition and description of smart contract rather than executable code. The ABI file is used by third-party applications to parse what functions are defined in a deployed smart contract and how to interact with them.

When a smart contract is "deployed" to a blockchain, a smart contract address is generated by calculating the Keccak-256 hash of the sender address and transaction nonce encoded with recursive-length prefix (RLP) serialization. A smart contract can also be deployed to different blockchains such as testnet or mainnet. The same smart contract address may refer to different blockchains.

It is important to know that "smart contracts" are used in different scenarios and contexts. In the following sections, we go into detail of smart contract programming.

What Is Solidity Programming Language

Solidity is the most popular programming language for Ethereum smart contracts. Solidity source code can be edited with a simple text editor or through IDE such as Remix or Microsoft Visual Studio. In order for Solidity code to run on Ethereum node, several things need to be done.

Firstly, the source code needs to be compiled into bytecode that can be interpreted and executed by the Ethereum Virtual Machine (EVM). Secondly, you need to deploy the smart contract bytecode to a blockchain or an EVM emulator for executions.

A bytecode is a program that can be executed by the Ethereum Virtual Machine. A bytecode program contains operands, data, and storage for each step. The EVM engine interprets instructions for each step and executes the instructions.

As mentioned in Chapter 6, Remix is a web-based integrated development environment (IDE), so developers can write code on the web page specified by the URL of remix.ethereum.org. This is very convenient for practicing smart contracting writing, compilation, and testing. The introduction of Remix has been mentioned in Chapter 6. This section will be focused on writing the Solidity programs.

Module 1: Hello World Solidity Example

Let's take the first example, HelloWorld.sol, as shown in the following:

```solidity
/**
 * SPDX-License-Identifier: MIT
 * @title HelloWorld
 * @dev Implements the hello world program
 */
pragma solidity >=0.7.0 <0.9.0;
contract HelloWorld {
    string helloworld = "Hello World";
    function justHelloWorld() public view returns(string
    memory) {
    return helloworld;
}

    function showHelloWorld(string memory me) public view
    returns(string memory) {
        string memory result = string(abi.
        encodePacked(helloworld, " from ", me));
        return result;
    }
}
```

In this example of helloworld.sol, it starts with comments that describe what the smart contract is about and then a HelloWorld smart contract where two functions are implemented. The first function, justHelloWorld(), simply outputs a string "HelloWorld", and the second function takes an input variable named "me" and then outputs "HelloWorld from [me]". This simple smart contract can be compiled, deployed, and executed on the blockchain. In the following, we describe the syntax of a smart contract Solidity code.

Solidity Comments

Comments are used extensively in Solidity to ensure that the smart contracts can be clearly understood by both programmers and third party users who need to use and trust the smart contracts. There are two kinds of comments that are supported with Solidity.

First is the double-forward slash "//" that is used to comment a whole line or a rear portion of a line as shown below.

```
//This is to comment a whole line
```

return "Hello World"; //This is to comment a portion of a line

Second syntax is to enclose the text with "/*" and "*/" to comment out the whole paragraph. To improve readability, each line in the commented paragraph might start with "**".

```
/**
** The HelloWorld program demonstrates a simple smart contract
   to return a "Hello World" string when a HelloWorld function
   is called.
** This program is an open source program that can be copied or
   modified without permission.
**/
```

Solidity Program and Version Declaration

Solidity source code starts with the "pragma" compiler directive followed by "solidity" and then a version specification. A compiler directive is an instruction for the compiler to parse and perform certain operations. The keyword "pragma solidity" instructs the compiler to treat the source code as a "Solidity" programming language.

```
// pragma: Tells compiler about the programming language and
    compiler version
pragma solidity ^0.5.2;              // specify an exact major version
pragma solidity >0.5.2;              // specify a newer version
pragma solidity >0.5.2, <0.6.2; // specify a range
```

Solidity programming language version has the syntax of x.y.z format such as 0.8.10. Here, x,y,z are numbers that can include 0. x is the major version number, y is the minor version number, and z is the patch number. For convenience, since x in Solidity has been "0" for a long time, "y" is referred to as "major version", and "z" is referred to as minor version.

Solidity language version section can have several forms such as the following:

~0.5.0 // This means an exact match of the Solidity.

^0.5.0 // This means a major version match. This version works with any 0.5.z but not 0.4.z or 0.6.z.

>0.5.2; // specify a newer version. This version works with any version that is newer than 0.5.2.

>=0.5.2, =<0.6.2; // specify a range of versions. Any version that is newer or equal to 0.5.2 but older or equal to 0.6.2 can be selected.

Versioning in Solidity is very important because Solidity programs run on blockchain and cannot be updated or patched to newer versions once they are deployed.

For developers, there are several things that can go wrong with the Solidity version. Because smart contracts cannot be upgraded or replaced, it is very important to make sure the source code is written in its "best" version as shown below

Exact latest version: This is recommended option. However, although specifying the exact version number is recommended, there are cases where flexibility is needed to address compatibility with other libraries.

Exact older version: This is used when the code is not compatible with the latest compiler and it takes too much effort to port it to the latest compiler.

Support of major versions: This provides more flexibility, particularly when the code is limited in scope and can be used as a library for various versions of smart contracts.

A range of versions: This is used when the code itself contains libraries of various versions and the smart contract is not mission critical.

It is very important to keep in mind that Solidity programming is progressing and the syntaxes are changing with different versions. Sometimes, a developer may have a source code working with version 0.5 but fail to compile with version 0.8. Therefore, it is a good practice to pay attention to version compatibility with Solidity source code or library.

Import a Solidity File

Right after Solidity and version declaration, there is normally an import statement where an external Solidity file is pulled into the source code. Solidity is an object orientation programming language and is very modularized. Developers separate source codes into different files and libraries and import the needed files to the main source code.

Many Solidity smart contracts are open source, and developers can import the library directly from open source repositories. One of the most popular open source smart contract libraries is from OpenZeppelin (`https://github.com/OpenZeppelin/openzeppelin-contracts`). Code such as SafeMath, ERC20, ERC721, ownership, and oracles can be reused from OpenZeppelin.

To import another source file, simply use the following formats:

import filename – This will import a file from the local directory.

import full_filename_with_path – This will import a file specified with an absolute path.

import github_location – This syntax will import a file from a GitHub location.

You can also import the file and give it a simple name to refer to such as following:

import filename as XYZ: Here, XYZ can be used to refer to the specific smart contract imported.

Constructor Function

A constructor is a special function that is executed during the deployment of a smart contract. This is to define parameters that are assigned during the deployment phase or to run an algorithm to dynamically set some parameters based on the deployment environment.

Function Modifier

A function modifier is similar to a macro that is defined once and can be used in multiple functions. For example, the following is a modifier that checks if the sender of the transaction is the owner. If yes, the validation is good, and if not, an exception is thrown. The "_" sign is the place where the function code will be inserted and executed.

```
modifier onlyOwner {
    require(msg.sender == owner);
    _;
}
```

```
function setMessage(string memory str)  onlyOwner {
//Do_Something
}
```

In the preceding code, the setMessage function has a modifier to check if the sender is the owner of the smart contract. If yes, the "Do_Something" code will be executed in the "_" location right after the require statement.

The best use of modifiers is for simplifying redundant codes of multiple functions in a smart contract. Once a modifier is defined, it can be used anywhere.

Blockchain Access Scope: Pure/View/Payable Functions

There are multiple scopes and permissions to define a function. The scope of a function describes the boundary of the function regarding whether the data can be altered and what part of the data can be accessed.

If a function is defined as pure, it is a self-confined function. The function variables are local, and the function will not access the blockchain. It simply takes an input, processes it, and returns an output. The "pure" functions do not have dependences on the blockchain states.

For the view function, the function may access the blockchain and get some read-only data from the blockchain to carry out the computation. The view function will not alter the state of the blockchain.

For payable functions, the blockchain state can be changed. For any function that will induce a transfer of assets, there should be a payable type assigned to the function and address.

One frequently asked question about pure, view, and payable functions is whether they all consume gas fees. It is obvious that a payable function always consumes gas fees as it changes the state of blockchain. For the view function, it only retrieves blockchain data, and the pure function does not even access blockchain state. The question regarding whether pure and view functions consume gas depends on how the function is called.

If a pure and view function is called through a transaction, there is a gas fee incurred to the transaction because running the function consumes CPU time. If the pure and view function is not called through a transaction, then there is no gas fee. A pure and view function can be called by directly attaching a client to an Ethereum node and instantiating a smart contract object in that local node and calling the function directly. Calling a smart contract function directly does not generate a transaction. The operation can be done by the local node without incurring gas fee. Therefore, the answer to the question about whether there is gas consumption for pure or view function depends whether there is transaction to the function call or not. Any function call that is triggered by a transaction will incur gas fee. The gas fee can be calculated by a gas fee consumption table in EIP-1559.

Function Access Scope: Public, External, Internal, and Private

The scope of functions defines who can access the functions. This is different from the function type of view/pure/payable, which defines whether the function will access the blockchain, and if yes, whether it reads or writes to the blockchain.

There are four access scopes in Solidity functions: public, external, internal, and private scopes. Public function means that you can call this function from an external blockchain client. If a function needs to be called through a Web3 client, it is defined as public. External functions can be called by another smart contract. Solidity supports importing an external smart contract and calling the functions defined in the other smart contract. The syntax to call an external smart contract is contractName. functionName(). If an external function is called by the same smart contract, use "this.functionName()" to refer to calling within the same contract.

Internal functions can be called by other functions in the same or derived smart contract. And finally, private functions can only be called by the functions in the same smart contract, which is the most restrictive.

254

Module 2: Solidity Data Types

A data type is a supported format and classification of data that tells the compiler and execution engine to interpret a programming language. Similar to any modern programming languages, Solidity has a good set of supported data types. In general, understanding data types can help programmers to improve code security and execution efficiency. For Solidity, there are additional reasons for knowing and paying attention to data types. Firstly, users who call smart contract functions need to pay gas fees for the storage and processing of computing steps. The gas consumption could be quite expensive, sometimes reaching $200 per transaction for Ethereum mainnet transactions. Secondly, smart contract functions are open to the world. Anyone can call the smart contract's public functions. If the data type for a variable is improperly defined such as allocating too much space, a malicious user may inject garbage to the data and cause some performance issue or even stall the process of smart contract function calls. Thirdly, Solidity only supports a limited set of data types when compared with Java programming language. Data types such as double and float are not supported in Solidity programming language.

Boolean

Boolean is the simplest data type for a programming language. It only uses one bit of storage to represent a true or false state of a variable. In Solidity, a variable can be declared as a boolean with bool keyword as shown in the following:

```
bool new_member;
```

There are several logical operators that can be applied to a boolean data type as shown in the following:

! (logical negation)

&& (logical conjunction, "and")

|| (logical disjunction, "or")

== (equality)

!= (inequality)

With the boolean data type, an exclamation sign ! can be used as a negation of the boolean type. A negation operation turns a true state to false and a false state to true. Other operations on a boolean type can be && or ||. An && operation of two boolean types will be true if both are true. A "||" operation of two boolean type variables will be true if either variable is true. Two boolean variables can also be compared. Two boolean variables are equal if they are both true or both false. Sometimes, a boolean variable can be conditionally checked in an "if" statement. If(variable) returns true if the variable is true, and false if the variable is false.

Since a boolean variable consumes only one bit storage and there are multiple operations that can be used to operate on boolean variables, it is recommended that developers use boolean type rather than other data types if possible for storage efficiency.

Integer Type

Integer data type is used to represent a positive integer (unsigned) or any integer (signed). In Solidity, the signed or unsigned integer can be in different sizes represented by the amount of bits allocated for an integer variable. For example, uint8 means an 8-bit unsigned integer. uint8 can hold values from 0 upto 2^8-1 (0–255). uint256 can hold values from 0 to $2^{256}-1$. Between uint8 and uint256, there are also various integer data types in incremental size increase of 8 bit (1 byte). Signed data types differ from unsigned ones as it can represent both positive and negative integers. For example, int8 can hold values from -128 to 127 (range of -2^7 to 2^7-1). int256 can hold values from -2^{255} to $2^{255}-1$. "int" can also have various sizes at an incremental step of 8 bit, such as int8, int16, int24, int32 up to int256.

If the bit number is not specified in the integer type, it is default to 256. uint and int are aliases for uint256 and int256, respectively.

Solidity also has built-in operators for integer type variables. This is shown in the following table (Figure 7-1):

Type of operator	Symbol	Remarks
Comparison	<=	A<=B returns true if A is smaller or equal to B
	<	A<B returns true if A is smaller than B
	==	A==B returns true if A is equal to B
	!=	A != B returns true if A is not equal to B
	>=	A >= B returns true if A is larger or equal to B
	>	A > B returns true if A is larger than B
Bit operations	&	The resulting bit is 1 when both bits are 1
	|	The resulting bit is 1 when either bit is 1
	^	Bitwise exclusive or
	~	Bitwise negation
Shift operations	<<	Left shift, equivalent to multiplication by 2
	>>	Right shift, equivalent to division by 2
Arithmetic operations	+	Arithmetic addition
	-	Arithmetic subtraction
	unary -	Negates a given signed integer
	*	Multiplication
	/	Division
	%	Modulo
	**	Exponentiation

Figure 7-1. *Operators for Integer Datatype*

Since smart contracts can be written to handle large sums of assets, it is important to ensure that the math is fully accurate. The boundary conditions and validity of inputs should be checked thoroughly. Many libraries have been written to let developers reuse the math components and to prevent hackers attacking smart contracts through security holes in math functions. For example, SafeMath is a good library to use to handle mathematics operations. Developers can download SafeMath libraries by OpenZeppelin and import the smart contract to use the class and functions in the library.

Address Type

Address is an unique identifier of a crypto account in blockchains. Address type is a data structure that is not defined in conventional programming languages such as C or Java but is essential in smart contract programming languages. Ethereum blockchain uses a 20-byte hex value to represent a crypto address.

When you create an account in Ethereum, three items are generated. The first item is a private key. This is the unique key to access the account and should be kept by the account owner and never revealed to other people. The second item is a public key that is used to represent the account and can be published. A public key can be used to encrypt a message, and only the private key can decrypt the message. The third item is an address derived from a public key. An address is actually a simplification of the public key. Simply apply Keccak-256 hashing to the public key and then take the last 20 bytes; the output is the address for the account. Since each byte can represent two hex numbers, it is actually a hex string with 40 digits such as *0x1F2D3A67b8E96039BbAC84EB4BC0913c0c16778c*.

In Solidity code, address data type is a representation of an asset account. When declaring an address variable, the developer needs to specify whether this address can receive external funds or not. This can be done by using the keyword **payable**.

If an address is declared payable, it can receive funds sent to this address. If not, the smart contract will reject any funds that are sent to this account. Payable keyword is an additional safeguard to ensure only valid accounts can receive assets transferred to it.

The following shows how to define a nonpayable and payable address example.

```
// address type is a twenty byte hex variable
address account_spending;
account_spending = 0x1F2D3A67b8E96039BbAC84EB4BC0913c0c16778c;
address payable account_receiving;
account_receiving = 0xDda897285Ce46CG78D786a9e993286AaC68c45bC;
```

In the preceding examples, there are two address variables defined. The first one, account_spending, is a nonpayable account. It cannot be used to receive any funds. It can, however, send out funds from its own account. The second one called account_receiving has the payable attribute and hence can send out or receive funds with the account.

One more thing to point out is that address can not only be an identification to an account, it can also point to a smart contract instance. A smart contract address is the entry point to a deployed smart contract. This address can be used to represent a deployed smart contract and call the functions inside the smart contract.

Byte Array

Byte array (Figure 7-2) uses array to represent a fixed amount of bytes from 1 to 32. The following defines various types of byte arrays and the bit operations that can be applied to the array.

Byte array name	Value range	Remark
byte1 or byte	00000000 to 11111111	This array holds 1 byte or 8 bits of data
byte2	0000000000000000 to 1111111111111111	This array holds 2 bytes or 16 bits of data
Up to byte32	128 bits of data	This array holds 32 bytes or 128 bits of data

Figure 7-2. *Byte arrays data type*

Note:

Byte is the same as byte1.

To define a byte array, use the following syntax:

byte1 b1;

byte2 b2;

Byte32 b32;

In the preceding example, b1, b2, and b32 represent a 1-byte, a 2-byte, and a 32-byte variable, respectively.

To retrieve an element of a byte array variable x, use x[i], where i ranges from 0 to byte size to get the byte at index i.

The following diagram shows the operations for byte arrays (Figure 7-3).

Type of operator	Symbol	Remarks
Comparison	<=	A<=B returns true if A is smaller or equal to B
	<	A<B returns true if A is smaller than B
	==	A==B returns true if A is equal to B
	!=	A != B returns true if A is not equal to B
	>=	A >= B returns true if A is larger or equal to B
	>	A > B returns true if A is larger than B
Bit operations	&	The resulting bit is 1 when both bits are 1
	|	The resulting bit is 1 when either bit is 1
	^	Bitwise exclusive or
	~	Bitwise negation
Shift operations	<<	Left shift, adding 0 bit to the right
	>>	Right shift, adding 0 bit to the left

Figure 7-3. *Byte array operations*

Fixed Size Array

Fixed size array is an indexed array of any data type such as the following:

data_type array_name[array_size]

Here, data_type is any data type such as integer, address, and byte, such as following:

```
uint balances[30];  // an unsigned integer array of fixed size
address students[25];
// an address array that holds 25 students' account address
```

A fixed size array can be initialized by assigning the data value during the declaration phase or later by assigning a value to the variable element.

```
uint balances[5] = [10, 20, 30, 40, 50]; // This declares a
balanced array of type unsigned integer and assigns values to
each element.
uint balances[] = [10, 20, 30, 40, 50]; // This declares a
balanced array of type unsigned integer and assigns values to
each element. The array size is omitted and it is equal to the
number of values assigned to the array.
```

To assign a value to an array element, simply use the following syntax:

```
array_name[index] = data_value;
```

Here, array_name is the array variable name, index is the index for the array element, and data_value is the value to be assigned to the element. An example is shown here:

```
balances[3] =300; // assigned value 300 to index 3 of
                          balances array.
```

Dynamically Sized Array

In Solidity, arrays have continuous addresses. The first element points to the lowest address, and the last elements points to the highest address. For a fixed size array, the size of the array is set during the compilation time. For a dynamically sized array, the array size is set during the runtime. To declare a dynamically sized array, use the following syntax:

```
data_type[] array_name;
```

Here, data_type is the name of the data type such as uint and address.

array_name is the array variable name such as balances and students_ addresses.

```
uint[] balances;
address[] students_addresses;
```

When a dynamic array is declared, its size will need to be set with a length in the code execution.

To set the array length, use the following syntax:

```
array_name = new data_type[](size);
```

Here, array_name is the array variable name. data_type is the data type name, and size is an uint that represents the intended size of the array. For example, the array variables mentioned earlier can be set to the following length:

```
balances = new uint[](9); // set balances array size to 9
students_addresses = new address[](10);
// set students_addresses array size to 10
```

Mapping Data Type

Besides address data type, another important one is mapping type. Mapping data type associates two variables like an associative array. Mapping type is an important data type because it correlates two or more variables.

To declare mapping types, use the following syntax:

```
mapping(key_type => value_type)
```

The key_type can be any elementary type such as built-in types like uint, address, bytes, and string.

The key_type can also be user-defined or complex types like contract types, enums, mappings, structs, and any array type.

value_type can be any type, including mappings.

The following defines a mapping of address array with balance for each array element:

```
address student_address;
uint score;
mapping(student_address => score) public scores;
```

The preceding example defines student_address as an address data type and a score as uint type. Then student_address is mapped to score. To assign a score to a student, use the following syntax as example:

```
student_1_address = 0x1B2E2A67b8E96039BbAC84EB4BC0913c0c16668D;
score_1 = 90;
scores[student_1_address] = score_1;
```

// This example sets the score for student 1 to be 90.

To retrieve the score of student 1, simply enter the student's address to the scores variable:

```
scores[student_1_address] // This will return 90.
```

A mapping is a versatile data type that associates two variables without a predefined size. This is used frequently in smart contracts.

Enum Data Type

Enum is a data type that enumerates a variable to have only some predefined values. By restricting the values in an enum variable, the chance to make mistakes is decreased.

The syntax for defining an enum is

```
enum enum_type_name{VALUE_LIST};
```

Here, enum is the data type keyword, and enum_type_name is the name of the enum type. VALUE_LIST is a list of values separated by comma.

Once an enum type is defined, it can be used to declare an enum variable.

```
enum_type_name variable_name;
```

For example, in order to limit the role of a decentralized organization, the role variable can be an enum data type such as

```
enum DAO_ROLES{SECRETARY, ACCOUNTANT, LEGAL, MEMBER};
DAO_ROLES newMember;
newMember = DAO_ROLES.MEMBER;
```

In the preceding example, DAO_ROLES is declared as an enum that can have the values of SECRETARY, ACCOUNTANT, LEGAL, and MEMBER.

The DAO_ROLES is used to declare a variable newMember. This new member is assigned a value of DAO_ROLES.MEMBER.

By using enum, it reduces the values for a variable to a limited list and hence is less error prone.

In the following, a code snippet is shown to illustrate how to use an enum to define variables:

```
pragma solidity ^0.6.0;

contract enum_example {
   enum DAO_ROLES{ SECRETARY, ACCOUNTANT, LEGAL, MEMBER};
   // define an enum type
   DAO_ROLES latestMember; // define an enum variable

   function setRoleSECRETARY() public {  // declare a function
   to set latestMember to be a SECRETARY role
      latestMember = DAO_ROLES.SECRETARY;
   }
```

```
function getRole() public view returns (DAO_ROLES)
{ // Query the role of the latest member
   return latestMember;
}
}
```

Struct Data Type

Struct is the abbreviation of structure. Similar to struct in other programming languages, Solidity supports struct data type to group a number of variables together. The group of variables can have different data types. A struct variable type is defined with the following syntax:

```
struct struct_type{
datatype_1 variable_1;
datatype_2 variable_2;
...
}
```

Here, struct_type is the struct to be defined. datatype_1, datatype_2, etc., are data types that are native with Solidity or defined by the user.

An example of defining a struct is shown here:

```
enum Experience{ENTRY, JUNIOR, SENIOR, EXPERT};
enum Skillset{SOLIDITY, PROTOCOL, BOTH};

struct Developer {
address addr;
Experience level;
uint hourly_rate;
Skillset skill;
 }
Developer guru1;
```

In the preceding example, a Developer struct is defined that contains four components: an account address of the developer, an enum of experience level, an hourly rate of uint type, and skill of enum type. The variable guru1 is declared as a Developer struct type variable.

To refer to components inside a struct, use "." symbol. For example, to set values to guru1 in the preceding example, do the following:

```
guru1.address = 0x1B2E2A67b8E96039BbAC84EB4BC0913c0c16668D;
guru1.level = Experience.EXPERT;
guru1.hourly_rate = 80;
guru1.skil = Skillset.SOLIDITY;
```

Besides setting values individually as shown earlier, a struct variable can be assigned values through struct constructor as shown in the following:

```
guru1 = Developer(0x1B2E2A67b8E96039BbAC84EB4BC0913c0c16668D,
    Experience.EXPERT,
    80,
    Skillset.SOLIDITY
)
```

If there are multiple developers such as guru1, guru2, and guru3, a mapping combined with struct can be used. For example, an uint can be mapped to a Developer struct to refer to a list of developers:

```
mapping(uint=>Developer) developers;
```

Here, developers is a mapping variable. Each developer can be referred to as developer[0], developer[1], etc.

Mapping combined with struct can provide very sophisticated data types that can address most of the data type tasks in Solidity programming.

In summary, Solidity provides a way to define new types in the form of structs. The following code snippet shows an example of Donor struct that contains an address and the donation amount:

```
contract Charity {
 // Defines a struct with two fields.
struct Donor {
address addr;
uint donation_amount;
 }
// define a mapping
mapping (uint =>Donors) donors;
//...
}
```

Blockchain Specific Variables

Frequently, smart contracts need to get information from blockchain itself and use blockchain data in the functions. Solidity actually defines some global variables to refer to the blockchain state and transaction data. The common ones are global variables and functions defined in the following table (Figure 7-4). There are two major variables: msg (message global variable) and block (the blockchain variable).

Special blockchain variables and functions		
Variable name	**Description**	**Unit**
block.coinbase	Current block miner's address	address payable
block.difficulty	Current block difficulty	uint
block.blockhash(uint blockNumber)	Hash of the given block – only works for 256 most recent, excluding current, blocks	bytes32
block.gaslimit	Block gas limit	uint
block.number	Current block number	uint
block.timestamp	Current block timestamp as seconds since Unix epoch of January 1, 1970 (midnight UTC/GMT)	uint
gasleft()	Remaining gas limit	uint
msg.data	Complete calldata passed in a transaction	bytes calldata
msg.sender	Sender of the message (or caller address for a smart contract)	address payable
msg.sig	First four bytes of the calldata	bytes4
msg.value	Number of wei sent with the message	uint
now	Current block timestamp	uint
tx.gasprice	Gas price for the transaction	uint
tx.origin	Sender of the transaction	uint

Figure 7-4. *Special blockchain variables and functions*

Most of the global variables listed in the preceding table are self-explanatory. There are a few variables that need further clarification.

The msg variable mainly defines the parameters and data inside a transaction. Every time when a transaction is sent to Ethereum blockchain, the msg object can be referred by a smart contract to extract the following information:

msg.value – This is the amount of Ether that is sent to the receiver. It is in the unit of wei.

msg.data – This is the data field in a transaction. It is the user input data that is sent to a smart contract to process.

msg.sig – This is the signature of the sender who sent the transaction.

msg.sender – This is the address of the sender. It is important to check the address of the sender to ensure that the sender is authorized to perform actions on the smart contract functions.

block.blockhash – The block.blockhash is a special function that takes in a block number and outputs its block hash.

block.difficulty – Outputs the difficulty of blockchain mining.

block.gaslimit – Defines the gas limit for the latest block.

block.number – The latest block number.

gasleft() – Returns the gas left for a transaction.

now – The current timestamp.

Another global variable is tx reserved for the transactions.

tx.gasprice – Shows the gas price of the transaction.

tx.origin – Original sender of the transaction. This is the same in single function calls as msg.sender.

Module 3: Events

What Is Ethereum Event

Ethereum events are important concepts that are related to how to message smart contract states and communicate with external programs. Event type is an inheritable member of smart contract that is built into Solidity programming language. Solidity provides syntaxes for defining an event format and emitting an event.

Where Are Events Stored

Once an event is emitted, the corresponding event data is stored in the transaction logs. The event data is the list of arguments passed to the emit event function. The transaction logs are accessible through smart contract addresses by external programs. Although events are stored in transaction logs, its content is not accessible by smart contracts. Smart contracts can emit events but cannot access events that are emitted.

How to Define an Event

Defining an event is very simple; just use the "event" keyword to define an event name with a list of attributes as the following:

event eventName(dataType_1 [indexed] attribute_1, dataType_2 [indexed] attribute_2, ..., dataType_n [indexed] attribute_n);

Here, event is the keyword to define an event.

eventName is a name of the event.

dataType_1, dataType_2, dataType_n are lists of data types defined in Solidity.

attribute_1, attribute_2, attribute_n are lists of attribute names specified by the developers.

271

indexed is a reserved keyword to allow a search for these events using the indexed parameters as filters.

For example, to define an event when a token is minted, use the following event definition as example:

```
event Mint(address indexed receiver, uint amount);
```

In the example above, a Mint event is defined with two attributes. The first attribute is the address of the receiver to which the minted token is sent. The address is indexed, meaning that this is a searchable attribute. The second attribute is the amount of token that is minted. The event does not need to specify the token name or mint time as these can be inferred from the smart contract address and the block time for the transaction.

In summary, an event definition basically defines an event name and a list of attributes. Once an event is defined, it can be called with parameters to emit an event.

How to Emit an Event

Once an event type is defined, it can be emitted and recorded in the transaction log as controlled by smart contract function. The syntax to emit an event is shown here:

```
emit eventName(parameter_1, parameter_2, ..., parameter_n);
```

Here, emit is the keyword to trigger an emission of an event.

eventName is the event type defined by the developer using the "event" keyword.

Parameter_1, parameter_2, parameter_n are the parameters for the attributes defined in the event type. The parameter data type should match the data type of the event attributes.

An event type can be called to emit as many events as needed. For example, the Mint event as defined in the last section can emit an event each time a mint operation is performed.

```
emit Mint(0x1F2D3A67b8E96039BbAC84EB4BC0913c0c16778c, 200);
```

In the example above, an event is emitted to show that 200 tokens have been minted to the specified address of 0x1F2D3A67b8E96039BbAC84EB4BC0913c0c16778c.

When an event is emitted, its data is actually saved onto the transaction log. The event can be viewed by using a block explorer to look into the transaction log section of a transaction. The log can be accessed through the address of the smart contract. The log cannot be accessed within the smart contract itself. A smart contract cannot emit an event in one function and then call another function to process the emitted event.

Events can only be accessed through external programs such as client programs. The Web3 library has some event access function calls that can be used to retrieve or search for the events.

Event Examples

Once we know the event definition and emission, coding events is very straightforward. The following shows a contract for DepositEvent that emits deposit records:

```
pragma solidity ^0.8.0;

contract DepositEvent {
    event Deposit(address indexed depositor_address, uint
    indexed deposit_id, uint deposit_amount);    // defines a
    Deposit event with depositor address, depositor_id (or
    deposit number), and deposit_amount as attributes
```

```
function deposit(uint deposit_id) public payable {
    emit Deposit(msg.sender, deposit_id, msg.value); //emit
    a Depositor event with sender address, positor_id, and
    depositor_amount equal to the ether transferred  in the
    transaction.
}

}
```

In this example, a snippet of the DepositEvent class is defined. In the class, a Deposit event is defined globally. There is a function deposit that takes in a deposit_id as input and emits an event with depositor_address, deposit_id, and deposit_amount. The depositor_address and deposit_amount are obtained from a special variable msg directly.

Event is a messaging method that allows smart contracts to communicate with external programs. Blockchain is very self-confined, and smart contracts cannot access external programs directly. In this case, events become a messaging mechanism between external programs and smart contracts. Since events are in transaction logs that are part of the state of Ethereum, emitting events will cause gas consumption and should be carefully designed.

Module 4: Security

Security is the most important aspect of Solidity programming.
In Chapter 8, we have one whole chapter describing blockchain security.
In this module, we will discuss security with Solidity programming.

Function Vulnerabilities
Function Visibility Error

This is a vulnerability where function visibility is not specified, or specified as public when it is supposed to be private.

In earlier versions of the Solidity compiler, the visibility of a function is default to public.

Functions should be properly specified as external, public, internal, or private.

One example of this vulnerability is shown in the following. The first function has an input check and calls the second function. The first function is declared as public, and it needs to be called by the client application with input from users. The second function has a vulnerability as it is declared as public but sends out funds without checking the validity of the senders.

```
pragma solidity ^0.4.24;

contract HashForEther {

    function withdrawWinnings() public {
        // Winner if the last 8 hex characters of the
            address are 0.
        require(uint32(msg.sender) == 0);
        _sendWinnings();
    }

    function _sendWinnings() public {  // security error. This
    function should be declared as private
        msg.sender.transfer(this.balance);
    }
}
```

To fix this vulnerability, simply declare the second function to be private.

Vulnerability: Function Call Return Value Not Checked

This is a vulnerability where the function call value is not checked. When a function is called and returns an error, the subsequent program still executes. It is important to check return values and exceptions and process the return value accordingly.

Vulnerability: Ether Withdraw Operation Not Protected

This is a serious vulnerability. It can happen in many cases. A withdraw function should be protected with many factors. Firstly, the visibility of the function should be right. Secondly, the input addresses need to be checked to make sure the sender has the authority to withdraw the funds. Furthermore, the constructor code will need to be protected. The constructor function runs in the runtime bytecode and can be called by a hacker to execute the code.

Vulnerability: Self-Destruction Functions

This is a vulnerability in which a user or hacker can call a function to destroy the functionality of a smart contract and make it unrecoverable. This happened with the famous parity "I accidentally killed it" bug where an anonymous user called a "kill" function in a parity multisign wallet component and destroyed the component. The vulnerability caused a total of 513,774.16 Ether inaccessible to the asset owners. In order to prevent this from happening, the use of kill function, denouncing ownership function, and destruct function should be kept minimum unless it is absolutely needed. The self-destruction functions include suicide or selfdestruct function.

```
// This is a selfdestruct function that will remove the
contract and send the remaining asset to the sender address
pragma solidity ^0.4.22;
```

```
contract SimpleSuicide {

  function sudicideAnyone() {
    selfdestruct(msg.sender);
  }

}
```

Vulnerability: Use of Solidity Deprecated Functions

Some of the functions in the older Solidity versions are deprecated and replaced with new ones as shown in Figure 7-5. When doing the compilation, watch the warnings and replace the deprecated ones with the new ones.

Deprecated	Alternative
suicide(address)	selfdestruct(address)
block.blockhash(uint)	blockhash(uint)
sha3(...)	keccak256(...)
callcode(...)	delegatecall(...)
throw	revert()
msg.gas	gasleft
constant	view
var	corresponding type name

Figure 7-5. *Deprecated functions in Solidity*

Vulnerability: Delegatecall to Untrusted Callee

Solidity supports delegatecall function that will call another smart contract with the same execution context of the calling contract. This means that msg.sender and msg.value are the same for the caller and callee. If the callee address is not trusted, it will cause security issues with the calling contract.

277

Vulnerability: DOS with Failed Function Calls

External calls may fail, and it should not halt the rest of the execution steps. Developers should avoid combining multiple calls in a single transaction. Contract functions should have logic to process failed calls. When sending funds to users, it is best to let users "pull" the funds by initiating a transaction rather than using smart contracts to push the asset to a group of users.

Vulnerability: Race Conditions and Transaction Order Dependence

Blockchain does not execute transactions in the order in which they are submitted. Transactions are packed by miners, and miners would like to package transactions with higher gas fees. It will cause issues for some smart contract functions when there are dependencies for function calls in different smart contracts. For example, ERC20 fungible tokens have an "approve" function to specify another user to use a certain amount of token. Then there is a transfer function that can transfer funds not exceeding the approved amount. Suppose Alice approves funds to Bob at the amount of m and then changes the approval amount to n, and during this time, Bob sends two transactions to transfer funds at amounts of n and m, respectively. Since the transactions are not in the exact order, it is possible that Bob first transfer falls between Alice approval 1 and approval 2, while Bob transfer 2 falls after approval 2. This will allow Bob to retrieve the m+n token rather than the expected amount of either n or m.

Fixing race conditions in function calls is not easy. One way to ensure function dependency is to use secret salt and hash methods. The sender will have a secret salt and produce a hash of the salt. Then the sender of the function will call the approved function with a hash and address. The smart contract will save the hash to the blockchain. The sender then sends the salt to the receiver. The receiver then calls the request function with a secret salt. The smart contract computes the hash from the salt and compares it with the one saved by the smart contract. If it matches, the request function will process the receiver's request. If not, it will be rejected. This ensures one-on-one mapping of two subsequent function calls.

Vulnerability: Assert Violation

Assert() is a function call to ensure the statement to be evaluated is always true. This is different from the require() function that is used to check the condition of the statement. Assert() result should never be false. If assert() function returns a false result, it means that there is a serious bug in the code.

Vulnerability: Cross Contract Call Enters into a Loop

Solidity smart contract supports calling another smart contract. If two smart contracts call each other's function, there is a possibility that the call might enter into a loop and consume all the funds as shown in the following example:

```
// security_callee.sol:
pragma solidity 0.8.0;
contract Bob {
    function ping(address c) public{
        //do something
        return;
    }
}
```

```
contract Mallory {
    fallback() external{
    Bob(msg.sender).ping(address(this));
    }
}
```

```
// security_caller.sol
contract Bob {
bool sent = false;
function ping(address c) external {
if (!sent) {
c.call{value:2}("");
sent = true;
}}}
```

The preceding example shows that a cross smart contract call might enter into a loop.

In this example, security_callee.sol and security_caller.sol are both deployed to the blockchain. The contract Bob in security_caller.sol invokes a function called ping and an input from an external program. The ping function then calls another smart contract with the Mallory contract address. Mallory contract has a fallback function that will take in the ping function call from Bob contract. In Mallory contract, the Bob contract is also called, hence causing a loop where Bob calls the fallback function in Mallory while Mallory calls Bob's ping function. Each step in the call will cause a value of 2 wei to be sent to the Mallory contract.

Data Type and Data Vulnerabilities

Vulnerability: Variable Value Overflow or Underflow

This happens when arithmetic operations cause the new value of a variable to exceed the maximum value or fall below the minimum value.

```
uint256 const PRICE_PER_TOKEN = 2;
function
buy(uint256 numTokens) public payable {
        require(msg.value == numTokens * PRICE_PER_TOKEN);

        balanceOf[msg.sender] += numTokens;
    }
```

To fix this vulnerability, check the value range. If possible, use the SafeMath library in which the boundaries of arithmetic operations are checked.

Vulnerability: Shadowing State Variables

For a smart contract, there are state variables and function-specific variables. The state variables can be referred to in each function as well. If a variable name is defined as both state variable and function variable, then the one defined in the function will have priority and shadow the one defined as state variable. Therefore, it is important to check the context and scope of the variables in a function. The following smart contract shows how state variables are shadowed in the functions:

```
pragma solidity 0.8.0;

contract ShadowingVariables {
    uint n = 2;
    address public x = 0x1f2D3A67B8E96039bbAc84eB4bC0913C0c16778c;

    function test_shadow1() public view returns (uint n) {
        return n; // Will return 0
    }

    function test_shadow2() public view  returns (address x) {
```

```
    address x = 0x1111111111111111111111111111111111111111;
     return x; // Will return
                 0x1111111111111111111111111111111111111111;
}

     function test_shadow3() public view  returns
     (address x) {

     return x; // Will return
                 0x0000000000000000000000000000000000000000
}

}
```

In the smart contract, state variables of uint n and address x are declared. The test_shadow1 function declared n as a return variable. It will return 0, and it is not assigned value and will take default 0.

The second function, test_shadow2, redefine address x and assigns a new address 0x1111111111111111111111111111111111111111 and will return this address.

The third function, test_shadow3, redeclared address x but does not assign the address value. It will therefore return the default address value of 0x0000000000000000000000000000000000000000.

It is very important to look at the same variable names appearing in different contexts and make sure correct values are associated with the variable.

Vulnerability: Authorization Through tx.origin

Solidity smart contracts can use tx.origin as a global variable to refer to the original sender of the transaction. Since a user or a smart contract can call a smart contract function that might be malicious, it is not a good practice to use tx.origin for authentication. Instead, msg.sender should be used for authentication as this is always the true address of the smart contract that calls another smart contract. For example, in the following programming, tx.origin is used to check if the sender is the owner of the smart contract. This might have vulnerability as the tx.origin account might call a malicious smart contract and then call this sendTo function to bypass the required check to send the fund to a receiver specified by the hacker.

```solidity
pragma solidity 0.4.24;

contract MyContract {

    address owner;

    function MyContract() public {
        owner = msg.sender;
    }

    function sendTo(address receiver, uint amount) public {
        require(tx.origin == owner); // This should be changed
        to tx.sender
        receiver.transfer(amount);
    }

}
```

Vulnerability: Using Block Values to Represent Time

Some smart contracts will need to handle operations such as asset locking or release that has dependency on time. Solidity has some special global variables such as block.timestamp and block.number that can be used to represent or infer elapsed time. However, since the block mining is not accurate and can be manipulated by miners, it is not recommended to use the block parameters as time stamps for functions that have time dependencies. Sometimes, it would be good to use time information from an Oracle implementation.

Vulnerability: Writing to Arbitrary Storage Locations

Ethereum EVM stores data in persistent locations for each account or smart contract address. It is important to protect the data storage location from malicious overwrites. Although Solidity does not support location pointers, there is still a possibility for writing data to wrong addresses. For example, in a dynamic array, if the array length is not set properly, the out-of-bound index will not be detected and cause the out-of-bound write to be valid. For example, in the following example, a dynamic length array bonusRecord is defined. The PopBonus function pops up one item at a time and decrements the length of the bonusRecord array. However, since "require(0 <= bonusRecord.length)" does not block length in 0 case, the next line of code "bonusRecord. length--" will cause an underflow, making the bonusRecord length to be 115792089237316195423570985008687907853269984665640564039457584007913129639935.

And since the array length is so large, the array index can be any number, and the value can be written to arbitrary storage locations:

```
uint[] private bonusRecord;
address private owner;

function PushBonus(uint c) public {
    bonusRecord.push(c);
}

function PopBonus() public {
    require(0 <= bonusRecord.length);
    // This is a bug.  Once the length is zero, it should
    not allow the PopBonus operation
    bonusRecord.length--;
}
```

```
function UpdateBonusRecordAt(uint idx, uint c) public
returns (uint){
    require(idx < bonusRecord.length);
    bonusRecord[idx] = c;
    return bonusRecord.length;
}
```

To fix the preceding arbitrary write issue, simply change "require(0 <= bonusRecord.length)" to "require(0 < bonusRecord.length)".

Vulnerability: Unused Variables

It is quite common for developers to have variables declared but not used. In Solidity, all computations and storage consume gas for the transactions. Therefore, it is best practice to remove all functions and variables that are defined but not used for the deployed smart contracts.

Compiler Vulnerabilities

Outdated Compilers

Compiler version compatibility is a complex issue. Solidity allows a smart contract to be declared as applied to a single version of compiler, or a range of compilers. Although it is recommended to use the latest compilers, there is a challenge of compatibility with older versions of libraries. Sometimes, libraries were written by third parties, or in the public domain, rewriting them to the latest version is not easy. Developers should look at both the compilation errors and warnings to ensure that the versions are compatible.

Randomness Vulnerability

Vulnerability: Weak Randomness from Blockchain Attributes

Smart contracts do not communicate with external programs directly and do not have a good source of random number generators. Sometimes, in applications such as gaming or lottery, there is a need for using random numbers. Developers need to know that some blockchain attributes are not as random as what they seem to be. For example, Ethereum miners might manipulate block.timestamp or blockhash by controlling block generation time or packaging different transactions.

For applications that require a high degree of randomness, it is recommended to use external randomness generators and Oracle to bring the randomness to smart contracts.

Signature Vulnerability

Vulnerability: Signature Manipulation

Sometimes, smart contracts implement cryptographic functions to verify signed messages and perform transfer operations accordingly. To ensure security, the smart contract functions need to ensure that the signed messages are authentic and the message cannot be replayed. When using a message, a private key and a message are supplied as input to create a signature. One important thing to note is that the signature is not unique. A hacker can manipulate (r,s,v) parameters to create a different yet valid signature for the same private key and message. Hence, signature or hash cannot be used as a unique identifier of a message transaction. Otherwise, hackers can take advantage of this by creating different valid signatures to replay previously signed messages.

For example, the following msgid is not unique and should not be used as an identifier for the signed message:

```
bytes32 msgid = keccak256(abi.encodePacked(getTransferHash(_to,
_value, _gasPrice, _nonce), _signature));
require(!signatureUsed[msgid]);
```

Here, msgid is supported to be unique for the same message signed by a private key. However, since _signature is not unique, msgid can be made different, and the same signed message can be replayed multiple times to trigger other actions that might involve asset transfer.

To fix this problem, simply remove _signature in the hashing function to make the msgid to be unique to block the replay of the message.

```
bytes32 msgid = keccak256(abi.encodePacked(getTransferHash(_to,
_value, _gasPrice, _nonce)));
require(!signatureUsed[msgid]);
```

Module Summary

Security is the most essential component for smart contract development. To ensure security, there should be a security framework in place, and developers should also focus on details for each line of code. There will be more discussion of security in Chapter 8.

Module 5: Tools, Test, and Debug

In Chapter 1, we discussed basic tools such as setting up a smart contract development environment by using Truffle and Remix to compile and deploy smart contracts. In this module, we continue to introduce useful tools such as smart contract visualization tools, security scanning tools, and gas estimation tools. We also discuss how to test and debug smart contract programs.

287

Tools

MythX: A Security Scanning Tool

MythX is a security scanning tool that is released as a fee-based service of mythx.io, or a CLI package, or a plug-in for other tools.

Here, we explain how to use MythX as a plug-in for Remix. To use Remix, follow the instructions in Chapter 6 and launch your application. To enable MythX, simply click the Plugin Manager icon to bring up the manager. Type "mythx" in the search box and you can see MYTHX SECURITY VERIFICATION plug-in. Click the Activate button to activate this plug-in (Figure 7-6).

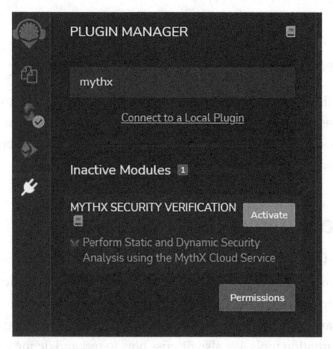

Figure 7-6. *Activation of MythX security scanning tool in Remix*

Once the MYTHX SECURITY VERIFICATION is activated, it needs to communicate with the MythX cloud service to perform the scanning. Developers need to apply for an API key from mythx.io website and enter the API token information in the plug-in setting (Figure 7-7).

Figure 7-7. *Sign in needed to use MythX APIs*

MythX security scanning also provides a plug-in for Truffle tool and an extension for Visual Studio vscode IDE tool. One thing to note is that MythX security verification is a fee-based service. Developers need to pay a subscription fee for the security scanning service.

Solidity Static Analysis: A Security Plug-in for Remix

Unlike MythX, which charges a subscription fee for security scanning, Solidity Static Analysis (SSA) plug-in for Remix is free and also provides basic features for static code scanning. To enable SSA, simply open the Plugin Manager and type in Solidity Static Analysis and click the Activate button to activate it (Figure 7-8).

Figure 7-8. *Using Solidity Static Analysis for security scan in Remix*

Once the plug-in is activated, click its icon on the plug-in panel and it will start to analyze the active Solidity program on the Remix screen. SSA not only scans source code for security vulnerabilities, it also perform checks on the gas consumption, ERC (Ethereum Request for Comment), and some miscellaneous analysis (Figure 7-9). Developers can filter what categories to analyze and show.

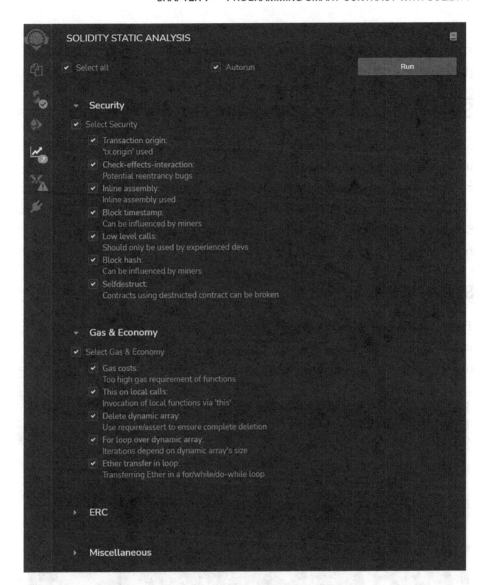

Figure 7-9. *Running Solidity Static Analysis scan*

Although Static Analysis tools are very helpful to catch some obvious vulnerabilities, they should not replace more complex security audits and penetration tests, especially for smart contracts that handle asset transfers.

Solidity to UML: Smart Contract Visualization Tool

Solidity is an object-oriented programming language that is easy to understand. Sometimes, when there are many functions and smart contracts for a dApp project, it becomes challenging to make sense of the workflow of smart contracts. In this case, it would be good to convert Solidity code to Unified Modeling Language (UML) to visualize the relationship of smart contracts and functions.

Solidity to UML for Remix

There are several tools to convert Solidity to UML. Remix provides a plug-in for this as well. Simply activate the Solidity UML and launch the plug-in to convert the Solidity code to UML diagram (Figure 7-10).

Figure 7-10. *Plugin for Solidity to UML conversion*

Once Solidity 2 UML plug-in is activated, it can be used to parse Solidity smart contracts and generate UML diagrams.

Solidity to UML Stand-Alone Tools

Besides Remix plug-in, there are also nodejs package or CLI package that can be used to generate UML diagram.

For example, sol2uml package is a versatile tool to generate UML from smart contract source code; it can also fetch UML for smart contract deployed to Ethereum blockchain.

To install sol2uml, simply type the following command by using node package manager (npm):

```
npm install sol2uml --only=production
```

Once sol2uml is installed, it can be run with various parameters as shown in the following help menu:

```
$ sol2uml -h
  Usage: sol2uml <fileFolderAddress> [options]

  Generates UML diagrams from Solidity source code.
  If no file, folder or address is passed as the first
  argument, the working folder is used.
  When a folder is used, all *.sol files are found in that
  folder and all subfolders.
  If an Ethereum address with a 0x prefix is passed, the
  verified source code from Etherscan will be used.

  Options:
    -v, --verbose                 run with debugging statements
    -f, --outputFormat <value>    output file format: svg, png,
                                  dot or all (default: "svg")
    -o, --outputFileName <value>  output file name
```

```
-d, --depthLimit <depth>        number of sub folders that
                                will be recursively searched
                                for Solidity files. Default
                                -1 is unlimited (default: -1)
-n, --network <network>         mainnet, ropsten, kovan,
                                rinkeby or goerli (default:
                                "mainnet")
-k, --etherscanApiKey <key>     Etherscan API Key
-c, --clusterFolders            Cluster contracts into
                                source folders
-h, --help                      output usage information
```

To generate UML diagram for smart contracts in a local directory, type the following command:

```
sol2uml ./contracts
```

Here, ./contracts is the directory location for smart contract files.

sol2uml can also fetch UML files for smart contracts deployed to Ethereum blockchain. For example, to get a UML for a particular address in the Ropsten blockchain, run the following command:

```
sol2uml smartcontract_address -n ropsten
```

Here, smartcontract_address is the address of the smart contract that has been deployed to Ethereum blockchain. "-n ropsten" means that this is for smart contracts in the Ropsten blockchain.

To understand a UML diagram, we use part of a smart contract for USDT ERC20 token. This UML diagram as shown in Figure 7-11 can be fetched by typing the following address in a browser URL:

```
https://etherscan.io/viewsvg?t=1&a=0xdAC17F958D2ee52
3a2206206994597C13D831ec7
```

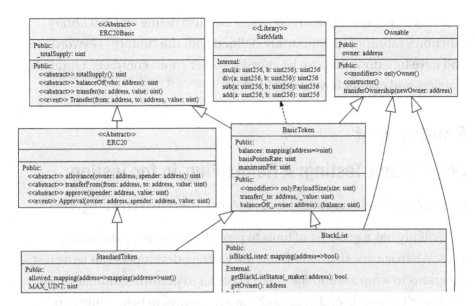

Figure 7-11. *UML diagram for USDT ERC20 token*

In this diagram, each box represents a smart contract class, an interface, or a library.

There are multiple sections for each box. The top bar is the smart contract name. Then each scope of variables and functions are grouped into their respective sections such as internal, public, and external. Each section contains a list of variable names, function names, and parameters.

Lines with arrows are drawn between boxes to represent entity relationships. If smart contract A uses smart contract B, meaning that B is a parent of A, then a directed line is drawn from B to A. If entity A is an abstract smart contract or an interface, then a dash line instead of a solid line is drawn.

In Solidity, an abstract class is a special smart contract in which functions are defined but not implemented. The contract that uses or inherits an abstract smart contract will need to implement those functions defined. Also interfaces are special smart contracts in which only function names are defined. There are no variables declared in interfaces.

Besides interfaces, smart contracts can also define and call library functions. Libraries in Solidity are defined with the "library" keyword and have functions that can be called by other smart contracts. Library is stateless and cannot have state variables.

Solidity Test

Solidity Unit Testing: A Remix Plug-in for Testing

`https://remix-ide.readthedocs.io/en/latest/unittesting.html`

Solidity has a good set of tools to provide unit tests or automatic tests. When source smart contracts are written, developers can write test programs to wrap around the smart contract to perform automatic tests. Tools such as Remix and Truffle all have test suites to help writing and executing test programs. In the following, we mention Solidity Unit Test as a Remix plug-in.

To activate Solidity Unit Testing plug-in, simply click at the Plugin Manager panel and type in Solidity Unit Testing to search. Then click the Activate button to activate the plug-in as shown in Figure 7-12:

Figure 7-12. *Plugin for Solidity unit testing*

One thing to note is that test files in Solidity Unit Test plug-in will not support functions with parameters. For smart contracts with parameters, there should be a wrapper test file that will call the functions with parameters from another function that does not have parameters.

To run Solidity Unit Testing, first, click at the plug-in icon to bring up the unit testing panel. Then choose a directory to store the test suite files. In the following screenshot, a directory of unit_test is chosen for the test files. Then developers need to generate a test file for the source smart contracts (Figure 7-13).

Figure 7-13. *Generation of Solidity unit test file*

To generate a test file for a source file, first, open the source smart contract and make it active in the file view panel. Then select the directory where the test file will reside. Click the "Generate" button to generate a test file in the specified directory for the file that is opened in the view panel.

Once a test suite file is generated, it is automatically opened in the file view panel. This test suite will have the basic code template for testing the source contract. It has code segments of test library import, target source files import, and testing function stubs. Developers can then initialize a target smart contract and simulate the function calls for the smart contract and then use the built-in logical checking function to assert the test results.

For example, the following code shows how to write unit test code to test if the global variables and local variables are the same. The source code is very simple. Variable x is declared as a global variable at the beginning of the code. And then x is also declared as a local variable in the function of localVariable.

```solidity
pragma solidity >=0.4.22 <0.9.0;

contract VariableScope {
    address public x = 0x1f2D3A67B8E96039bbAc84eB4bC0913C0c16778c;

    function localVariable() public view  returns (address x) {

        address x = 0x1111111111111111111111111111111111111111;
        return x; // Will return
                    0x1111111111111111111111111111111111111111;
    }

    function globalVariable() public view  returns (address) {

        return x; // Will return
                    0x1f2D3A67B8E96039bbAc84eB4bC0913C0c16778c;
    }

}
```

The unit test is to check if the variable x is the same at the global scope
and local scope. To test this, the following test suite is generated and
modified:

```solidity
pragma solidity >=0.4.22 <0.9.0;

// This import is automatically injected by Remix
import "remix_tests.sol";

// This import is required to use custom transaction context
// Although it may fail compilation in 'Solidity
Compiler' plugin
// But it will work fine in 'Solidity Unit Testing' plugin
import "remix_accounts.sol";
import "../variable_scope.sol";
```

```
// File name has to end with '_test.sol', this file can contain
more than one testSuite contracts
contract testSuite {
    VariableScope vs;
    /// 'beforeAll' runs before all other tests
    /// More special functions are: 'beforeEach', 'beforeAll',
    'afterEach' & 'afterAll'

    function beforeAll() public {
        // <instantiate contract>
        vs = new VariableScope();
        // Assert.equal(uint(1), uint(1), "1 should be
        equal to 1");
    }

    function checkNotEqual() public {
        // Use 'Assert' methods: https://remix-ide.readthedocs.io/
        en/latest/assert_library.html
        address x1 = vs.x.address;
        address x2 = vs.localVariable();
        Assert.notEqual(x1, x2, "variables are supposed to be
        not equal");

    }
}
```

In the test suite code, source file is imported, and VariableScope smart contract vs is instantiated. Then checkNotEqual() function is called to generate a local and global variable x in the vs and then make a comparison.

The test suite is run in Remix and shows that it passes the Unit Test (Figure 7-14), meaning that the global variable and local variable are indeed different even though they have the same name.

Figure 7-14. *Unit test run example*

Using the Remix Solidity Unit Testing plug-in, it is very easy to write scripts to test smart contracts.

It is important to note that test files in Solidity Unit Test plug-in will not support functions with parameters. For smart contracts with parameters, there should be a wrapper test file that will call the functions with parameters from another function that does not have parameters.

Besides the Remix plug-in for unit testing, Truffle also has good unit test modules that support manual and automatic testing. The workflow and functionality are similar to the Remix plug-in.

Solidity Debug

Sometimes, Solidity smart contracts might encounter issues during executions. It would be good to step through the execution of each source code and analyze various debugging information such as call stacks and local variable values. Solidity does have some debugging tools that can help with this. Here, we introduce the Debugger plug-in for Remix.

Enable the Debugger

To enable Remix debugger, simply open the Plugin Manager and type in debugger in the search box and enable this plug-in (Figure 7-15).

Figure 7-15. Enabling debugger plugin in in Remix

Launch the Debugger

Once the debugger is enabled, a bug-like icon will show up in the plug-in panel. To debug a Solidity program, developers need to compile a contract source code, deploy the smart contract to a local EVM, and then create a transaction to get a transaction hash. After that, developers can enter the transaction ID to the debugger configuration panel and start the debugging process (Figure 7-16):

Figure 7-16. *Launching Solidity debugger*

Debug the Smart Contract

When the debugger is started, a debugging window as shown in the following will pop up, and developers can step through the code to see the execution of each line of code. Debugger supports steps functions such as step into, step over, and step into breaking point.

The debugger shows all the EVM execution context, storage, and calling stack information including function stacks, Solidity locals, Solidity state, step details, stack, memory, storage, call stack, call data, global variables, return value, and full storage changes. Some of the information might not be available, but the debugger generally gives a good amount of bytecode execution information (Figure 7-17).

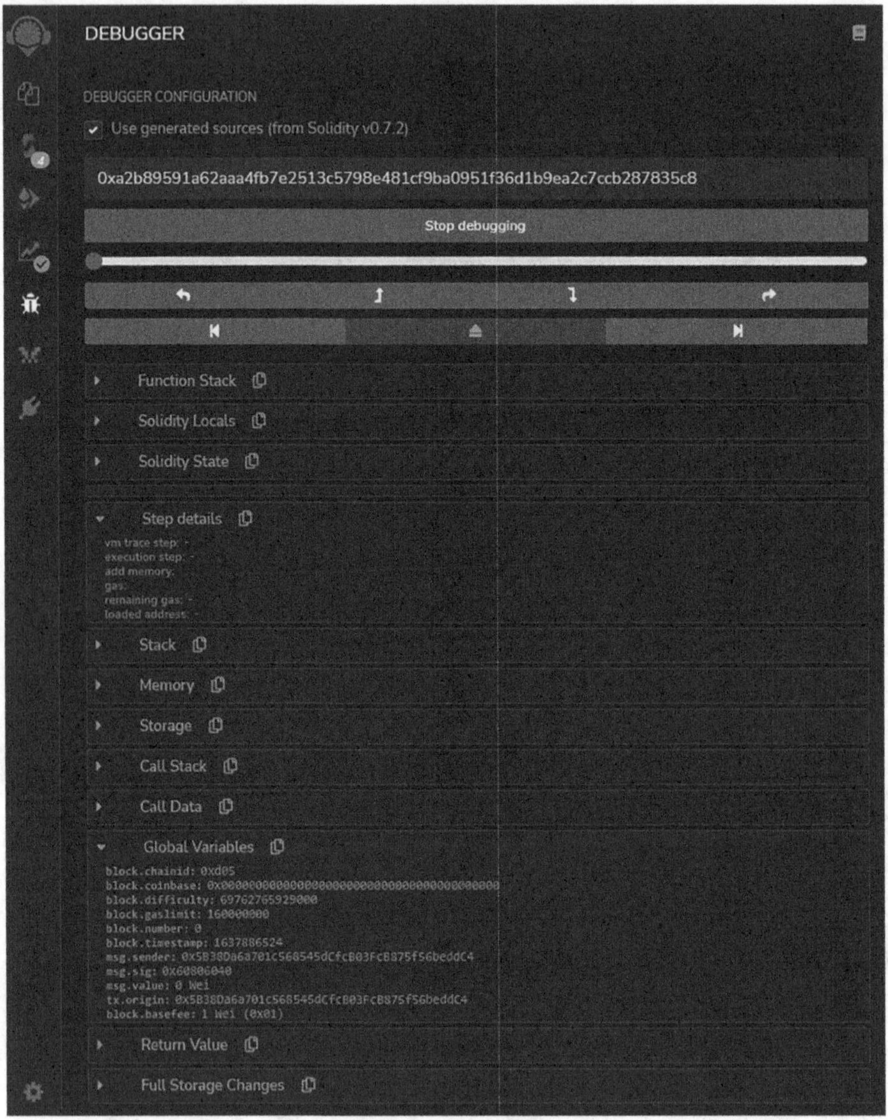

Figure 7-17. *Stepping through a debugging program*

One thing that is not obvious with the debugger is how to add a breakpoint for the debugger. To add the breakpoint, simply open the source code in the edit window and click at the line number (not the source code itself). A blue dot will show up beside the line number to indicate that a breaking point is inserted to that line (Figure 7-18).

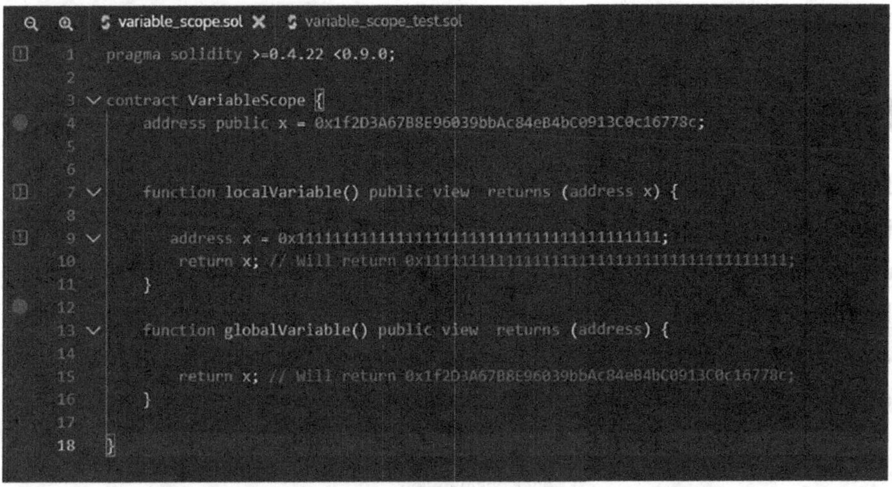

Figure 7-18. *Adding a breaking point in the source code*

Although the debugger is a great tool to debug a Solidity program, we find that when debugging a more complex smart contract, there is still some information that cannot be seen in the debugging windows. It is a good practice to modularize smart contracts to simplify unit tests and debugging.

Module 6: Client Considerations

In Chapter 6, and previous modules of Chapter 7, we discussed how to program Solidity smart contracts and deploy them to blockchains. Once smart contracts are deployed to a blockchain, they are accessible publicly and will never be removed or altered once the blocks are finalized. Smart contracts are bytecodes that are not user-friendly. To interact with dApps, clients need to be developed to facilitate user interaction with smart contracts. The clients for dApps can be web browsers, mobile application, desktop application, or command-line interface (CLI). In this module, we will discuss the pros and cons of these clients and also give examples for building a dApp client.

Types of dApp clients

dApp clients can be in a graphic user interface (GUI) format or command-line interface (CLI) format. The GUI format can be web-based app, mobile app, or desktop app that requires user inputs and operations as shown in the following figure. CLI formats are normally for automatically scripting to perform testing or for application programming interfaces. In the following diagram (Figure 7-19), we describe different kinds of clients.

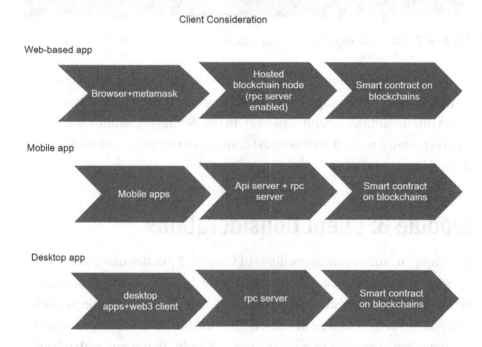

Figure 7-19. *Types of clients for decentralized applications*

Browser Client

Browser client is the most basic user experience for a decentralized application. Users are directly introduced to a website to use the dApp. For example, to access CryptoKitty dApp, users just need to point their web browser to www.cryptokitty.com. As shown in the client topology diagram, the browser needs a web extension/plug-in to connect to an Ethereum node through RPC protocol. The most common web extension is MetaMask. MetaMask serves as a crypto wallet for web applications.

To design a web application with a crypto account interaction, developers need to develop web pages that connect to MetaMask or other wallets. When a user connects to a URL through a browser, the browser script will check if MetaMask is installed and prompt users to install it if not found. This is normally called "Connecting Wallet." Normally, JavaScript scripts are written to use the Web3 library to connect to Ethereum nodes. We will have a detailed coding example later in this module.

One of the challenges of browser-based dApp is the security of wallet. Since browsers are prone to hacker attack, it is possible that MetaMask storage and private keys might be hacked in some browsers. It is recommended that when storing large amounts of crypto assets, hardware wallets should be used. MetaMask does support connecting to hardware wallets to sign transactions to ensure safety of the wallet.

Mobile Clients

Mobile apps can also be developed to interact with smart contracts in the Ethereum blockchain. Since mobile apps normally do not have a large footprint, they rely on API or RPC to communicate with blockchain nodes. Similar to web wallet, mobile wallet does not have hardware grade security, and it should not be used to store large amounts of crypto assets.

Desktop Client

Both web client and mobile client need to connect to external nodes to interact with the Ethereum blockchain. Desktop clients have enough storage and computing power and might be able to run an Ethereum node by itself. This means the desktop client might carry its own RPC server and does not have dependency on third-party RPC nodes. One disadvantage is that desktop apps need installation and need to have a desktop to run the application.

CLI Client

CLI client is to use a command-line interface to run the scripts that interact with Ethereum blockchain. This is typically done in unit tests or automatic scripting of projects. CLI is handy for those who like to use text-based typing rather than GUI-based browsing.

Each client has its own pros and cons, and we have seen that web clients are becoming more and more popular. In the following, we provide a use case for designing web pages for a deployed smart contract.

Web Client Example for Interacting with Smart Contract

In this example, we demonstrate how to write a web page to interact with a deployed smart contract. To make the demo an end-to-end experience, we do the following to deploy the smart contract to the development environment.

Step 1: Create an Ethereum development blockchain

An Ethereum development blockchain is created by downloading geth application and running the following commands:

```
./geth --datadir test-chain-dir --http --dev --http.corsdomain
"https://remix.ethereum.org,http://remix.ethereum.org"
```

This command creates a private development blockchain and allows Remix development tools to interact with it. The data storage is located in test-chain-dir, and a development account will be generated by default. The location of the keystore of this account is located in the test-chain-dir/ keystore directory. This address and keystore can be used to manage the account.

For more details, refer to http://geth.ethereum.org/docs/getting-started/dev-mode. Use geth attach <IPC_LOCATION> to attach to the node and use eth.sendTransaction to send from coinbase to the target account.

Once the development blockchain is started, the next step is to deploy a smart contract to it. Here, we develop a smart contract with two functions: storeMessage and retrieve.

```
// SPDX-License-Identifier: GPL-3.0

pragma solidity >=0.7.0 <0.9.0;
/**
 * @title MessageStorage
 * @dev Store & retrieve value in a variable
 */
contract MessageStorage {

    string message;

    /**
     * @dev Store value in variable
     * @param messageInput value to store
     */
```

```solidity
function storeMessage(string memory messageInput) public {
    message = messageInput;
}

/**
 * @dev Return value
 * @return value of 'message'
 */
function retrieve() public view returns (string memory){
    return message;
}
}
```

Step 2: Compile and deploy the smart contract to the development blockchain

Once the smart contract is written, use Remix or Truffle to compile it. To use Remix, simply go to `http://remix.ethereum.org` and create a file for the preceding smart contract. Upon a successful compilation, an Application Bytecode Interface (ABI) file and bytecode file are generated. The bytecode file will be deployed to the blockchain. The ABI will be used for dApp clients to interact with the smart contract. The ABI will need to be copied by clicking at the ABI button and saved to client code. In the example, the following ABI file describes the format of the functions and variables defined in the smart contract:

```
[
    {
        "inputs": [],
        "name": "retrieve",
```

```
            "outputs": [
                    {
                            "internalType": "string",
                            "name": "",
                            "type": "string"
                    }
            ],
            "stateMutability": "view",
            "type": "function"
    },
    {

            "inputs": [
                    {
                            "internalType": "string",
                            "name": "messageInput",
                            "type": "string"
                    }
            ],
            "name": "storeMessage",
            "outputs": [],
            "stateMutability": "nonpayable",
            "type": "function"
    }
]
```

Step 3: Deploy the smart contract

Once the smart contract is compiled, go to deploy panel and deploy to the
development blockchain (Figure 7-20):

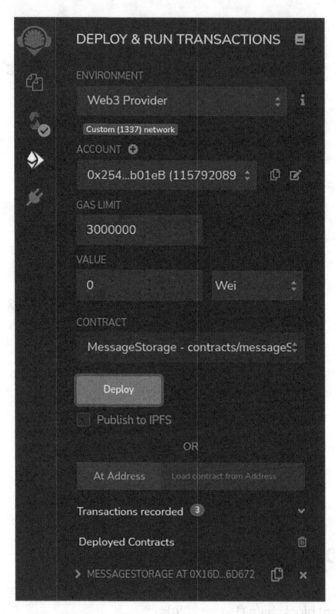

Figure 7-20. Remix smart contract deployment panel

Here, Environment should specify Web3 provider and point to `http://127.0.0.1:8545`, which is the endpoint of the development chain.

Once the smart contract is deployed successfully, a smart contract address will be returned as shown in the bottom of the screen:

0x16d29C0A07dcDBe6e1097257Ee39DEe18136d672

Developers can copy this smart contract address for the web browser to interact with.

Step 4: Write web client to interact with the smart contract

For a web client to interact with a smart contract, several parameters are needed, including the following:

> **An RPC endpoint of the blockchain** – This is the entry to the blockchain. In this example, it is `http://127.0.0.1:8545`. Web wallets such as MetaMask will need to connect to the blockchain through this RPC endpoint.

> **ABI for the smart contract** – This is created when the smart contract is compiled.

> **Smart contract address** – This address is returned after a successful deployment of the smart contract.

In the following, we have an HTML/JavaScript page to show the UI for interacting with the smart contract. The HTML portion shows the layout of the buttons. The JavaScript portion shows the scripting code to interact with the smart contract.

The following shows the web UI of the HTML/script code (Figure 7-21). On the left side of the GUI, there are three buttons that allow users to connect to a wallet and get the wallet address, to set a message to write to

313

blockchain, and then a button to retrieve the message. The top right is a
pop-up of MetaMask that allows users to sign transactions to interact with
blockchain.

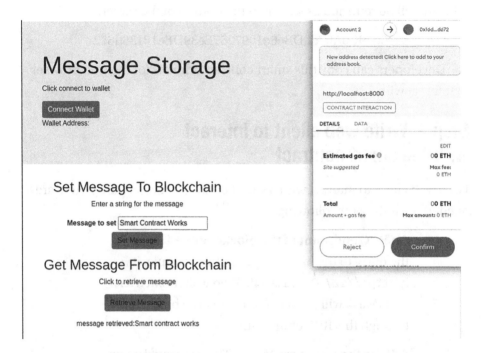

Figure 7-21. *Example of a user interface to interact with smart
contract*

A code snippet for the three HTML buttons is shown below:

"Connect Wallet" button will trigger enableEthereumButton and get
the wallet account address.

```
<DIV class="container">
  <H1 class="display-4">Message Storage</H1>
  <P>Click connect to wallet</P>
  <P><BUTTON class=
```

```
"btn btn-secondary enableEthereumButton">Connect Wallet
</BUTTON><BR>
Wallet Address:<span class="showAccount"></span></P>
</DIV>
```

"Set Message" button will trigger the setMessage() function in the JavaScript.

```
<P>Enter a string for the message</P>
<DIV class="cluegene">
  <LABEL for="cluegene"><B>Message to set</B></LABEL>
  <INPUT type="text" class="ignore-form-control" id=
  "cluegene" placeholder="" value="[My_Message]"
  size="20"
  required="">
</DIV>
<P><A class="btn btn-secondary" onclick="setMessage()"
role="button">Set Message</A></P>
```

"Retrieve Message" button will trigger the getMessage() function:

```
<DIV class="row" id="getmessagerow">
  <DIV class="col-lg-6 text-center">
    <H2>Get Message From Blockchain</H2>
    <P>Click to retrieve message</P>
    <P><A class="btn btn-secondary" onclick="getMessage()"
    role="button">Retrieve Message</A></P>
    <DIV id="GetMessageValue"></DIV>
  </DIV>
</DIV>
```

The three functions are implemented in JavaScript code.

For getting the address of the wallet, an eth_requestAccounts request is sent as an Ethereum request to fetch the accounts enabled by the MetaMask.

```
async function getAccount() {
const accounts = await ethereum.request({ method:
'eth_requestAccounts' });
const account = accounts[0];
        account0 = account;
showAccount.innerHTML = account;
}
```

For setting the message, the following workflow is coded:

- The setMessage function first checks if the MetaMask is installed. If it is installed, get the account associated with the MetaMask.

- JavaScript code creates a smart contract object with the specified contract address and ABI information. The ABI can be in a separate file to be imported.

- Package data for the transaction. This step takes the message to be set from the input field and package with embedded encodeABI() function.

- Send the transaction with the sendTransaction function.

```
function setMessage() {
if (!ethEnabled()) {
    alert("Please install an Ethereum-compatible browser or
    extension like MetaMask to use this dApp!");
}
web3.eth.getAccounts(function(err, accounts) {
    var myContract = new web3.eth.Contract(messagestorage_abi,
    messagestorage_contract.toLowerCase());

    var gene = $('.cluegene input').val();
    var auctionData = myContract.methods.storeMessage(gene).
    encodeABI();
```

```
var tx_genescience = web3.eth.sendTransaction({
  from: accounts[0].toLowerCase(),
  to: messagestorage_contract.toLowerCase(),
  data: auctionData
}, function(err, transactionHash) {
  document.getElementById("SetMessageValue").innerHTML =
  "setMessage tx:" + transactionHash;
})

})

}
```

Similar to the setMessage function, the getMessage function also creates a smart contract object and a call retrieve function in the smart contract. Since getMessage is a function that does not write to blockchain, a call() function is called directly. This call() function does not need MetaMask to sign the transaction and does not cost gas fee.

```
function getMessage() {
  if (!ethEnabled()) {
    alert("Please install an Ethereum-compatible browser or
    extension like MetaMask to use this dApp!");
  }
  var myContract = new web3.eth.Contract(messagestorage_abi,
  messagestorage_contract.toLowerCase());

  var tx_getmessage = myContract.methods.retrieve().
  call(function(err, result) {
    document.getElementById("GetMessageValue").innerHTML =
    "message retrieved:" + result;
  })
}
```

Summary

In this chapter, we describe Solidity programming with examples, syntax, data structure, functions, events, client applications, security, test, debug, and deployment. This should lay down a good foundation for basic Solidity programming for decentralized applications.

CHAPTER 8

Security Considerations

Introduction

We went through many aspects of Solidity smart contract programming already in previous chapters. We covered Solidity programming syntax, using Remix or Truffle to compile source code, and deploying bytecode to an embedded EVM or development blockchain. We also mentioned the token economy and token design such as choosing fungible or nonfungible tokens and using the tokens to represent assets and elements for business use cases.

On the storage and communication side, we talked about the importance of Ethereum blockchain state and event concepts as well as different networks such as mainnet, Rinkeby testnet, and Ropsten testnet.

On the architecture side, we talked about building end-to-end solutions with building blockchain nodes to connect to the Ethereum blockchain, deploying smart contracts, developing web clients or mobile apps, and using Web3 to connect clients with blockchains.

In this chapter, we are going to cover Ethereum blockchain and smart contract security. Security is one of the most critical aspects of software development. It plays an even larger role in the Ethereum blockchain for the reasons shown below in Figure 8-1:

© Weijia Zhang and Tej Anand 2022
W. Zhang and T. Anand, *Blockchain and Ethereum Smart Contract Solution Development*,
https://doi.org/10.1007/978-1-4842-8164-2_8

Figure 8-1. Complexity of blockchain security as compared to conventional IT security

- **Decentralized nature of blockchain** – Any code written and deployed to the blockchain is going to run in thousands of machines. Anybody can access and run blockchain code.

- **Constraints of patches and upgradability** – Due to the immutability of blockchains, smart contracts deployed to blockchains cannot be modified. This increases the difficulty for upgrading decentralized applications. When security flaws are detected in blockchain applications, the cost of patching the applications is high, and sometimes, a fork of the blockchain is needed.

- **Trustless and permissionless environment** – For public blockchains, both the client nodes and decentralized applications are open to global participants. There is no centralized authority to check the qualifications of participants. There is no security perimeter to block bad players from participating.

- **Privacy and anonymous nature of blockchain** –Blockchain users can remain anonymous. Smart contract functions do not have a way to check the profile of the users. Hackers can carry out blockchain attacks, get the assets, and remain unidentified.

- **High value impact on business** – Smart contracts
  normally have a small footprint. Bigger projects might
  have over thousands of lines of code, while others may
  only have a few hundred. Smart contracts manage
  high value crypto assets, and each attack might bring
  catastrophic results to the decentralized application.
  Some decentralized applications have suffered huge
  losses due to simple errors in smart contracts.

Several smart contract breaches have been found in the past. We can classify these security issues as functional security holes and attackable security holes. Functional security holes are obvious code errors and can cause loss of funds with normal transactions and by bona fide users. The functional security holes for smart contract contain the following.

Functional Security Holes in Smart Contracts

Fund Deadlock

This is a security hole where a smart contract can take in fund transfer but will lock the funds in a smart contract indefinitely. For example, a smart contract can implement a receive function to take in funds but not to implement functions for send or transfer. In this case, funds sent to the smart contract will be owned by the smart contract, but there is no way to transfer funds out. Similar to a blackhole, this is a case that takes in everything with nothing going out.

Fund Leakage

This is a functional security hole that can cause leak of funds by an unprivileged user. This is normally due to a lack of access rights and privilege checking. For example, a security hole can be caused by a function that has fund transfer capabilities but is declared public without authenticating the user's ownership of the fund. In Solidity smart contract programming, there are several places where the security can be enforced, including setting the scope of a function to be public or private, setting the ownership access rights, and using require and assert to make sure access conditions are met before proceeding to the next line of code for execution. When a token is minted or transferred, the smart contract needs to make sure the caller of the function is the owner, or administrator, and an authorized user for the function. It is very important to define roles in smart contracts, and each role will have limited access rights. In CryptoKitty's example, there are four roles defined including owner of smart contract, CEO of the project, COO, and CFO. For the mint function, the smart contract defines the mint right to COO. You have to be a COO of this project to mint an NFT token. There is also a pause/unpause function to handle emergency situations by halting the execution of smart contracts, and this right is given to the CEO. The CFO can do other things related to auctions. The owner of the smart contract is also a critical role. Normally, whoever deploys a smart contract to the blockchain is the owner of the smart contract by default. This owner can then transfer the ownership to another user, or to a smart contract address, or even renounce the ownership. Because the owner of a smart contract has the highest access privilege, it is very important to protect the private keys for the owner account.

Disabled Smart Contract

This is another functional security hole where a nonprivileged user can call a function to kill the smart contract. This is another thing that needs to be watched. In a smart contract, there might be a function that can be executed to disable the whole smart contract by clearing the states, storage, and settings. If this function is incidentally called, it will completely ruin the smart contract.

Orphan Smart Contract

When a smart contract is deployed, the account that sends the deployment transaction is the owner, and it has high privilege administration rights to the smart contract. Sometimes, to increase the degree of decentralization, the owner might transfer the ownership to another owner account, a smart contract, or denounce the ownership. Once ownership of a smart contract is transferred or denounced after the deployment, the original owner does not have the right to administer the smart contract anymore. It is thus important to come up with a smart contract ownership plan during the design process. Once the smart contract is deployed and ownership transferred or denounced, there is no way to pause or upgrade the smart contracts when an emergency situation arises in the decentralized applications.

Attackable Security Holes in Smart Contracts

This kind of security breach is caused by users with malicious intent. It is less obvious than functional security holes and very difficult to be discovered. Hackers will normally need to construct artificial transactions and carry out multiple steps of attacks. The attackers also remain anonymous and have methods to transfer the funds. These kinds of breaches can also include attacking blockchain nodes and Web3 clients and environments outside the smart contracts. Other breaches have also happened with hackers doing the following: (1) calling faulty internal functions with malicious transactions; (2) changing outside parameters and conditions for a function call; (3) changing whitelist addresses and names; and (4) attacking Oracle. The following are some examples of attackable security holes:

Example 1: Pay bill to arbitrary accounts

The following is a code snippet with a security hole:

```solidity
pragma solidity ^0.8.6;

contract PayIssue {

function payBill ( address payable recipient, uint256 x_amount ) public payable {

    recipient.transfer(x_amount);

}

}
```

In the preceding code, there is a function called payBill(address payable recipient, uint256 x_amount) public payable.

This payBill function when called will simply transfer "x_amount" of Ether to the recipient address specified in the function. This function is payable, which allows the funds to transfer to a receiver. Payable is a new keyword in Solidity to specify whether a function or an address can transfer or receive funds.

One main functional security error with this smart contract is that it does not check the privilege of the users calling the function. As this function is public and payable, anyone can call this function and transfer funds to an arbitrary address they specify. In fact, users can call this smart contract to deprive all the funds owned by the smart contract and send them to the hackers address. A simple error in function access scope can cause loss of assets and destroy an otherwise promising project.

Example 2: No guarding of kill or selfdestruct function

There was a security incident in which a "kill" function is coded in a smart contract but does not have privilege checking and eventually caused 300 million in loss of funds. In a community Telegram chat group, a transaction hash is posted. The message sender claimed to be a newbie in Ethereum but had just sent a transaction to call a kill function in a smart contract. Because the kill function does not check user privilege, the function call was executed and effectively reset the storage of the smart contract and destroyed the smart contract. The funds locked by this smart contract are 300 million, and there is no way to recover it once the kill function is executed.

Functions such as kill, destroy, selfdestruct, or renounce are highly privileged operations that have the potential to invalidate a smart contract. It is critical to implement thorough checks on the calling parameters to ensure there is no security risk when these functions are executed.

Best Security Practices for Smart Contracts

In previous sections, we described functional and attackable security holes and some examples. As shown in Figure 8-2, we are now switching to the discussion of good security practices for designing smart contracts and writing code.

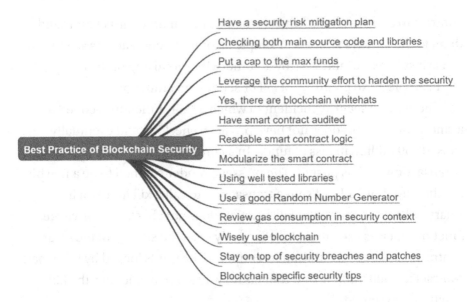

Figure 8-2. Best practice of blockchain security

Have a Security Risk Mitigation Plan

Ethereum and any public blockchains are open and permissionless systems where bad players have the same access to the smart contracts as good players. It is essential to have a mindset that there could be bugs and security holes in the smart contract, and some mitigation plans should be prepared. For example, in the smart contract of CryptoKitty, there is a pause function implemented, and only the CEO can pause or unpause the smart contract. If there is a security hack of smart contracts, the CEO can send a transaction to call the pause function and halt the minting and auction of CryptoKitties.

In addition, it is important to consider the trade-off between decentralization and upgradability. Blockchains are supposed to be immutable, and therefore, the smart contracts by default should be unalterable. On the other hand, there is no way to write Solidity code that is free of bugs or vulnerabilities. A better practice is to classify the smart contracts into two classes – one is stable and cannot be updated, while the other is dynamic and can be upgraded by privileged administrators. The smart contracts that are called by Web3 clients can be proxy smart contracts that are not upgradable and have a fixed address, while the other contracts that are called by the proxy smart contract can be upgraded. Once a smart contract is upgraded due to bug fixes, the address of the newly deployed smart contract is updated in the proxy smart contract, and there is no need to change the Web3 clients.

Checking Both Main Source Code and Libraries

Not only can security vulnerabilities happen in the code you write, but also they can exist in the libraries imported to your smart contract. The library's code might also be written in different versions of Solidity and hence increase the complexities of integration and security risk. For example, some of the libraries are written in Solidity version 0.4, while the main smart contracts that you are working on might be in version 0.8. Solidity version 0.4 does not support certain security features, and modifications are needed to integrate the libraries. This in turn increases vulnerabilities for the whole smart contract. Therefore, it is important to have compatible versions of main code and libraries, and the security review, audit, and test should include library code as well.

Put a Cap to the Max Funds

Due to the complexity of smart contracts, sometimes, it is good to set a maximum amount of asset values a smart contract function can handle. A smart contract can have a global cap, and each function with asset transfer capability will compare the amount of assets to be transferred with the cap. If it exceeds the cap, the function will not execute the transfer. This provides an additional safety guard to prevent asset loss. In fact, the ERC20 smart contracts have an "approve" function to set the maximum amount of funds that can be transferred by a user calling a transfer function.

Because total values of cryptocurrency processed by smart contracts are growing exponentially, projects such as Uniswap and Compound have billions of dollars of assets managed by smart contracts. If there is a security breach with the smart contract code, the impact is huge. It is always a good practice to have a design to put a threshold on the amount of funds that can be impacted if there is a security breach.

Make Your Smart Contract Open Source and Leverage the Community Effort to Harden the Security

Smart contracts are used to power the DeFi world where there are no central authorities and big IT teams to bring trust and security to the platform. It is therefore important for the project community to play a critical role in hardening the smart contracts. Unlike legacy financial applications where software vendors use their engineering resources and services to ensure security and quality, smart contracts are normally open sourced so that the community and users can review the codes to make sure that the business logics are accurately encapsulated in the source code. Community developers are encouraged to review the source code, and big bounties are provided for experts who are able to find any functional, cosmetic, or security defects. Smart contracts are also deployed to testnets first with alpha and beta releases, and communities are requested to find defects and rewarded with bug bounties. Because dApps powered with smart contracts are normally projects that can issue tokens, sometimes, community developers are rewarded with project tokens when they find security issues or defects. Healthy and growing projects that manage billions of dollars of crypto assets always have enthusiastic community developers who work hard to improve the security of smart contracts.

Yes, There Are Blockchain Security Whitehats

Sometimes, smart contracts get hacked with different endings. It happened several times that "hackers" did not have intention to steal the fund, but rather to teach a lesson to the project team. So if a security breach does happen, it is important to watch where the funds get moved to. Hackers who have intention to use the stolen funds will normally transfer the fund to a "mixer" to hide the identity and remove the traceability of the fund. Whitehat hackers will just move the fund to a security location, tell the project team about the security breach, let the project team fix issues, and then move the fund back. So if a security breach does happen, don't panic; the result might not be as bad as it looks.

Have Smart Contract Audited

Smart contracts auditing is a good practice to harden security. A security audit is a practice to hire an external professional company to evaluate and review token economy, smart contracts design, and code implementation. Auditors use automatic security scanning tools and manual penetration testing to produce a thorough report of the smart contracts. The security scan of smart contracts can reveal static security errors in syntax and programming styles. More in-depth review of smart contracts will require experts to go through each smart contract in UML diagrams and figure out the relationship between functions and inspect potential vulnerabilities. Sometimes, meetings are held by the project team and audit team to go through the smart contract design to figure out if the end-to-end flow has security issues. Any issues found are labelled with severity levels, and critical issues will need to be fixed in order for the product to be released. A security audit can not only improve security of smart contracts from catastrophic failure, it is also required when the project team later decides to work with other partners or wants to license their smart contracts to other companies. Security audits have been a growing business in the blockchain industry, and there are often backlogs with audit requests. Expedited audit normally requires much higher fees; therefore, security audit time should be built into the project release schedule.

Readable Smart Contract Logic

We mentioned that smart contracts have high VLC (value per line of code). It is extremely important to make sure smart contract logic is straightforward and easy to read. If you read smart contract codes of good projects, you will probably find out that often there are more comments than source code itself. The comments are there to help readers to review and make sense of the source code. If you strip the code out of the Solidity file, you will find that the comments are actually good design and documentation for the smart contract functions. Good smart contracts are written and documented in a way that both technical and business experts can read it and get a good picture of the business logic.

Modularize the Smart Contract

Solidity is an object-oriented programming (OOP) language where you can use hierarchy, inheritance, and polymorphy mechanisms to define classes and functions similar to Java and JavaScript. A good practice of modularizing smart contracts is to mimic the real-world scenarios and build the smart contracts as the components of the corresponding business logic.

Using Well-Tested Libraries

Relevant to modularization, using well-tested libraries is another way to increase security. Since the majority of smart contracts are open source, there are many handy and secure libraries that have been built and available for use. For example, OpenZeppelin provides a good set of libraries such as SafeMath, ERC20, and ERC721, while Oraclable provides Oracle libraries to use.

Well-established library code normally has better boundary checking for their smart contract functions. For example, SafeMath libraries have checks on the arithmetic data type ranges and division checks for denominators equal to zero case. Using library code from a well-tested project decreases the uncertainty of the main code.

Use a Good Random Number Generator

In gaming applications, sometimes, smart contracts use a Random Number Generator (RNG) to generate a random number to pick a winner from a group of users. RNG is also used to enhance security by grouping actors randomly to prevent collusion. It is generally not a good idea to roll out your own RNG without a sound mathematical validation and thorough testing of the degree of randomness in RNG. For example, using the hash value of a blockchain block might seem to be random for some applications. However, if the smart contract of the dApp is handling large-scale and high-value gaming similar to Powerball, the randomness of blockchain hash is attack prone. A block producer can add or remove transactions in a proposed blockchain block and provide a manipulated hash. At this time, there is not a perfect RNG onchain, and full randomness has to be introduced through offchain computing and brought into blockchain by using Oracle.

Review Gas Consumption in Security Context

Gas usage and fees are designed as a way to compensate miners and increase the cost of deliberate attack on the Ethereum network. In a smart contract transaction, each function and storage will consume gas, and the gas cost is paid by the user who sends the transactions to the smart contract. There are several security factors to consider when dealing with gas consumptions in smart contracts. In a dApp application, if a proxy is used to send transactions for users, then it is important to review the functions to see if the gas consumption is a fixed value and if there is a potential for the function to get into an infinite or large loop and deprive the Ether of the sender's account. In general, smart contracts should be designed and written in a way to minimize gas consumption. To achieve these, special attention should be given to avoid while-loops for long operations, large dynamic arrays for data storage, and complex function calls across smart contracts. When writing smart contracts, there are some gas estimate tools to help check the usage of gas in the code. There is also a gas consumption table published by the Ethereum Foundation as a guide to optimize gas performance for smart contracts.

Wisely Use Blockchain

Some people have misconceptions that blockchain can solve all problems that conventional IT technologies cannot solve today. To some extent, blockchains do solve challenging problems such as consensus, decentralization, permissionless, and token economy. However, today, there are still many drawbacks for blockchain technology. For example, when a smart contract is executed, it runs on thousands of machines simultaneously. In fact, the Bitcoin blockchain has over 20,000 mining nodes, and Ethereum has thousands of nodes. All Ethereum nodes will have the same deployed smart contract and will run smart contracts to process the transactions. With this scale of redundancy in the blockchain, it drastically decreases overall performance and increases risks when something actually goes wrong.

So from a security point of view, in a dApp architecture and design, it is a better practice to use blockchain for the system that requires decentralization, multiparty consensus, immutability, and transparency. For components such as UI (User Interface), dynamic content storage, temporary data, and heavy computations, these can be done offchain. Take the example of CryptoKitty; the minting, gene generation, and management of kitty auctions are done onchain, while the UI and rendering of kitty are done offchain. Well-balanced onchain and offchain components of decentralized applications increase usability, upgradability, performance, and security.

Stay on Top of Security Breaches and Patches

Blockchain is far away from a stabilized state, and security breaches happen quite often. So it is helpful to subscribe to blockchain security news alerts and evaluate any hacks that might impact your projects. Blockchain hacks always get to the headline of the media. In the Ethereum community, workaround, security vulnerabilities are discussed and shared quite timely. It is important to have action plans if the security breaches impact your smart contracts deployed in the production network.

It is also best practice to upgrade the smart contract code to the latest version of Solidity as soon as possible. This is easy to say but is very difficult to actually do. Once the smart contracts are deployed, they cannot be patched due to immutability of blockchain. An upgrade will require abandoning the old smart contract and deploying a brand new one. Also there are various versions of Solidity programs coexisting in smart contract libraries and production codes. There are incompatibilities among different versions of Solidity compilers. Before deploying a smart contract, it is best to upgrade all source code for both main smart contracts and libraries to the latest version.

Also there are some good security analysis and visualization tools that can be used to help developers write secure smart contracts. Security scanning tools can help developers to spot static security vulnerabilities and follow good security coding practice. Visualization tools help developers and reviewers to see the whole picture of the smart contracts and analyze potential attacking points from hackers.

Blockchain Specific Security Tips

For programmers who used to develop stand-alone applications or web services, it should be noted that blockchains have some special properties and pitfalls to watch and avoid.

When doing cross smart contract function calls, the calling function will take in the address of another smart contract and call the bytecode of a target function. Sometimes, that target function might contain malicious codes and alter the control flow of the calling function. It is very important to inspect the source code of the target smart contract to ensure it is free of security vulnerability. If the address of the target smart contract is passed in from outside, it is vital to ensure that only privileged users can pass in the target address.

Ethereum blockchains are public, decentralized, and permissionless. If there is any function in a smart contract that is declared as public, anybody in any part of the world can call that function and pass in arbitrary parameters. So it is important to double-check the scope of function and have parameter check for all permutations that might cause security breach. Public functions in smart contracts are globally public and can be called in any order with any data. Therefore, it is extremely important to check the following attributes for a smart contract function:

- **Scope of function** – Declare whether it is public or private, or view.

- **Scope of access** – Check who can call the function, maybe only owner, or only a predefined user role.

- **Parameter permutation** – Check parameter range of data. Check validity of inputs.

Ethereum blockchain's intrinsic security has some constraints. When a variable is declared in a smart contract, it can be a private variable. However, a private variable is really not private as the Ethereum Virtual Machine (EVM) installed on blockchain nodes can reveal it. To ensure privacy of data in smart contracts, the data should be encrypted before sending to blockchain and then decrypted after receiving from the blockchain. Because of the transparency of public blockchain, onchain data encryption and decryption are not secure in smart contracts. The execution steps and internal data are viewable with an EVM with debugger enabled. The encryption and decryption should be performed through offchain computing.

For decentralized applications that need to use time sequence in computing, it is important to know that timestamps in blockchain are not accurate because miners can manipulate the block time by delaying or accelerating block computation and proposal. It is not a good practice to use block timestamp to check for sequencing execution and ordering transaction steps. The timestamp of blockchain or transactions should not be used as a unique identifier for multiple events as there is no guarantee of block timestamp collision within the range of seconds.

Security needs to be considered in all life cycles of smart contract development, from conceptions, requirements, token design, architecture, to implementation and operations. One important security factor to consider is safe-guarding private keys in the deployment process. Crypto assets are stored in accounts, and each account is represented by a private and public keypair. Private keys are used to sign transactions to send assets from one user to another. Whoever has the private key of an account owns the asset of that account. When deploying a smart contract to a blockchain,

335

there needs to be a user who sends the deployment transaction to the blockchain. To sign a transaction, the user needs to unlock the account with its private key. If an account is unlocked in a blockchain, its private key is open and can be stolen by a spoofer. This has happened many times in the cryptoworld.

There are several secure ways to deploy smart contracts. For example, users can use a hardware wallet or use an offline wallet for the deployment. In both cases, the private keys are kept in separate devices, and only signed transactions are copied to the online system to be sent out to the blockchain. Since a private key will never leave a dedicated device without network communication, it is completely secure unless the device is physically tempered.

Security Impact of Quantum Computing

The security impact of quantum computing has been a major concern of the blockchain community. People worry if the supremacy of quantum computing will nullify blockchain advantages and bring cryptocurrency value to zero. Quantum computing is a revolutionary technology that takes advantage of quantum physics' amazing principles and phenomena such as superposition, entanglement, and measurement uncertainty. In quantum computing, a qubit is used to represent the "0" and "1" state of a quantum system, similar to bits in conventional computing. Multiple qubits can be built into a register to become a compute and storage unit for quantum computing. Quantum computing provides much higher computing power and is going to impact blockchain in the following areas.

The hashing algorithm of sha-256 or sha-3 will no longer be valid. A hashing algorithm is a one-way function that takes in an input string and produces a fixed length output string. One important requirement for hashing is that different inputs should generate different outputs. Also, there should not exist a way to reversely compute an input from its hash value. With quantum computing, these rules will be broken, and any system that relies on hashing such as SHA256 will need to be overhauled.

The asymmetric public key–private key signature algorithm such as ECDSA or DSA that uses elliptic curve cryptography will no longer be secure. Quantum computing can compute private keys from public keys or break a signed message from a private key.

The impact of quantum computing on cryptography will in turn impact the security of blockchain in areas as shown in Figure 8-3.

Figure 8-3. *Impact of quantum computing on blockchain security*

The fundamental immutability of blockchain will be impacted. Blocks in blockchains are uniquely identified by their block hashes. If hashes are no longer secure and can be manipulated with quantum computing, then blockchain can be altered with data changed inside but still keeps its hashes on the chain.

The crypto assets are no longer secure because the private keys that control asset accounts can be hacked with a quantum computer.

The P2P network layer communication will no longer be secure. Ethereum uses secp255k1 for nodeKey and nodeId generation. As secp256k1 will no longer be secure, the client node identification and communication mechanism will need to be changed.

The smart contract of Ethereum blockchain is no longer valid because the owner of the smart contract can be hacked as well.

All transactions signed with private keys with ECDSA and SECP256 are no longer valid, and new algorithms will need to be used.

Even the proof-of-work (POW) consensus will be impacted. The POW is based on computing a matching hash to validate a miner who proposes a block. With quantum computing, the computation is so fast, and those with quantum computing power will build the longest chain, hence breaking the 51% computing power role.

To mitigate quantum computing supremacy, there are several key items to consider.

Firstly, Ethereum 2 is moving from POW to POS (proof of stake). This will mitigate the impact of quantum computing on consensus.

Secondly, there are quantum-resistant signature schemes developed already, including Lamport, XMSS, and SPHINCS.

Thirdly, the security compact of quantum computing is not just on blockchain, it is on all cryptography and network computing. The quantum solutions worked out in the general field can be ported to blockchain.

Fourthly, the solution for the impact of quantum computing on blockchain security might go beyond the technology side of blockchain. There might be some legal regulations to prohibit using quantum computing power to hack information and blockchain systems. Similar to the nuclear nonproliferation policy, there might be some restriction on quantum devices released to the public domain.

It is very important to follow the development of quantum computing and stay on top of the mitigation plans and get ready to make critical decisions. With IBM on the way to release 1000 qubit devices and Google making the leap jump on quantum computing, it is inevitable that computing will challenge and threaten the security of blockchain. It is highly recommended to learn about quantum computing technology and get ready to accept quantum-resistant technology for Ethereum blockchain.

Summary

In summary, we just cannot overemphasize the importance of security in blockchains. Security breaches and bad things have happened in the past, are happening now, and will happen in the future. So when you write Solidity smart contracts, make sure the security procedures are followed; always go above and beyond to let the community test the smart contracts out before rolling them out to the blockchain mainnet.

Summary

CHAPTER 9

Layer 2 and Ethereum 2

Problem with Ethereum Mainnet

The Ethereum mainnet is designed as a public blockchain rather than an Enterprise platform; hence, it lacks privacy, performance, scaling, and permissioning capacities.

With regard to privacy, Ethereum mainnet stores all data in a permissionless fashion, and everyone has access to the data. All sensitive data will need to be encrypted before being sent to the blockchain, and transactions need to be obfuscated through smart contracts. Some institutes and states will not allow certain categories of data to be published to the public blockchain. Thus, the use of the public mainnet is limited to storing hashes or URLs of data resources. The original data are stored in private blockchains or nodes, and verified through public chains and channels.

For performance and scalability, Ethereum mainnet has already hit a bottleneck. The release of CryptoKitties has caused congestion in the Ethereum blockchain. Transaction fees have reached over $100 per transaction and hence limit feasible transactions to high-value and low-frequency applications. In order to speed up transactions, sometimes,

© Weijia Zhang and Tej Anand 2022
W. Zhang and T. Anand, *Blockchain and Ethereum Smart Contract Solution Development*,
https://doi.org/10.1007/978-1-4842-8164-2_9

users have to set high gas prices to increase the chance for their transactions to be included by miners to their proposed blocks.

For permissioning, public blockchains are designed as permissionless, but there are use cases where applications do want to have access control due to security and regulation considerations. The "public" nature of Ethereum mainnet deters some uses such as certificate issuance and personnel database.

To solve the issues in Ethereum mainnet, many Ethereum Improvement Proposals and solutions have been proposed, including layer 2 and Ethereum 2. In this chapter, we discuss new scalability technologies for Ethereum, including layer 2 and Ethereum 2. The following illustration (Figure 9-1) shows the classification of scalability solutions of Ethereum, and they are explained in detail in their respective sections.

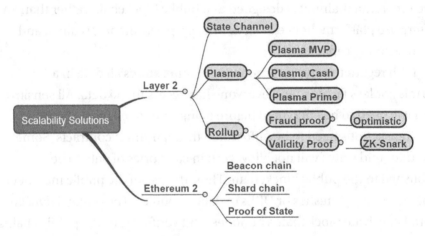

Figure 9-1. *Overview of scalability solutions for Ethereum blockchain*

Layer 2 Technology

Layer 2 is a suite of technologies to improve the performance and scalability of Ethereum layer 1 mainnet by moving the computing and storage of transactions from onchain to offchain through smart contracts. Onchain transactions require running EVM on all nodes and storing all states on Ethereum blockchain, hence decreasing performance and scalability. The mechanism for the layer 2 solution is to move some of the transactions off the main chain and only record the vital information on the mainnet to ensure security and transparency. One major difference between layer 2 and Ethereum 2 is that layer 2 uses smart contracts to connect offchain resources to the mainnet and thus does not require the mainnet blockchain to have a hard fork. Layer 2 solutions can be implemented by third-party projects using the existing Ethereum mainnet. There are several L2 mechanisms that are available, including state channel, plasma, and rollup; each has its own unique features.

Ethereum State Channel

State channel is one of the layer 2 solutions that allow two or more participants to send transactions among themselves offline and only send the beginning and final transactions of the state channel cycle to the mainnet blockchain. This way, mainnet is used as an escrow and auditing platform for the trusted channel between two or multiple parties. For example, a state channel can be built as a proof of authority (POA) or Byzantine Fault Tolerance private blockchain that is permissioned for the participants only. To make it simpler, the private blockchain can be replaced with a smart wallet that can connect with other wallets and record the transactions among them. Participants use the private blockchain or smart wallet as a state channel to do fast and low cost transactions.

To illustrate a use case of a state channel, we use a payment system of a construction company in which the builder needs to record contracting employees earning on daily bases and pay them on a monthly basis. If the daily transactions are recorded on the blockchain, that would increase transaction fees dramatically as the cost for gas fees could reach $100 per transaction. Using the state channel, the owner of the company can pay daily transactions with the state channel and only pay employees the lump sum each month. This will save the cost at roughly 1/30 of the original cost.

The topology and workflow of a state channel is shown in the following diagram (Figure 9-2):

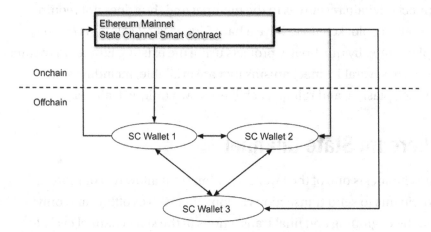

Figure 9-2. *Topology and workflow of state channel solutions*

The preceding diagram shows the schema of a state channel that has the following components:

- State channel smart contract is deployed to the mainnet.

This smart contract is multisigned, and not a single user can alter or delete the smart contract.

The state channel smart contract can accept deposits for users and create a state channel for a group of users. The depositor needs to specify the participants' account addresses.

The state channel smart contract also has functions to (a) process multisign signatures and distribute funds to participants and (b) process audit requests from any of the participants by accepting evidence sent by any participants.

- Each user can have a state channel wallet (SC wallet).

The wallet can interact among participants by sending transactions, requesting receipts, or multisigning a transaction for the main chain. The wallet also has storage to store local copies of the transaction history and receipts.

The workflow is as follows:

- A payer uses a crypto wallet to deposit ether assets to the state channel smart contract and specify the payees' accounts who will receive payments.

- The smart contract creates a record and returns a deposit record with balance and payee addresses. The payee addresses are also recorded by the smart contract to process claims or audit requests.

- The payer gets the deposit receipt and starts sending payments through offchain signed transaction to payees. For each transaction, the state channel wallet will update the account balance offchain and have signed receipt for both sender and receiver. These transactions are offchain and hence have a low transaction fee or even no fee.

- Once the operation of the state channel is completed, the offchain transactions will need to be transferred to the mainnet, and each participant's balance will need to be updated. Each participant will check the local copy of their transaction receipt and sign the exit state channel transaction. Once the exit transaction is multisigned by all parties, it is sent to the mainnet state channel smart contract for processing. The mainnet smart contract will verify the information and then distribute the deposited funds to respective participants.

- If any of the participants does not sign the transaction, the other participants can send a transaction to call the smart contract's claim or audit function and provide the needed local receipt as proof. If the state channel smart contract verifies the payer frauds, the deposited balance of the payer can be slashed.

There are different implementations for layer 2 state channel solutions. In the aforementioned, we have offchain computing and storage built into the state channel wallet. This will increase the footprint of the wallet and need to customize the crypto wallet. Another solution is to implement the state channel offchain computing through a private blockchain using permissioned consensus such as proof of authority (POA) or Byzantine Fault Tolerance (BFT) blockchain. The private blockchain can process and record transactions among state channel participants. Only the entry and exit transactions of the state channel will be sent to mainnet for security and persistent record. The wallet can be a regular wallet such as a MetaMask wallet that can switch from mainnet chain to private chain for state channel transactions.

Although state channels can improve scalability for Ethereum by moving transactions offchain, there are some limitations for this mechanism. First, state channel participants need to actively participate in the transactions. Their accounts will need to be registered in the state channel smart contract. A sender cannot send transactions to an arbitrary address not in the channel. Secondly, all state channel participants will need to be actively involved in the transactions by verifying transactions and multisign exit transactions. Thirdly, since the mainnet only has the initial state and final state, it will need to rely on the offchain participants to provide proof if there are discrepancies with the state channel transactions. Needing participants to be involved to secure state channels is a big drawback and makes it difficult to develop a generalized solution for state channels.

Plasma As a Layer 2 Technology

Ethereum Plasma is another layer 2 scaling solution that uses smart contracts to link external blockchains with Ethereum mainnet as a security and arbitration platform. These children blockchains are called plasma chains, and their blockchain transaction records are merkelized, and the roots of the Merkle tree are sent to mainnet to be stored as proofs.

The preceding diagram (Figure 9-3) shows the components and workflow of plasma blockchain working as a layer 2 solution.

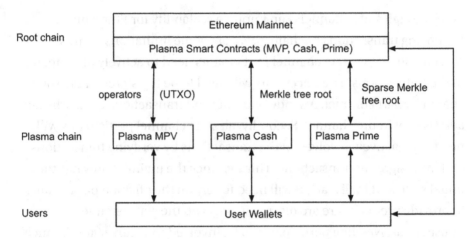

Figure 9-3. *Components and workflow of plasma scalability solutions*

Plasma Smart Contract on Ethereum Mainnet

The top layer is the layer 1 or root blockchain, which in this context is Ethereum mainnet. Plasma smart contracts are deployed to Ethereum mainnet, and it has the following functions.

Deposit function for users to deposit assets to use in layer 1: This deposit function will allow a user to send a transaction to a plasma smart contract with a certain asset value. The asset sent by the user through the deposit function will be locked in the mainnet by the plasma smart contract. A record will be created by the smart contract, and a new token related to this deposit will be created. After that, the deposit function can emit a deposit event to notify plasma blockchain. The token and its value will be replicated in the plasma blockchain and used as assets for the layer 2 blockchain.

SubmitPlasmaTxRecord function for layer 2 plasma blockchain to submit the transaction Merkle tree to the layer 1 root chain: The transactions in the plasma blockchain are recorded in a Merkle tree structure, and the root of the Merkle tree is sent to the parent or root blockchain.

StartWithdraw function that allows users to withdraw assets from the layer 2 chain to the layer 1 blockchain: The function is normally called by users directly or by operators that connect with both layer 1 and layer 2 blockchains. The caller of this function should provide plasma block number, transaction indexid, transaction record, Merkle proof, and signatures. When users withdraw assets from the plasma blockchain, the assets in the plasma chain will be burned, and then the assets originally deposited on the layer 1 chain will be distributed to the target user. To ensure that the burning operation and unlock operation are secure, there will be a wait period for the StartWithdraw function to distribute the funds to the users. This is to ensure that the assets in layer 2 are burned before the same value of asset in layer 1 is distributed. During this wait period, anyone can challenge this withdrawal by providing proofs from the plasma blockchain.

ChallengeWithdraw function that allows any user or operator to provide evidence to challenge the withdrawal transaction waiting to be validated: The caller of this function needs to provide a withdrawal ID that is challenged and other inputs such as Merkle root and proofs that are similar to the StartWithdraw function. The inputs from StartWithdraw function and ChallengeWithdraw function are compared and validated. If the challenge is successful, then the StartWithdraw transaction will be voided.

Operators

Operators connect plasma blockchain with layer 1 root chain. It watches deposit events in layer 1 and then generates a new token ID to represent the one in the mainnet and then mint the same value of tokens in the plasma chain. Once the new token is generated on the plasma blockchain, the depositor owns the token and can send the token to any user in the layer 2 chain. Operators will also submit plasma blockchain Merkle tree root records to the layer 1 blockchain. Users can withdraw their assets to layer 1 using smart contract functions calls on blockchain. If the withdrawal is requested in layer 2, the operator will also pass the request to layer 1 for processing.

Transactions or Smart Contracts on Layer 2

In the plasma layer 2 chain, users can send regular transactions among each other. The plasma chain can also implement smart contract capability to withdraw assets to the layer 1 blockchain. The transactions in the plasma chain are packaged into a Merkle tree and saved as a blockchain state. The root of the Merkle is sent to the layer 1 chain for record.

Plasma Chain

Plasma chains can be implemented in various ways. Since the security of the plasma chain is coupled with the root chain and receipts of transactions are sent to the receiver, plasma chains do not need to have full consensus to ensure security. The plasma chain can be implemented in various ways. In one implementation, a plasma chain can be implemented as a server that takes user transaction inputs and also has a Merkle tree structure or a database to store transactions. The plasma chain can also be implemented as a POA (proof of authority) or BFT (Byzantine Fault Tolerance) blockchain. In this POA or BFT plasma blockchain, a couple of permissioned nodes create a blockchain to accept plasma layer transactions. The root of the transaction Merkle tree is then calculated and sent to the root blockchain for record and verification. The plasma chain can also be implemented as a POS (proof of stake) chain where anyone can run a node by staking an asset to a smart contract on the root chain. The assets staked in the plasma chain are to secure the plasma chain. If there is a collusion of nodes in the plasma chain, the stakes of these nodes get slashed through a smart contract on the root chain.

Transaction Merkle Tree Example

Ethereum blockchains leverage the Merkle tree extensively. A Merkle tree
is a data structure that arranges data/message and its respective hash
in a hierarchical tree structure to ensure data integrity and processing
efficiency. There are multiple Merkle trees. A standard Merkle tree is the
one that records the elements and their hash in a binary tree structure as
shown in the following diagram (Figure 9-4):

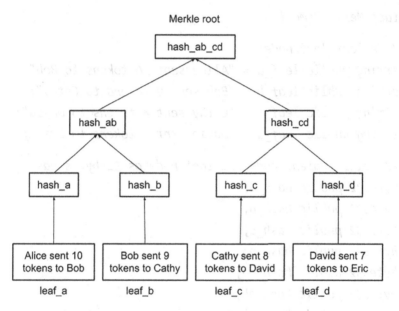

Figure 9-4. *A standard Merkle tree example*

The leaf nodes are data nodes, and the nodes on top of leaf nodes
store the hash of the data element. Here, H(A) means a hash of data A. The
hashing function can be sha256 or keccak256, which are commonly used
in Ethereum. With these Merkle trees, the integrity of each node can be
verified by providing root hash and hashes of the "uncle's" node. For
example, in the preceding diagram, to prove transactions of A element
are valid, users need to provide hash_b, hash_c, and hash_d to compute

the root node hash and compare with the root hash as recorded in the root chain.

The following code snippet demonstrates how the Merkle tree in the preceding diagram is implemented in Solidity. The source code for this Merkle tree demo program is located at the GitHub location.

```
/**
 * @title MerkleDemo for 4 leaf nodes
 */
contract MerkleDemo {

    //declear leaf nodes
    string public leaf_a = "Alice sent 10 tokens to Bob";
    string public leaf_b = "Bob sent 9 tokens to Cathy";
    string public leaf_c = "Cathy sent 8 tokens to David";
    string public leaf_d = "David sent 7 tokens to Eric";

    //declare parent node and root node as 32 bytes hash.
    bytes32 public hash_a;
    bytes32 public hash_b;
    bytes32 public hash_c;
    bytes32 public hash_d;
    bytes32 public hash_cd;
    bytes32 public hash_ab;
    bytes32 public hash_ab_cd;
    bytes32 public hash_root;
```

In the preceding code snippet, four leaf nodes – leaf_a, leaf_b, leaf_c, and leaf_d – are defined as string type variables that record simplified transactions. The content of the leaf nodes is hashed and stored in variables of hash_a, hash_b, hash_c, and hash_d of bytes32 data type.

hash_a and hash_b are combined to form a parent hash named hash_ab. Hash_c and hash_d are combined to form parent node hash_cd. And finally, hash_ab and hash_cd are combined to form hash_ab_cd. Hash_ab_cd is the top node equivalent to hash_root.

The constructor of MerkleDemo smart contract constructs the Merkle tree as shown in the following:

```
/*
 * Constructor function to construct a merkle tree.
 */

constructor() public {
    // construct a Merkle tree with sha256 hash function.
    // abi.encodePacked concatenate two child hashes
    hash_a = sha256(abi.encodePacked(leaf_a));
    hash_b = sha256(abi.encodePacked(leaf_b));
    hash_c = sha256(abi.encodePacked(leaf_c));
    hash_d = sha256(abi.encodePacked(leaf_d));
    hash_ab= sha256(abi.encodePacked(hash_a, hash_b));
    hash_cd= sha256(abi.encodePacked(hash_c, hash_d));
    hash_ab_cd= sha256(abi.encodePacked(hash_ab, hash_cd));
    hash_root = hash_ab_cd;
}
```

In the preceding code in the constructor, the sha256 Solidity function is used to hash a leaf or nonleaf node. abi.encodePacked function is to concatenate two elements and hash the merged result to get the parent node. Once the hash_root is generated, it is saved to the root blockchain and can be used to validate nodes in the Merkle tree as requested by the users or operators.

To check if a transaction represented by a leaf node is in the Merkle tree, simply use the following checkMerkleTree function:

```
/**
 * Check if a leaf is valid
 * @param _leaf Leaf to check.
```

```
     * @param _index Index of the leaf in the tree.
     * @param _rootHash Root of the tree.
     * @param _proof Merkle proof showing the leaf is in
     the tree.
     * @return True if the leaf is in the tree, false otherwise.
     */
    function checkMerkleTree(
        string memory _leaf,
        uint256 _index,
        bytes32 _rootHash,
        bytes memory _proof
    ) public pure returns (bool) {
        // Check _proof to be one or multiple bytes32
        require(_proof.length % 32 == 0, "proof length not
        valid.");

        // Compute the merkle root.
        bytes32 proofElement;
        bytes32 parentHash = sha256(abi.encodePacked(_leaf));
        uint256 index = _index;
        //loops through each bytes32 element in the proof
        for (uint256 i = 32; i <= _proof.length; i += 32) {
            assembly {
                proofElement = mload(add(_proof, i))
            }
            if (index % 2 == 0) {  // leaf node is on the left
                parentHash = sha256(abi.
                encodePacked(parentHash, proofElement));
            } else { //leaf node is on the right
                parentHash = sha256(abi.
                encodePacked(proofElement, parentHash));
            }
```

```
        index = index / 2; //Go to the next level
    }

    // If parentHash equal _rootHash, then it is validated.
    return parentHash == _rootHash;
}
```

The checkMerkleTree function takes a leaf node contract (i.e., a transaction), an index that shows the location of the leaf node, a root hash, and then a proof to compute if the root hash as computed by the leaf node and proof matches what is recorded. If the computed hash root and the recorded one match, the leaf and proof are considered as valid. Otherwise, the leaf node or the transaction that it represents is considered as tempered.

And then we have a testcasedemo function to verify leaf nodes c and d for the untempered and tempered cases as shown in the following:

```
// test some leaf nodes in the Merkle tree
function testCasesdemo() public payable returns(string
memory, string memory, string memory, string memory){

    //valid and invalid transaction message to be validated
    string memory test_leaf_c = "Cathy sent 8 tokens
    to David";
    string memory test_leaf_d = "David sent 7 tokens
    to Eric";
    // These two are tempered and should not be validated
    string memory test_leaf_c_tempered = "Cathy sent 100000
    tokens to David";
    string memory test_leaf_d_tempered = "David sent 100000
    tokens to Eric";

    // leaf_a, leaf_b, leaf_c, lead_d have index = 0, 1, 2,
    3 respectively.
```

```
// Use test_index variable to represent index
uint test_index = 2;
// construct Merkle proof for leaf_c
bytes memory merkle_proof = abi.encodePacked(hash_d,
hash_ab);
bool result = checkMerkleTree(test_leaf_c, test_index,
hash_root, merkle_proof);
string memory return_leaf_c = string(abi.
encodePacked(test_leaf_c, ": ",result?"true":"false"));
//Do the same validation for tempered leaf_c
result = checkMerkleTree(test_leaf_c_tempered, test_
index, hash_root, merkle_proof);
string memory return_leaf_c_tempered =
string(abi.encodePacked(test_leaf_c_tempered, ":
",result?"true":"false"));

// Do the same leaf_d, similar to leaf_c
test_index = 3;
merkle_proof = abi.encodePacked(hash_c, hash_ab);
result = checkMerkleTree(test_leaf_d, test_index, hash_
root, merkle_proof);
string memory return_leaf_d = string(abi.
encodePacked(test_leaf_d, ": ",result?"true":"false"));
result = checkMerkleTree(test_leaf_d_tempered, test_
index, hash_root, merkle_proof);
string memory return_leaf_d_tempered =
string(abi.encodePacked(test_leaf_d_tempered, ":
",result?"true":"false"));

//Return and output results
return (return_leaf_c, return_leaf_c_tempered, return_
leaf_d, return_leaf_d_tempered);
}
```

This test method constructs test_leaf_c and test_leaf_d transactions that are valid. Also, it modified the two transactions to test_leaf_c_tempered and test_leaf_d_tempered and changed the transferred token to a larger amount. The proof for each node is also constructed and the index for the transaction specified. The leaf node, index, root hash, and proof are sent to checkMerkleTree function for verification. The result is shown here:

```
//Output of testCasedemo
{
    "0": "string: Cathy sent 8 tokens to David: true",
    "1": "string: Cathy sent 100000 tokens to David: false",
    "2": "string: David sent 7 tokens to Eric: true",
    "3": "string: David sent 100000 tokens to Eric: false"
}
```

The output shows that the untempered transactions are validated as true and the tempered ones are validated as false.

Transaction Merkle Tree for Plasma MVP

In the last code example, we showed a standard Merkle tree with simple transaction messages of "User A sent x tokens to user B" recorded in the leaf nodes. Although we are able to show that these transaction messages can be proved with a root hash recorded in the root chain and a proof submitted by a user or operator, a simple message format is not sufficient enough to be used practically for plasma transactions. More complex Merkle tree formats have been proposed for both fungible and nonfungible tokens. In the following, we describe Plasma MVP and Plasma Cash.

Plasma MVP uses a standard Merkle tree that uses UTXO to record transactions and send the root hash to the root chain. Vitalik proposed using the following unspent transaction output (UTXO) format for the Merkle leaf node:

```
[blknum1, txindex1, oindex1, sig1, # Input 1
blknum2, txindex2, oindex2, sig2, # Input 2
newowner1, denom1,                # Output 1
newowner2, denom2,                # Output 2
fee]
```

This leaf node format uses two inputs and two outputs. The two inputs allow a user to combine two UTXOs to send to one address. The two outputs allow a user to send partial UTXO to one user and the others to another user. In this leaf node format, blknum1, txindex1, and oindex1 represent blockchain number, transaction index, and output index for input 1. This uniquely identifies the leaf node of the transaction Merkle tree. The sig1 is used to sign the transaction to ensure the sender is the owner of the UTXO. Similarly, blknum2, txindex2, oindex2, and sig2 represent the block number, transaction index, output index, and signature of input 2. For the outputs, newowner1 and denom1 represent the amount of token to be allocated to the new owner 1. And newowner2 and denom2 represent the amount of token to be allocated to the new owner 2. And finally, the fee in the transaction is the amount of token to pay for the plasma transaction.

Using UTXO format for Merkle tree nodes, the transactions can be uniquely identified, and there is no need to traverse the Merkle tree to query other transactions. To make the query even more efficient, the blknum, txindex, and oindex can be merged to become a uint256 integer.

This way, one integer can be used to uniquely identify a UTXO transaction using the following conversion:

```
utxo_index = blknum*1000000000+txindex*10000+oindex;
```

To retrieve blknum, txindex, and oindex from utxo_index, use the following:

```
Blknum = utxo_index/1000000000;
Txindex = (utxo % 1000000000)/10000;
oindex = utxo_index - blknum*1000000000-txindex*10000;
```

Using the UTXO format, Plasma MVP can record fungible tokens with a UTXO format efficiently on the plasma chain. Users can also withdraw their assets or UTXO on the root chain. To submit a withdrawal request, simply send a utxo_index to identify the location of the UTXO, the transaction itself, the Merkle root, and the signature. The smart contract will do the following to distribute the funds to the new owner of the root chain:

- Check that the sender for the withdrawal request is the same as the owner of the UTXO.

- The transaction has been signed by the sender.

- The output 1 and output 2 amount plus the transaction fee is the same as the sum of input 1 and input 2.

- The UTXO for the sender is not spent yet. This would require some time to confirm.

Once all validity checking passes, the plasma smart contract on the root chain will distribute the assets on the root chain to the new owners.

Transaction Merkle Tree for Plasma Cash

With Plasma MVP mentioned earlier, users can send fungible assets through UTXO to the end users. However, the Plasma MVP does not solve the problem for nonfungible tokens. UTXO has a denominator for transactions but does not require a unique ID. Plasma Cash is an extension of UTXO where each token is assigned a serial number for record and transfer.

Although cash or money is normally considered as fungible, Plasma Cash is actually best for dealing with nonfungible tokens similar to ERC721 or assets that are uniquely identifiable.

To allow Merkle trees to work with nonfungible tokens, a sparse Merkle tree is proposed to ensure uniqueness of a token. The following diagram (Figure 9-5) is an illustration of how a sparse Merkle tree works for a nonfungible token.

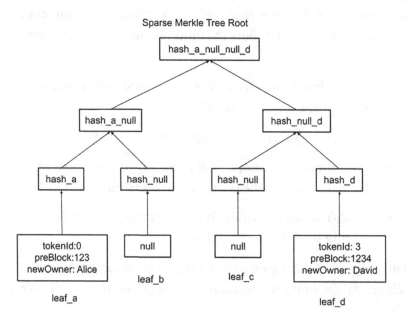

Figure 9-5. *A Sparse Merkle tree example*

For ERC721 NFT token, there is an NFT identifier to represent the tokenId to represent the index of the token. This uint32 tokenId can be casted to a smaller size integer such as uint32 and uint64.

A Merkle tree can be constructed to represent the tokenId of an NFT. In this Merkle tree structure, echa token is represented by a leaf node. For a tokenId of size n of uint, the number of leaf nodes will be 2^n. For example, the tokenId of uint8 will have a leaf number of $2^8=256$. Similarly, the leaf numbers for uint16, uint32, and uint64 are 65536, 4294967296, and 18446744073709551616, respectively.

The location of the leaf node is equivalent to the tokenId. The leaf indexes from left to right are arranged from 0 to (2^n-1). The content of the leaf node is a byte32 data that is the hash of a transaction of NFT token. The Plasma transaction format is a tuple of (slot, previousBlock, denomination, owner, hash). Here, slot is the same as tokenId that represents to the index of the leaf node, previousBlock is the block number that contains this tokenId's owner transfer, denomination is default to 1 for NFT case, owner is the new owner for this token transfer, and hash is a sha256 or keccak256 hashing of the other parameters. Once the hash is computed, its value is inserted to the leaf node at the location of the slot or tokenId.

For a tokenId range of 0 to 2^n-1, there needs to be n level of nodes from root node to leaf node. If we label the leaf nodes to be at level 0, then the root node will be at level n-1. For tokenId with size of uint16, there will be 16 layers, and uint64 will have 64 layers.

The merkle tree can be initialized as an empty Merkle tree where the leaf nodes are all hash of null.

For level zero, the hash content of the node will be hash_null = H(null) = sha256(null)=e3b0c44298fc1c149afbf4c8996fb92427ae41e4649b934 ca495991b7852b855.

Level 1 hash_null_null = H(H(null), H(null))

Level 2 hash is hash_null_null_null_null = H(H(H(null), H(null)), H(H(null), H(null)))

And so on until it gets to the root of the Merkle tree.

Here, H(x) is a hash function such as sha256 or keccak256 that takes a string as input and produces a bytes32 hash. H(x, y) is a function that packs x and y and then gets its hash.

These precalculated values can be used for the proof computation to improve efficiency.

When there is a transaction, a bytes32 hash will be calculated and stored in a leaf node. Accordingly, all the parent nodes of this leaf node will be updated up to the root node of the Merkle tree. If there are n levels for a Merkle tree, each update of a leaf node will trigger n-1 updates to the parent nodes.

Each block will have a Merkle tree. Since the number of transactions for each block is much less than the number of possible tokenIds, the Merkle tree will be sparsely populated. Majority of the nodes will be null. The parent nodes that go from a leaf node to the root node will be the default value calculated in the preceding table and can be represented by a bit rather than a full 32-byte hash. The fact that nodes that are affected with transactions are scattered in the Merkle tree gives the storage structure the name of sparse Merkle tree.

Different from the Plasma MVP, the proof for Plasma Cash uses two lists: one is a simplified bit list for the precalculated hashes of null or its parents; another one is the concatenated bytes32 hash list. The reason for using a bit list is to save storage space and computation effort as most of the nodes are not altered and have predefined values.

The mechanism for providing proofs for a leaf node for Plasma Cash is different from that of Plasma MVP. In MVP Merkle tree, a proof is a list of node hashes that can be used to compute with a leaf node to derive the root node hash. It is normally the concatenated list of hashes by the sibling nodes of the target leaf node or its parent nodes. For Plasma Cash, since it is a sparse Merkle tree, most of the sibling nodes will be null or predefined. These nodes can be presented by a bit=0 to mean that the default hash value should be used. If the bit is set to 1, then the changed hash value should be used. In the simple sparse Merkle tree shown earlier, for the tokenId=0 leaf_a node, the proof is hash_b and hash_c_d. Since hash_b is hash_null, which is already known, the proof can have a bit proof showing 01 uses first bit=0 to mean that the first hash is hash_null, which is already known, and the second bit is 1 to mean that the modified hash should be used. This cuts down the proof size almost by half. If there are more nodes and the data is sparsely populated, the proof size can be decreased dramatically.

Overall, with sparse Markle trees, the proof size is decreased, and the computational workload is decreased as well.

There are many alterations in implementing plasma layer 2 technology. With both plasma and state channels, layer 1 does not have full information about layer 2. Therefore, the security of plasma or state channel depends on layer 2 providing proof and transactions to the layer. This dependency on layer 2 limits the usage of state channel and plasma.

The third type of layer 2 technology is called rollup. This is different from plasma or state channels. In layer 2 rollup, the transactions are actually repackaged and then performed in the layer 1 blockchain. With rollup, the layer 1 blockchain no longer needs to ask users or layer 2 operators for proof and transaction data. In the following, we describe how rollup works.

Layer 2 Rollup

In previous sections, we discussed layer 2's state channel and plasma. State channel has the advantage of only interacting with layer 1 when opening or closing the state channel. However, state channels will require participants to be enrolled in the channel and cannot send transactions to an arbitrary address. Layer 2 plasma solved this problem by using operators to send layer 2 transaction Merkle tree root to the layer 1 storage. However, plasma layer 2 has the limitation of relying on layer 2 to store and provide proofs and challenges. In this section, we introduce a third layer 2 technology called rollup. Rollup is a technology that repackages transactions in layer 2 and sends them as a batch transaction to layer 1. The parameters in the batch transactions are optimized to save gas fee and increase scalability. There are two kinds of rollup technology that are being developed. One is using fraud proof that allows participants to challenge layer 2 to layer 1 transactions. Typical fraud proof solutions are called optimistic layer 2 solutions such as Arbitrum, Polygon, and Optimism. Another kind is called validity proof that uses validation methods such as zero knowledge proof to interact between layer 2 and layer 1. Validity proof layer 2 solutions include zk-rollup, zksync, etc.

Optimistic Layer 2

An overview of optimistic rollup is shown in the following diagram of Figure 9-6. The top layer shows the layer 1 blockchain such as Ethereum mainnet. An optimistic rollup smart contract is deployed to the layer 1 mainnet. There are several major functions for the rollup smart contract. For example, the smart contract has a function to receive transactions from layer 2 blockchain in a Merkle tree format and process these transactions on layer 1.

On layer 2, there is a similar blockchain built with OVM (Optimistic Virtual Machine). OVM supports smart contracts and can process transactions. The transactions on layer 2 are arranged based on the transaction time. The ordering of transactions is done by sequencers. The ordering of transactions is very important as there might be dependencies among these transactions.

When transactions in layer 2 are repackaged and rolled up to layer 1, there will be a wait period as layer 1 does not have enough information to prove that the transactions are valid. During this wait period, the optimistic rollup smart contract allows third parties to provide fraud proof to disqualify a rollup and to claim reward tokens. The reward to

fraud prover comes from the rollup transaction stakes deposited by
the aggregators. If an aggregator provides valid faulty proof, the stake
deposited by the aggregator will be forfeited.

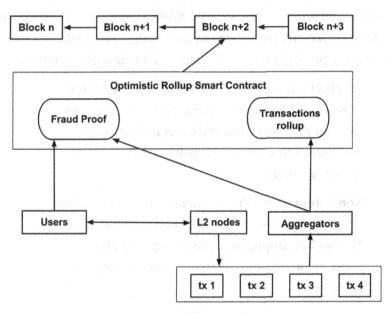

Figure 9-6. *Overview of Optimistic Rollup*

Since optimistic rollup relies on fraud proof to ensure that the
transactions in layer 2 are properly propagated to layer 1, there is an
overhead of several days to one week for the rollup transactions to be
finalized in layer 1. This means that to claim assets in layer one, users
will need to wait for up to one week to clear all the challenges posted
on the rollups. This is a bottleneck for optimistic rollup. To overcome
the limitation of fraud proof mechanism, the validation proof method is
proposed to allow transactions to use rollup proof to prove their validity.
In the following, we describe zk-SNARK (Zero-Knowledge Succinct Non-
interactive Argument of Knowledge) for validation proof rollup.

zk-SNARK Layer 2

zk-SNARK is a layer 2 rollup scalability solution that uses zero knowledge proof to ensure the rollup transactions from layer 2 to layer 1 are always in a valid state. Zero Knowledge proof is a technology for a party to prove that a statement is true without revealing what information is processed and how the conclusion is derived. zk-SNARK stands for Zero-Knowledge Succinct Non-interactive Argument of Knowledge. zk-SNARK is a special zero knowledge proof whose mechanism has the following characteristics:

> **Succinct** – The proof is short and easily verifiable. This is best for onchain verification, where the gas costs for the Ethereum, and other networks are expensive and many nodes will need to verify the same statement.

> **Non-interactive** – Proof generation and verification do not require users' manual interventions. The offchain applications can programmably generate proofs, and onchain smart contracts can verify proofs.

> **Argument of Knowledge** – Meaning that the statements can be confirmed or falsified with zero knowledge proof system. The communications parties gain knowledge of the other party without the need to disclose the private information and knowledge.

Zero knowledge proof is viewed as no private knowledge leak proof. It means that a person can prove that a knowledge is possessed without revealing it. Normally, in order to convince another person that you know something, you have to reveal that knowledge. Zero Knowledge proof is a privacy-enhanced crypto computation that can prove beyond reasonable doubt about a statement without leaking that statement.

Example: Alice wants to show to Bob that she knows how to do square root. If the test is just to supply an input and an output such as input=16 and output=4, the third party can know this is about square root. If the input and output are hashed, then the third party will not know that the rule of square root is used.

Zero knowledge proof can be used in privacy computing and layer 2 rollup. With zero knowledge proof such as zk-SNARK, the rollup transactions between layer 1 and layer 2 can be validated without the need of third-party challenges. In the following figure (Figure 9-7), we explain who zk-SNARK can be used for layer 2 rollup solution:

Workflow of zk-SNARK proof and verification key generation

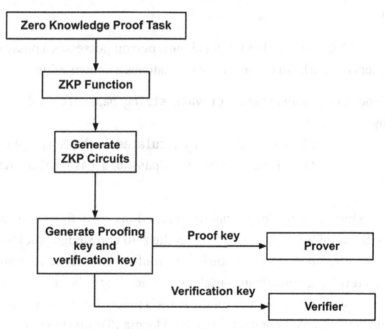

Figure 9-7. *zk-SNARK work flow*

To use zero knowledge proof, first is to define the tasks. This could be proof a person is over a certain age, a person possesses a password, a transaction is signed with a private key, the transactions in a Merkle tree are all valid, etc. Then variables will need to be defined, and functions will need to be written to ensure the proofing conditions are met. For example, the functions for the preceding tasks will be as follows:

//Define a function to check the age is over certain age such as drinking age

```
function proveAge(private age) {
    const Drinking_Age = 21;
    require (age >= Drinking_Age);

}
```

//Define a function for checking a person possesses a password by checking the hash of the password matches a known value

```
function provePassword(private string password, public
bytes32 hash) {
    bytes32 password_hash_calculated = sha256(password);
    require( password_hash == password_hash_calculated);
}
```

Once the knowledge statement functions are defined, they will need to be simplified or reduced to meet the zero knowledge proof format. This is because the zero knowledge proof has some requirements such as not revealing any private variables and needing to be stateless. There are many ways to do this. One of the ways is to rewrite the functions to meet the R1CS (rank-1 constraint systems) format. This is done by writing the functions using circuit models. Once R1CS are defined, a QAP (Quadratic Arithmetic Program) is used to represent the knowledge statement. Using QAP, the system can generate a proof key and a verification key. The proof key is given to a prover, and the verification key is given to a verifier.

As shown in the following figure (Figure 9-8), the prover uses the proof key, public inputs, and witness to generate a proof. The proof is then sent to the verifier. The verifier uses public knowledge or public variable data and the proof to verify that the knowledge statement is true or false.

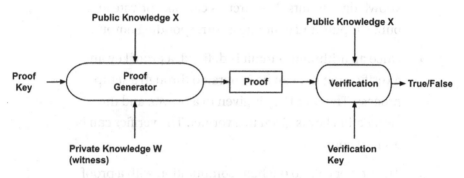

ZK-SNARK proof and verification

Figure 9-8. *zk-SNARK proof and verification*

Fully understanding zero knowledge proof and zk-SNARK requires a strong mathematical background. Here, we summarize conceptually how zk-SNARK works:

- Zero knowledge proof allows two parties to verify a statement without disclosing private information.

- zk-SNARK is a subset of zero knowledge proof that meets the succinct, non-interactive, and augment of knowledge requirements.

- Layer 2 zk-rollup uses zk-SNARK because this is computationally feasible onchain. The heavy duty computing is carried out offchain to generate a proof. The verification step is efficient and succinct and can be carried out onchain with smart contracts.

- To design a zk-SNARK, the first thing is to define a proof task. This task is to define a function to verify a statement.

- The defined verification function is then flattened and reduced to multiple steps of arithmetic operations. Sometimes, these arithmetic operations are called zero knowledge circuits. The circuits can take private and public inputs and generate a corresponding output.

- Once an arithmetic circuit is defined, a proof key and a verification key can be generated through a setup process. The proof key is given to a prover, and the verification key is given to a verifier. The verifier can be a smart contract.

- The prover can do offchain computation with a proof key and generate a proof.

- The proof and the public data are then sent to a verification smart contract to verify.

zk-SNARK is still under development, and it is foreseeable that more research will generate better zk-SNARK mechanisms for layer 2 rollup.

Ethereum 2
Major Changes in Ethereum 2

Both Ethereum 2 and layer 2 are developed to solve scalability problems in Ethereum mainnet and improve energy efficiency. In fact, sometimes, the layer 2 solution is jokingly called Ethereum 1.5. Ethereum 2 is a promising network improvement to Ethereum 1 with the following new components and features.

Transferring from POW to POS

Compared with proof-of-work (POW) consensus, proof of state (POS) has the advantages of energy efficiency, higher scalability, better incentive, and shorter block time. POS allows one system to have additional computing power to do extra work such as hosting multiple staking accounts or running services to connect with beacon chains or sidechains.

Beacon Chain

Ethereum beacon chain is an essential proof-of-stake blockchain that connects stakers and shards. The stakers are from Ethereum 1 mainnet accounts that send their ether asset to a staking smart contract to participate in the beacon chain block generations. The shards are storage and computational blockchains that expand the features of EVM and state storage of the mainnet.

Sharding

Sharding is a new architecture of Ethereum blockchains that allow a hierarchical set of blockchains to process transactions independently and then aggregate block hashes to its parent shard and eventually store the hash on the beacon chain. Sharding allows a cluster of blockchains to process transactions and execute smart contracts simultaneously and hence dramatically improve the scalability of Ethereum 1 mainnet.

Ethereum 2 Architectural Overview

Ethereum 2 is an extension of Ethereum 1 with added beacon chains and sharding chains. The following diagram (Figure 9-9) shows an overview of Ethereum 2's architecture.

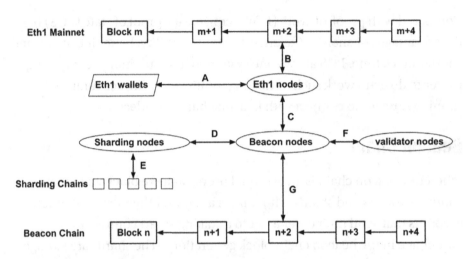

Figure 9-9. *Ethereum 2 topology and workflow*

There are three blockchains in Ethereum 2 including the legacy
Ethereum mainnet. The Ethereum mainnet provides the staking assets for
Ethereum 2's proof-of-stake mechanism. The beacon chain is a proof-of-
stake-based blockchain that records the staking information, generates
random numbers, proposes validators, and connects with sharding
blockchain to record the data and transaction Merkle tree of sharding
blockchains. Then there are also multiple sharding blockchains that are
used to store Ethereum 2 data and carry out EVM computations and
process transactions.

To generate and validate blocks for the three types of blockchains
mentioned earlier for Ethereum 2, there are four types of client nodes that
we want to mention. The first one is the Ethereum 1 client nodes such as
geth client that generate blocks for Ethereum 1 mainnet. The second one
is beacon nodes that propose blocks for the beacon chain. The third one is
validation nodes for the beacon chain. The validator node will generate or
validate beacon chain blocks through beacon chain nodes. Then the fourth

one is the sharding nodes that are responsible for blocks of the sharding blockchains.

The blockchain nodes mentioned earlier connect and communicate with one another through peer-to-peer or RCP protocols. Several interactions/edges in the diagram are labeled as A, B, C, D, E, F, and G.

The edge A is an interaction of an account owner wallet with Ethereum 1 node. The interaction allows a user to construct and sign a transaction in a wallet and then send the signed translation to an Ethereum 1 client node. The client node then validates the transaction and packages to a new block. In the diagram, the wallet is only connected to an Ethereum 1 node as there is currently no Ethereum 2 wallet to interact with the beacon chain yet.

The edge B represents Ethereum 1 client nodes to view Ethereum 1 mainnet blocks and transactions or write blocks to the blockchain. In the context of Ethereum 2, the interaction B is mainly for a staker to stake an asset to the Ethereum 2 staking smart contract deployed on Ethereum 1 mainnet. Once an asset is deployed as a stake, the smart contract function will emit an event to show the staking address and amount.

The edge C is an interaction between an Ethereum 1 client node and a beacon node. The staking information in Ethereum 1 blockchain should be visible to the beacon nodes. Beacon nodes use RPC to connect with a client node and get all the events emitted by the staking smart contract. When the new staking information is retrieved from Ethereum mainnet, the beacon node generates a block to keep the new staking information.

The edge D is for interaction between the beacon nodes and Sharding nodes. The edge E is for sharding nodes to propose blocks for sharding blockchain. Sharding nodes are to carry out the data storage and transaction processing.

The edge F is for interactions and communications between a validator node and a beacon node. Proof-of-Stake (POS) miners need to run client nodes to request tasks from the beacon chain, package transactions, validate blocks, and propose blocks. Ethereum 2 architecture separates beacon nodes from validator nodes. The beacon node does the work of managing communications and management of epoch, slots, random number generation, and validator selections. The validator nodes do the processing of transactions and blocks. The miner-specific information such as miner credentials is only stored in validator nodes, not in the beacon node. The communication between beacon nodes and miner nodes is done through RPC protocol.

The edge G is beacon nodes to propose beacon blocks to the beacon chain. Each beacon node will synchronize with the beacon chain, manage stakers registry, organize validators into committees, manage epoch and slots, generate a random number, assign validator roles, and propose new blocks to the beacon chain.

From Ethereum 2 architectural topology and interactions, it is clear that Ethereum 1 mainnet is still an essential component of Ethereum 2. The staking power of POS comes from the assets designated by owners to participate in the POS consensus for Ethereum 2. It is important to understand the process for Ethereum 1 to migrate to Ethereum 2.

Migrating from Ethereum 1 to Ethereum 2: POS Deposit, Staking, and Slashing

The migration from Ethereum 1 to Ethereum 2 has been done in a phased approach. The first phase of Ethereum 2 is to build a beacon chain based on proof-of-stake consensus. In the following, we mention some important concepts and steps for staking Ethereum 1 asset to migrating to Ethereum 2.

The assets of the proof of stake are deposited in Ethereum 1 mainnet through a deposit smart contract. In the following, a snippet of deposit contract interface is shown.

// Deposit contract interface based on the following specs for Ethereum 2:

```
// https://github.com/ethereum/eth2.0-specs
interface IDepositContract {
    /// @notice A processed deposit event.
    event DepositEvent(
        bytes pubkey,
        bytes withdrawal_credentials,
        bytes amount,
        bytes signature,
        bytes index
    );

    /// @notice Submit a Phase 0 DepositData object.
    /// @param pubkey A BLS12-381 public key.
    /// @param withdrawal_credentials Commitment to a public
    key for withdrawals.
    /// @param signature A BLS12-381 signature.
    /// @param deposit_data_root The SHA-256 hash of the SSZ-
    encoded DepositData object.
    /// Used as a protection against malformed input.
    function deposit(
        bytes calldata pubkey,
        bytes calldata withdrawal_credentials,
        bytes calldata signature,
        bytes32 deposit_data_root
    ) external payable;

    /// @notice Query the current deposit root hash.
    /// @return The deposit root hash.
    function get_deposit_root() external view returns (bytes32);

    /// @notice Query the current deposit count.
```

```
/// @return The deposit count encoded as a little endian
64-bit number.
function get_deposit_count() external view returns (bytes
memory);
}
```

The deposit smart contract uses a sparse Merkle tree to store the stake deposit records and use a deposit event to notify external programs such as beacon nodes. Major functions supported by this smart contract include deposit, get_deposit_root, and get_deposit_count. When depositing a stake, users need to supply information such as public key, withdrawal credential, owner signature, and deposit data root hash. The deposit amount is in msg.value and hence is not a function parameter. The deposit ID is incremented automatically and does not need to be supplied.

When depositing assets to the deposit smart contract, one key point to remember is that Ethereum 1 public key and private key pair curve has been replaced with BLS12-381 curve that is more versatile. The Ethereum 2 key pair will need to be generated through a new tool with a 24-word mnemonic phrase. Different from Ethereum 1, Ethereum 2 has both withdraw keys and validator keys for an account. One set of mnemonic phrases can generate multiple withdraw public keys, and one withdraw key can derive multiple validator keys.

Run an Ethereum 2 Validator Node with POS Staking

Running a validator node will get rewards from Ethereum 2 blockchain. Unlike Bitcoin or Ethereum mining, Ethereum 2 is based on proof of stake, and hence, all the nodes will get rewarded if the nodes are online and function correctly. The reward return rate is about 3–8% APR at ether value. The following shows major steps to build an Ethereum 2 mining node.

Firstly, Ethereum 2 depends on Ethereum 1. Therefore, an Ethereum 1 node is still needed. This node can be built with geth or can be a stable public node with a static IP.

Secondly, users need to allocate staking funds. A minimum of 32 ethers is needed to run a validator node. Users also need to consider that if their node goes down, there is a penalty that will decrease the staking balance.

Thirdly, users need to prepare a deposit account. There is a deposit tool that can be used to generate mnemonic phrases and derive withdrawal keys and validator keys. These keys are extremely important and should be safeguarded. If the mnemonic phrases and withdrawal keys are lost, the locked ether for Ethereum 2 will be lost.

Fourthly, download and run beacon nodes and validator nodes. There are multiple vendors who provide the packages to run beacon and validator nodes.

And finally, use scripts or third-party tools to deposit assets to deposit contracts. The deposited event will be detected by the beacon node. The deposit will be in pending state for a certain time and then become active.

One important factor to consider is that unlike proof-of-work consensus, the proof-of-stake mechanism implements penalties for validators. The Ethereum beacon chain implemented two penalties for validators. One is the inactivity penalty that punishes validator nodes that are offline or do not propose/attest a block. Another one is slashing that punishes validators that construct or attest malicious blocks. It is recommended that validators run a monitoring program to ensure that their nodes are working actively and correctly.

Many tools and solutions have been developed on this. Users can check the Ethereum 2 website to see the recommended ones.

Uncertainties with Ethereum 2

Although Ethereum 2 has been viewed as a promising solution for Ethereum mainnet scalability solutions, there are still some uncertainties about this project. For example, the sharding chain is still not finalized. There has been a lot of debates on sharding regarding security and the staking economy. It is recommended that readers keep an open mind on the road map, implementation, and rollout of Ethereum 2.

Summary

In this chapter, we explained various layer 2 scalability solutions including state channel, plasma, rollups, as well as Ethereum 2 technology. Each technology has its pros and cons. When designing decentralized applications, it is important to consider the usage models of the applications and choose the most feasible technology to scale out the solutions.

CHAPTER 10

Fund a Project: Tokens and Gas Fees

Introduction

In previous chapters, we went through the technical aspects of smart contract coding, development, and deployment as well as blockchain security and scalability.

In this chapter, we will discuss how to fund a project from both the business and technical aspects of smart contracts.

Ethereum has achieved several milestones relevant to project funding, such as the Initial Coin Offering (ICO), Nonfungible Token (NFT), decentralized finance (DeFi), and Decentralized Autonomous Organization (DAO). It is foreseeable that the Security Token Offering (STO), Central Bank Digital Currency (CBDC), and other decentralized applications will soon gain popularity. All of these use cases have one common and essential element: the token. In the following, we describe how tokens are used to represent assets to fund a project and how to use smart contracts to program tokens.

© Weijia Zhang and Tej Anand 2022
W. Zhang and T. Anand, *Blockchain and Ethereum Smart Contract Solution Development*,
https://doi.org/10.1007/978-1-4842-8164-2_10

Tokens for Funding Ecosystem Projects

Tokens in ICO and DeFi

An ICO in Ethereum is a fundraising mechanism that was popular around the year 2017. It is enabled by the ERC20 token, which allows tokens to be programmable, distributed, and traded in the Ethereum ecosystem. The ERC20 token is fungible, meaning that it only has value and cannot be distinguished among each other. The ERC20 token follows the specification of EIP-20 located in the following URL:

https://eips.ethereum.org/EIPS/eip-20

In the ERC20 specification, several standard functions as well as two events are defined, and all smart contracts that issue ERC20 tokens will need to implement them accordingly. The function specifications are as follows:

```
// Returns the name of the token
function name() public view returns (string)

//Returns the name of the symbol. Normally several capitalized
letters, optional.
function symbol() public view returns (string)

// Returns the number of decimals the token uses.
function decimals() public view returns (uint8)

// Returns the total supply of the token

function totalSupply() public view returns (uint256)

// Returns the account balance of another account with
address _owner.
function balanceOf(address _owner) public view returns (uint256
balance)
```

```
//Transfers _value amount of tokens to address _to, and MUST
fire the Transfer event.
function transfer(address _to, uint256 _value) public returns
(bool success)
```

```
// Transfers _value amount of tokens from address _from to
address _to, and MUST fire the Transfer event.
function transferFrom(address _from, address _to, uint256 _
value) public returns (bool success)
```

```
//Allows _spender to withdraw from your account multiple times,
up to the _value amount. If this function is called again it
overwrites the current allowance with _value.
function approve(address _spender, uint256 _value) public
returns (bool success)
```

```
//Returns the amount which _spender is still allowed to
withdraw from _owner.
function allowance(address _owner, address _spender) public
view returns (uint256 remaining)
```

Events
```
// this event MUST trigger when tokens are transferred,
including zero value transfers
event Transfer(address indexed _from, address indexed _to,
uint256 _value)
```

```
//this event MUST trigger on any successful call to
approve(address _spender, uint256 _value)
event Approval(address indexed _owner, address indexed _
spender, uint256 _value)
```

There are two smart contract packages that have been implemented for the EIP-20 standard: the OpenZeppelin package and the ConsenSys package. Developers can extend these packages and make their own ERC20 tokens with a few customized lines of code. For example, by importing the OpenZeppelin ERC20 package, a developer can create an ERC20 token named "DEVELOPER_TOKEN" with a symbol of DEV and a customizable total supply as input for the constructor:

```
// contracts/DEVToken.sol
// SPDX-License-Identifier: MIT
pragma solidity ^0.8.0;

import "@openzeppelin/contracts/token/ERC20/ERC20.sol";

contract DEVToken is ERC20 {
    constructor(uint256 initialSupply) ERC20("DEVELOPER_TOKEN",
    "DEV") {
        _mint(msg.sender, initialSupply);
    }
}
```

When the preceding smart contract is deployed with an initialSupply specified, the deployed token will have totalSupply equal to the initialSupply.

Once an ERC20 token is created, another smart contract can be written to handle the minting and distribution of the token. This smart contract is sometimes called the crowdsale smart contract when used for ICOs. A smart contract for crowdsale normally contains the following functions:

Ratio of token and ether – The ratio of ether and the target token.

Time of the crowdsale – The start time and end time when the token is available for distribution.

KYC/AML – The crowdsale can have a white list for senders who can participate in the crowdsale.

382

Refunds – The smart contract can also implement the functions to refund the token.

Besides crowdfunding, ERC20 tokens are extensively used in other decentralized finance (DeFi) projects such as Compound for lending, Uniswap for exchanges, and USDC for stablecoins.

In the Ethereum community, there are also some discussions on whether the ERC20 token is a utility token or a security token. These are country or state specific and should be consulted with legal professionals.

Token in NFT

Different from ERC20 tokens, nonfungible tokens (NFT) are distinguishable and can be used to represent ownership. For example, birth certificates, diplomas, and rental contracts are all nonfungible and have clear ownership. An NFT is specified as an EIP-721 standard to represent

- Physical assets such as houses, cars, and artwork

- Virtual collectables such as digital art and collectable cards

- "Negative assets" such as loans and debt

The detailed specification of the EIP-721 is located in the following URL:

```
https://eips.ethereum.org/EIPS/eip-721
```

Similar to the ERC20 token, the ERC721 NFT also defines the token name, token symbol, and total supply. There are some major differences for the NFT:

- Each NFT token has an index that is unique.

- Each NFT token has an owner.

- Since NFTs can point to a physical or virtual asset outside the blockchain, there is an interface ERC721Metadata that defines a function called tokenURL.

```
function tokenURI(uint256 _tokenId) external
view returns (string);
```

This tokenURL function takes an input of _tokenId and returns a Universal Resource Identifier (URI) that points to an NFT item defined in a conventional digital system.

- Each NFT token can be transferred from one owner to another with the following function:

```
function transferFrom(address _from, address
_to, uint256 _tokenId) external payable;
```

- There are also other functions or interfaces that help NFT tokens to be assigned, transferred, or identified.

NFT tokens based on the EIP-721/ERC721 standard have been implemented by several projects. For example, 0xcert and OpenZeppelin have implemented ERC721 token smart contract packages. Developers can easily extend the ERC721 package and create their own ERC721 nonfungible tokens.

For example, for a college to create an NFT for their students' diplomas, the smart contract can be written with the following sample code:

```
// SPDX-License-Identifier: MIT
pragma solidity ^0.7.0;

import "https://github.com/OpenZeppelin/openzeppelin-contracts/
blob/release-v3.4/contracts/token/ERC721/ERC721.sol";

contract TTCDiploma is ERC721 {
    uint private _tokenIds;
    address admin;
```

```
constructor() ERC721("TexasTechnologyCollegeDiploma",
"TTC") public {
admin = msg.sender;
}

function issueDiploma(address student, string memory
tokenURI) public returns (uint256) {
    require(msg.sender == admin); // only admin can issue
    diploma.
    _tokenIds++;

    uint256 newDiplomaId = _tokenIds;
    _mint(student, newDiplomaId);
    _setTokenURI(newDiplomaId, tokenURI);

    return newDiplomaId;
}
}
```

In this program, the TTCDiploma smart contract is written to issue diplomas for students. When the smart contract is deployed, the token name and token symbol are provided. Also, the smart contract deployment address is assigned as the admin address. Only admin can perform privileged actions such as issuing diplomas. In the issueDiploma function, the sender is checked to see if it has admin permissions. If it does, the tokenId is incremented, and a new diploma ID is generated. This new diplomaId is then assigned a tokenURI that points to an external source for retrieving the diploma for that ID. When students want to retrieve the diploma, they simply sign a message and send it to the URI specified by the diplomaId. The diploma server pointed by the URI will check the signed message to verify that the requester is the legitimate owner of the diploma and will then output the diploma to the request.

NFT tokens can be used in many fields. There have been many projects that provide marketplaces for NFT artwork and collectables. Projects such as OpenSea and Decentraland are popular for the NFT marketplace.

Tokens in DeFi (Compound, Uniswap, and Stablecoins)

In Chapter 1, several DeFi projects such as the decentralized lending platform, decentralized exchange, and stablecoins are mentioned. All DeFi projects use one or multiple ERC20 tokens as asset tokens or governance tokens. In the following, we mention several examples.

Compound is a project for a decentralized lending platform that allows users to lend or borrow cryptocurrency without the need for going through intermediaries such as banks. Lenders can send their asset tokens to a Compound smart contract and receive cTokens to represent the amount of assets that are deposited to the lending pool. cTokens can earn interest and can also be traded. Borrowers can borrow cryptocurrency from the Compound protocol. In order to borrow a crypto asset, borrowers need to supply other crypto assets as collaterals. The collateral calculation is based on the token price feed and a published formula. If the borrowed asset cannot be paid back and the collateral values fall below the threshold to secure the borrowed balance, the collateral can be liquidated based on the rules written in the smart contract.

The cTokens represent crypto assets supplied in the lending protocol. In addition, Compound has issued a governing token named COMP. COMP can be earned by supplying or borrowing assets in the lending protocol. The COMP token can be used to vote on proposals. All cTokens and COMP tokens are ERC20 tokens.

Uniswap is a decentralized exchange platform using the Automated Market Maker (AMM) mechanism. Different users can trade their crypto assets without a dependency on centralized exchanges. Uniswap liquidity providers provide pairs of crypto assets as trading pairs for the liquidity pool. Traders then trade their assets with the assets in the liquidity pool. There are two kinds of tokens that are designed for Uniswap and other similar decentralized exchange platforms. The first kind of token is called a liquidity provider (LP) token, which represents the supplier's contribution to the liquidity pool. The LP token is an ERC20 token that is trading pair specific. Each trading pair will have its own LP token. Another Uniswap token is a UNI token that is an ERC20 token as well. The UNI token is a governance token that can be used to vote on proposals within the Uniswap ecosystem.

Stablecoins such as DAI, USDT, and USDC are all ERC20 format tokens that can be traded or transferred. Additional functions such as automatic minting and burning based on supply and demand are built on top of the ERC20 format to make its value stable. Stablecoin values can be kept stable with several mechanisms such as fiat-collateralization, crypto-collateralization, or algorithmic mechanism.

Although most of the DeFi tokens are ERC20 tokens, they are not the same as each DeFi builds additional functions on top of the standard ERC20 tokens. DeFi projects are all open source, and the code for their tokens can be viewed and inspected in public source code repositories.

Tokens for Enterprises/Standardized (Pervasive) Tokens

The ICO is enabled by an ERC20 token, which enables tokens to be programmable, distributed, and traded in the Ethereum ecosystem. An ERC20 token is a fungible token that is not distinguishable between individual tokens. An NFT milestone is empowered by ERC721, which allows a token to be unique, traceable, exchangeable, and tradable. STO is empowered by ERC1400 that allows owners to own a portion of an entity asset. Tokens are inseparable from decentralized applications.

Tokens in public blockchains are open, permissionless, and intended for large-scale distribution. For enterprises, there is a need to have a more structured and formal framework for tokens that can propagate through different private blockchains and are easy to design and customize. Enterprise tokens have potential uses in many areas including the following:

Supply chain tokens

In a supply chain, assets can correspond to parts, inventory, orders, shipment, loans, and bills of lading. All these assets can be tokenized and recorded in the blockchain. Operations on these assets can be modeled as transactions in the blockchain. Enterprises such as IBM, FedEx, Microsoft, and Accenture are all building blockchain solutions to help solve supply chain problems to increase efficiency, enhance traceability, and maximize transparency. The types of tokens used in the supply chain are broader than ERC20 or ERC721 that are commonly used in DeFi. In a supply chain system, all identifiable items can be tokenized and recorded in the blockchain.

Industry-Specific Tokens

Tokens can be expanded to represent all identifiable items and can be used in all industries for physical, digital, or virtual assets. For example, in the renewable energy domain, solar or wind power generation can be tokenized and traded. Below we describe how carbon credit tokens can be used to characterize and tokenize CO_2 emission and how these credits can be traded in the marketplace (Figure 10-1).

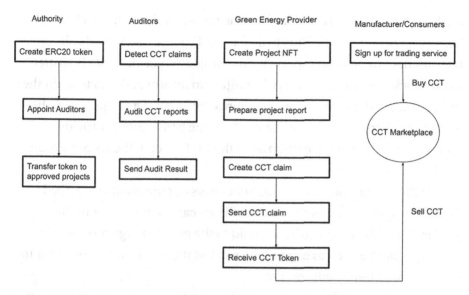

Figure 10-1. *Overview of Carbon Credit Token (CCT)*

To establish a carbon credit market, the authority will first need to mint and issue an ERC20 token to represent CO_2 reduction. The carbon credit authority first creates a Carbon Credit Token (CCT) by using a name such as "United Groups' Carbon Credit," a symbol of "CCT," and a total amount for CO_2 reduction. The initial carbon credit is minted and owned by the authority account. Only the authority has the privilege to transfer or grant the carbon credits.

To manage the carbon credits, the authority will appoint auditors to review and audit the requests from green energy providers to decide whether the claims can be granted. If the claims are granted, an event is emitted to show the projectId and the credit amount.

To claim a carbon credit, green energy providers will first create an NFT token to represent the project. This NFT token is unique and points to the project records. The project team then files a claim that contains information about the CO_2 reduction amount and the carbon credit requested. The NFT related to the project will also have a Unified Resource Location that points to an external source that records all relevant documents and reports for the project. Once this data is written to the blockchain, a Claim event is emitted to inform auditors to audit the information in the claim. After the claims are audited and approved, the authority will transfer the carbon credit to the green energy providers' accounts. The provider can then send the CCT asset to the carbon credit marketplace for trading.

On the consumption side, manufacturers or consumers who need the carbon credit to meet the quota will buy carbon credits from the marketplace. The cryptocurrency paid to the green energy provider for CCT asset can be used to expand the work of the green energy provider to produce more renewable energy.

For a carbon credit project example, refer to the following repository:

```
https://github.com/masaun/tokenized-carbon-credit-marketplace/
blob/main/smart-contract/contracts/GreenNFT.sol
```

Token Taxonomy Initiative

Carbon credit token, solar token, electricity token, parts token, system token, and water token can all be classified as enterprise tokens and can be designed using a more formal definition of tokens. Organizations such as the Enterprise Ethereum Alliance (EEA) and InterWork Alliance (IWA) have been working on Token Taxonomy Initiatives (TTI) to develop a token framework that can be formalized and used to tokenize all identifiable assets in complex enterprise use cases.

The token taxonomy infrastructure and framework have the following goals and key features:

- Blockchain agnostic, meaning that it is not dependent on Solidity, Haskell, WASM, or Java programming languages for different blockchains

390

- Understandable for both business and technical professionals

- Descriptive as well as programmable

- Address broad usage scenarios for the enterprise and public blockchains

- Aim for ease of use, improved interoperability, easier communication, and faster and more secure development

The following picture (Figure 10-2) shows the hierarchy of token taxonomy. Different from ERC20 and ERC721 where tokens are defined in specification and coded into smart contract, the Token Taxonomy Framework (TTF) defines tokens in three layers. The first layer is the template layer where the property, formula, and behavior of the tokens are defined. The token templates can be generic, such as the loyalty token template or inventory token template. The second layer is the class layer when templates are assigned parameters to create token classes. For example, loyalty token templates can be applied with airline loyalty or hotel loyalty parameters to create an airline loyalty token class or hotel loyal token class. The token class can then be instantiated into instances such as a Delta or AA airlines loyalty token.

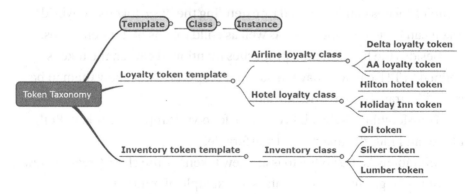

Figure 10-2. *Token Taxonomy example*

When using this framework for an Ethereum smart contract, the template layer is similar to ERC20 or ERC721 specifications. The class layer extends the ERC20 smart contracts into airline loyalty tokens or hotel tokens. The instance layer constructs specific tokens with the token smart contract constructor function during deployment.

TTF also defines several fundamental attributes for a formalized token, including the following:

Token unit – The unit of a token that can be Fractional, Whole, or Singleton.

Fractional means that the token can be divided into fractional units.

Whole means that the token cannot be divided but can have multiple copies.

Singleton means that the token cannot be divided and has a quantity of 1.

Value type – If the token has value, its value type is Intrinsic. If a token is a representation of a physical or digital item that has value, its value type is Reference.

Representation type – Tokens that do not have individual identities are called common or fungible tokens. Tokens that have an index or serial number are called unique or nonfungible tokens.

Template type – Templates describe the basic characteristics of tokens. Primitive tokens such as ERC20 or ERC721 are single tokens. More complex tokens can be created by extending the basic tokens. A hybrid token can have a parent token as well as child tokens of different types.

Besides the fundamental properties mentioned earlier, the tokens defined in TTF can also have behavioral properties that allow them to be mintable, transferable, and burnable.

Transferability is the ability to transfer ownership of the token. Both ERC20 and ERC721 tokens are transferable.

Mintability is the ability to issue new tokens of the class. Creating new diplomas for graduating students is an example of minting.

Burnability is the ability to remove tokens from the supply. Some projects can burn project tokens to decrease the circulating number of token supply.

The TTI might seem to be abstract when viewed from the framework point of view. It is actually quite useful to build generic tools such as a token designer that can be used to create tokens through a GUI that supports drag-and-drop features. Developers or users do not need to write smart contract code for tokens. The code will be automatically generated when users define tokens through text or GUI tools. The work of TTI is still in progress and is currently not accepted as a standard yet.

Token Economy Consideration
Token Allocation

When reward tokens are proposed and designed, they need to be awarded to those who contribute to the projects. Normally, stakeholders such as project teams, funders, and communities will need to be considered. For example, the Filecoin project is a blockchain-based decentralized storage network. The project team built a persistent storage service on top of the IPFS protocol that allows data users to use Filecoin to incentivize miners to provide long-term data storage and availability. Filecoin tokens are designed as a fungible token that uses the percentage chart, shown in the following diagram (Figure 10-3), to allocate Filecoin tokens.

Filecoin Token Allocation

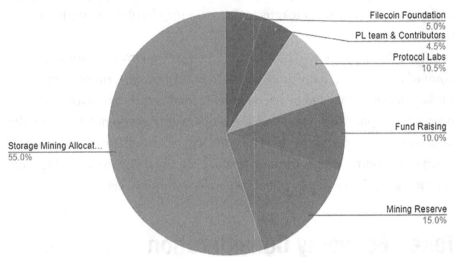

Figure 10-3. *Filecoin token allocation*

For the Filecoin project, the maximum number of tokens created will be 20 billion. Five percent of the tokens are allocated to the Filecoin Foundation to facilitate governance of the Filecoin network, fund critical development projects, support the growth of the Filecoin ecosystem, and advocate for Filecoin and the decentralized web. Another 4.5% of the tokens are allocated to the Protocol Labs team and contributors, and 10.5% are for the Protocol Labs company. The Filecoin project allocates 10% of their tokens for the fundraising. The majority of tokens are allocated to miners to support storage mining rewards, block rewards, and other operations such as faucets and storage incentives. The final 15% of the tokens are reserved for future mining services and rewards.

Token Distribution

Once the tokens are allocated, there are different ways to distribute the tokens to the receivers, as shown in the following diagram (Figure 10-4):

Through direct transfer	This is a regular asset transfer in which both sender and receiver have an Externally Owned Account (EOA). The EOA senders are authorized personnel who have secure methods such as hardware wallets to manage the transfer of assets.
Through smart contract	This is a distribution where funds are locked and smart contracts are distributed to entities who made contributions to the project and should be rewarded based on the token allocation algorithm coded in the smart contract.
Through block mining protocol	This is a blockchain level protocol that will reward miners based on the blockchain proposal and verification. For Filecoin cases, the storage provider can also be rewarded with the block mining protocol.
Through airdrop	Airdrop is a process for the distribution of tokens to community members who have performed tasks and meet the criteria. For example, to expand the community and ecosystem, the Filecoin project can provide airdrops to users who use Filecoin to store their data within a certain time frame.
Through faucet service	Faucet service is used to provide a small amount of tokens to first time token users. Users normally post a social media message to prove their identity and then use a faucet to receive the tokens.

Figure 10-4. Token Distribution methods

Gas Fee Consideration

When funding a project, there are many factors to consider.

The Ethereum blockchain has been made sustainable with a gas economy in which each transaction is paid by senders to blockchain miners. If a project is building a new blockchain, then the gas fee mechanism should be considered thoroughly to ensure a sustainable network system. For projects that build decentralized applications, the cost of gas consumption should be examined to make sure the high gas cost of transactions will not become a showstopper for the applications. In the following, we discuss how Ethereum gas works and if there exist ways to lower gas fees in smart contract development.

What Is Ethereum Gas?

In the Ethereum blockchain, gas can be viewed as the cost of performing transactions or as the mechanism to power the blockchain ecosystem. When a transaction is sent to the blockchain, a small amount of ether needs to be specified and paid to the miner in order for the Ethereum blockchain node to take in the transaction to a block. The higher the gas fee, the higher the possibility for mining nodes to include the transaction. In addition to rewarding miners, the gas mechanism also increases the cost of network attacks by malicious users. In a public blockchain, everyone can access the network and send transactions to the miners. Without an appropriate gas fee, tremendous amounts of transactions may be sent to the network, causing congestion issues or even halting the network. The gas fee is a well-designed mechanism to maintain a sustainable network and balance decentralized application ecosystems.

Understand Ethereum Gas with Gas Station Analogy

Gas in Ethereum is a complex concept. It is difficult to grasp its meaning and implication for the blockchain network and application ecosystem. In this section, we will use a gas station analogy to help readers better understand gas usage in Ethereum (Figure 10-5).

Terms	Gas Station	Ethereum
Gas use	Power transportation	Power Ethereum network
Tasks	Transportation • Move goods from one location to another	Transactions • Transfer balance • Deploy smart contract • Small contract calls
Payment	Need to pay for gas	Need to pay for gas
Gas price	Gas price Price per gallon	Gas price Price per gas unit
Gas unit	Gallon	CPU cycle and storage unit (more)
Gas limit	Gas tank • Max amount of gas to use	Gas limit • Max amount of gas to use for one transaction
Gas fee	Gas price * gas consumed	Gas price * gas consumed
Max gas fee	Gas price * tank size	Gas price * gas limit
Gas exceed max	Task abandoned	The transaction reverted. Gas fee paid to the miner
Common transactions	NA	Gas unit used: 21,000
Max block gas limit	NA	Max amount of gas unit for one block 8,000,000 No transaction can consume this max number of gas.

Figure 10-5. *Gas Station Analogy*

Gas in transportation is used as fuel to power vehicles to move people and goods from one location to another. On the other hand, gas in Ethereum is used to power the Ethereum network to make it more secure and less congested and to incentivize blockchain miners. Gas in Ethereum is used to pay for transferring assets, deploying smart contracts, or calling smart contract functions.

In a gas station, the gas price is normally marked as dollars per gallon, while in Ethereum, the gas price is also used to refer to the unit price of gas. The concept of the gas price is not that straightforward. The gas price unit in Ethereum is wei per gas unit, where wei is the smallest unit of ether. One ether is equal to 10 to the power of 18 wei. The gas unit refers to the mining cost in Ethereum. It is manually defined in the gas cost table in the Ethereum yellow paper. For example, an addition operation has a gas cost of 3, and multiplication has a gas cost of 5. The total gas fee will be equal to the gas price multiplied with the gas consumed.

In the Ethereum gas mechanism, there is also the concept of gas limits. This is the maximum amount of gas a single transaction can consume. The reason to have a gas limit is to protect the sender account. Sometimes, a smart contract might go into a computation loop and drain the whole account balance if there is no gas limit set. For a car, the gas limit is the gas tank capacity. When a gas limit is set and the consumption of gas exceeds that limit, the transaction will be marked as failed, and the state is reverted back to its original state.

There are two kinds of transactions, the first of which is a simple asset transfer to move assets from one account to another. These asset transfers will consume 21,000 Gwei gas. The second transaction type is the smart contract call. The gas consumption is much more than the common asset transfer.

Furthermore, for the Ethereum blockchain, there is also a maximum block gas limit. This is the limit of gas for all transactions in a block.

Finally, the gas consumed here is in the unit of wei. Normally, the actual cost is measured in USD in which the gas consumed is multiplied by the price of ether to get the fiat cost.

Quantize Gas Expenses in a Smart Contract Program

When a decentralized application is deployed, one of the biggest costs for the users is the gas fee. The gas fee for Ethereum mainnet transactions has been skyrocketing and sometimes reaches over 200 USD for a single transaction. Hence, the feasibility study of the project will need to include a gas fee expenses analysis to see if the project is financially sustainable. For example, some people have proposed using blockchain to build a decentralized music service. Quantitative analysis can help determine the cost feasibility for storing musical data, both for musical bits and metadata.

As explained in Chapter 7, Solidity smart contracts are compiled into bytecodes and then deployed to and executed on the blockchain. Each bytecode command contains an opcode and operands. The gas costs for various opcodes are shown in the Ethereum yellow paper with some added opcodes and modification in EIPs. The following is the summary of the gas costs for categories of opcodes (Figure 10-6).

Opcode	Gas used	Note
Stack-manipulating opcodes		
POP	2	Remove stack item
PUSH, DUP, SWAP	3	Store, duplicate, swap stack items
Arithmetic/comparison/bitwise opcodes		
ADD, SUB, GT, LT, AND, OR	3	Arithmetic addition, subtraction, or logical comparison
MUL, DIV	5	Arithmetic multiplication or division
Environmental opcodes (CALLER, CALLVALUE, NUMBER)		
CALLER	2	Get caller address
CALLVALUE	2	Get ether sent by the caller
NUMBER	2	Get block number
Memory-manipulating opcodes (MLOAD, MSTORE, MSTORE8, MSIZE)		
MLOAD, MSTORE, MSTORE8	3	Load word, save word, or save bytes in memory
MSIZE	2	Get byte size of the active memory
Storage-manipulating opcodes (SLOAD, SSTORE)		

Figure 10-6. *Gas costs for various opcodes*

SLOAD	200	
SSTORE	20000, 5000	20000 when setting the value to nonzero, 5000 when setting the value to zero

Program counter–related opcodes (JUMP, JUMPI, PC, JUMPDEST)

JUMP	8	Alter program counter
JUMPI	10	Conditionally alter program counter
PC	2	Get program counter
JUMPDEST	1	Mark destination counter for jump

Halting opcodes (STOP, RETURN, REVERT, SELFDESTRUCT)

STOP, RETURN	0	Halt execution or return output data
REVERT	NA	Undo all changes and return unused gas fee
SELFDESTRUCT	5000+	Halt execution and register account for later use

Figure 10-6. (*continued*)

As we can see from the gas cost table, arithmetic operations such as addition, subtraction, multiplication, division, and logical operations such as AND/OR only cost about 2 to 5 gas units and can be viewed as low gas fee operations. Environment operations such as getting sender address, ether value, and block number are also low gas operations that only consume 2 gas units. The memory manipulating operations are more complex. The operation on a single 256-bit word is only 2 for loading and 3 for storing. However, memory storage also has an additional memory expansion cost. When more data is stored, there is a cost for memory. The cost for memory storage operations is not linear. We will explain this further with the next table.

The most expensive opcode operation is storing to the blockchain. When storing data to the blockchain, the cost per word is 20,000 gas units for a nonzero value and 5,000 for a zero value. Loading data from blockchain is 200 gas units per word.

There are program counter–related operations such as JUMP, JUMPI, PC, and JUMPDEST defined in the table as well. They cause 1 to 10 gas units, respectively.

Halting program operations have very different gas costs. Opcode STOP or RETURN is used to halt the execution of a function. The RETURN opcode also returns output data to the calling function. Both opcodes do not consume gas.

REVERT is an operation that encounters an issue and has to undo all changes to the blockchain. The remaining unused gas allocated to the transaction is returned to the sender. The SELFDESTRUCT operation halts the execution and registers an account for later use. This opcode costs at least 5000 gas units.

The preceding table shows the gas cost at the opcode and word payload level. For storage operations, the cost is not necessarily linear. For example, for memory storage operations, there is an additional memory expansion cost. The total cost for MSTORE and MSTORE8 is defined as the sum of memory expansion and static store operations as shown in the following:

gas_cost_operation = (new_mem_size_words ^ 2 // 512) + (3 * new_mem_size_words)

The following table (Figure 10-7) shows the cost of storage for stack, memory, and persisted storage for word, kilobyte, and megabyte data sizes.

ZONE	EVM Opcode	Gas/Word	Gas/KB	Gas/MB
STACK	POP	2	64	65,536
	PUSHX	3	96	98,304
	DUPX	3	96	98,304
	SWAPX	3	96	98,304
MEMORY	MLOAD	3	96	98,304
	MSTORE	3	98	2,195,456
	MSTORE8	3	98	2,195,456
STORAGE	SLOAD	200	6,400	6,553,600
	SSTORE	20,000	640,000	655,360,000

Figure 10-7. *Gas cost of storages for various categories and sizes*

For the stack operations, there is no additional memory expansion cost. The gas per word for POP, PUSHX, DUPX, and SWAPX is defined as 2, 3, 3, and 3 per word, respectively. In Ethereum, a word has 256 bits or 32 bytes in size. Since one kilobyte is equal to 32 words (1024 bytes/32 bytes), the gas cost per kilobyte is 32 times the gas cost per word. Hence, the gas per KB for POP, PUSH, DUP, and SWAP is 64, 96, 96, and 96, respectively. Similarly, since 1MB is 1024 times of 1KB, the gas per MB for POP, PUSH, DUP, and SWAP is 65,536, 98,304, 98304, and 98304, respectively.

For memory operations, it is more complex when scaling it to KB and MB.

The first MLOAD does not have a memory expansion cost. The gas cost for 1KB is equal to 32 times the gas cost per word, which is 96, and the cost per MB is 1024 times the cost per KB, which is 98,304.

For both MSTORE and MSTORE8, there are memory expansion costs with the formula shown in the preceding equation. The cost per KB and MB for MSTORE and MSTORE8 is shown in the following:

For 1KB MSTORE or MSTORE8, there are 32 words for new_mem_size_ word. The following memory expansion equation is used:

gas_cost_operation = (new_mem_size_word $^\wedge$ 2 // 512) + (3 * new_mem_size_words)

The result is

gas_cost_operation_per_KB = ($32^\wedge2$)/512+3*32 = 98

Similarly, for 1MB MSTORE and MSTORE8, there are 32*1024=32,768 words.

The result becomes

gas_cost_operation_per_MB = ($32768^\wedge2$)/512+3*32768 = 2,195,456

Therefore, the calculation shows that the memory storage operations are not linear. It increases dramatically when the stored data size increases.

For the persisted storage with SSTORE and SLOAD, the gas cost grows linearly with data size. The cost per word for SLOAD is 200. Hence, the MLOAD gas cost per KB and MB is 6,400 and 6,553,600, respectively. Similarly, since cost per word for SSTORE is 20,000, the cost for KB and MB is 640,000 and 655,360,000, respectively.

From the preceding calculations, it is shown that the quantitative calculation of gas usage and cost is quite complex. In general, storing data in the blockchain and using large amounts of memory in the running nodes are also expensive and should be minimized as much as possible. Gas estimation should be built into project proposals to seek proper funding in order to make the project sustainable.

Summary

In this capture, we describe core components for funding a decentralized application project, including token design, token allocation, distribution, and gas cost. For the Ethereum blockchain, the significant gas cost is still a big challenge. There are alternatives such as using a similar blockchain with EVM and Solidity support but a lower gas fee. There is also a possibility to build a blockchain that does not require a gas fee. These solutions are all technically possible and can be evaluated to see if it fits with the business model.

CHAPTER 11

Building Team Projects

Problem Statement and Brainstorming

When the Ethereum blockchain was first built, there was no chainId in the blocks. The concept of chainId was introduced after a DAO attack in 2016 that resulted in 3.6 million ethers stolen and made Ethereum blockchain to fork into two blockchains, that is, Ethereum mainnet (ETH) and Ethereum Classic. The following diagram (Figure 11-1) shows how the fork happened. In the diagram, block m is a block where the DAO attack happened. The Ethereum foundation had a vote, and the community decided to patch the Ethereum node client and invalidate the hacker accounts. This is not a rollback but rather an update of all client nodes to force a change of the state of Ethereum. There are some miners who believe that blockchain should be immutable and should not be changed due to attack. These miners continue to append blocks to the DAO attacked blocks and retain the immutability of the Ethereum blockchain. They called this blockchain Ethereum Classic (ETC). Since then, there have been two forked Ethereum blockchains that share the same blocks until the block of 1920000.

© Weijia Zhang and Tej Anand 2022
W. Zhang and T. Anand, *Blockchain and Ethereum Smart Contract Solution Development*,
https://doi.org/10.1007/978-1-4842-8164-2_11

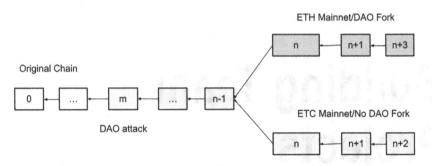

Figure 11-1. *Overview of ETH and ETC fork*

With Ethereum blockchains forked into ETH and ETC, there is a double spend or replay attack issue. If Alice has 50 ethers at block M, she actually has 50 ethers for ETH chain and 50 ethers for ETC chain. Suppose Alice signs a transaction to transfer 50 ethers to Bob on the ETH chain, since the ETC and ETH are almost identical, Bob can take the same signed transaction and send it to the ETC chain and receive 50 ethers on the ETC chain as well.

To overcome double spend/replay attack on two blockchains, Vitalik proposed EIP-155 (simple replay attack protection) to assign an integer to each blockchain and sign the transaction with a chainId. This way, the transaction signed by Alice for Ethereum mainnet (ETH) cannot be resent to Ethereum Classic (ETC) chain to cause double spend.

In EIP-155, some chainIds are preallocated as shown in the following table (Figure 11-2). To obtain a new chainId, an administrator on behalf of the blockchain community will need to go to `https://github.com/ ethereum-lists/chains` to submit a pull request to register for a new chainId. The assignment of the chainId is on the first-come first-serve basis to ensure there is no collision of the chainIds.

CHAIN_ID	Chain(s)
1	Ethereum mainnet
2	Morden (disused), Expanse mainnet
3	Ropsten
4	Rinkeby
5	Goerli
42	Kovan
1337	Geth private chains (default)
Other chainIds	

Figure 11-2. *Chainids defined in Ethereum mainnet and testnetst*

Although EIP-155 solves the replay attack for various blockchains, there are some drawbacks including that the chainId is self-defined and not bundled with blockchain property. A malicious user may construct a blockchain with a chainId of another blockchain. This can cause crosschain transaction being sent to a wrong target blockchain. Another drawback is that when a blockchain is forked into two blockchains such as the case of ETH and ETC, the two blockchains will have the same chainId to cause conflict.

Specifications and Solutions

To overcome the drawback of simple number-based chainId, a crosschainId with 32 bytes can be used to add more information to the crosschain ID to make it more versatile. The crosschainId can have a genesis block hash and a checksum so that third-party application and user can verify that the crosschain ID is valid for a particular blockchain.

The specification of the crosschainId is published as Ethereum Improvement Protocol (EIP) 3220 and is shown in the following.

EIP-3220: Crosschain Identifier Specification

Simple Summary

A self-verifying unique blockchain identifier that deals with forks.

Abstract

The crosschain ID is a 32-byte hex string and with some bytes extracted from blockchain hash and some manually defined to characterize a blockchain. We also propose a registration and lookup service to retrieve blockchain metadata from the crosschain ID.

Motivation

With the success of Bitcoin and Ethereum, various blockchains such as EOS, Ripple, Litecoin, Besu, Wanchain, and the like have been developed and are growing at a fast pace. There are also other private and consortium blockchains such as Hyperledger Fabric, Hyperledger Besu, Stellar, Corda, and Quorum that only allow nodes with permitted identities to join the blockchain network. The growth of public and private blockchains imposes challenges for interchain interoperability, particularly when these chains are heterogeneous and incompatible. The Enterprise Ethereum Alliance formed the Crosschain Interoperability Task Force (CITF) to look into common crosschain problems and solutions. CITF team noticed that there is a lack of unique identifiers to characterize and describe a blockchain. Several proposals were discussed in EEA Crosschain Interoperability Task Force meetings and discussions.

EIP-155 provides a unique identifier to a blockchain to provide simple relay attack protection. This specification defines an integer for chainId for a blockchain and signs the chainId into a transaction data and hence prevents attackers to send the same transaction to different blockchains. This specification will require blockchains to define a chainId and register the chainId in a public repository.

The challenge of using an integer for chainId is that it is not broad enough to cover all blockchains and it does not prevent different blockchains using the same chainId. Also, it does not address the issue for two forked blockchains having the same chainId.

Hence, there is a need for a more robust blockchain identifier that will overcome these drawbacks, especially for crosschain operations where multiple chains are involved. A blockchain identifier (crosschain ID) should be unique and satisfy the following requirements:

- *Should provide identification, description, and discovery of blockchains*

- *Should provide unique identification of each blockchain in the crosschain service ecosystem*

- *Should provide descriptions for blockchain identities such as chainId, name, type, consensus scheme, etc.*

- *Should provide a discovery mechanism for supported blockchains and also for new blockchains in the ecosystem*

- *Should provide a mechanism for a joining blockchain to register to the ecosystem*

- *Should provide a mechanism for a blockchain to edit properties or unregister from the crosschain ecosystem*

- *Should provide a mechanism to get some critical information of the blockchain*

- *Should provide a mechanism to differentiate an original blockchain and a forked blockchain*

- *Should provide a mechanism to verify a chainId without external registration service*

Specification

The following diagram (Figure 11-3) shows the definition of a 32-Byte Crosschain ID.

Name	Size(bytes)	Description
Truncated Block Hash	16	This is the block hash of the genesis block or the block hash of the block immediately prior to the fork of a blockchain. The 16 bytes is the 16 least significant bytes, assuming network byte order.
Native Chain ID	4	This is the **Chain ID** value that should be used with the blockchain when signing transactions. For blockchains that do not have a concept of **Chain ID**, this value is zero.
Chain Type	2	Reserve 0x00 as an undefined chain type. 0x01 as mainnet type. 0x1[0-A]: testnet, 0x2[0-A]: private development network
Governance Identifier	2	For new blockchains, a governance_identifier can be specified to identify an original **owner** of a blockchain, to help settle forked/main chain disputes. For all existing blockchains and for blockchains that do not have the concept of an **owner**, this field is zero.
Reserved	7	Reserved for future use. Use 000000 for now.
Checksum	1	Used to verify the integrity of the identifier. This integrity check is targeted at detecting Crosschain Identifiers mistyped by human users. The value is calculated as the truncated SHA256 message digest of the rest of the identifier, using the least significant byte, assuming network byte order. Note that this checksum byte only detects integrity with a probability of one in 256. This probability is adequate for the intended usage of detecting typographical errors by people manually entering the Crosschain Identifier.

Figure 11-3. Definition of a 32-byte crosschainId

Rationale

We have considered various alternative specifications such as using a random unique hex string to represent a blockchain. The drawback of this method is that the random ID cannot be used to verify a blockchain's intrinsic identity such as the block hash of the genesis block. A second alternative is simply using a genesis block hash to represent a blockchain ID for crosschain operations. The drawback of this is that this ID does not have information about the property of the blockchain and it has problems when a blockchain is forked into two blockchain.

Backward Compatibility

CrosschainId can be backward compatible with EIP-155. The crosschain ID contains a 4-byte segment to record the chainId based on EIP-155.

Security Considerations

Collision of crosschain ID: Two blockchains can contain the same crosschain ID and hence mistakenly transfer assets to a wrong blockchain.

This security concern is addressed by comparing the hash of the crosschain ID with the hash of the genesis block. If it matches, then the crosschain ID is verified. If not, the crosschain ID can be compared with the forked block hash. If none of the block hash match the crosschain ID hash, then the crosschain ID cannot be verified.

Preventing relay attack: Although crosschain ID by itself is different from chainId and it is not signed into blockchain transaction, the crosschain ID can still be used for preventing relay attack. An application that handles crosschain transaction can verify the crosschain ID with its block hash and decide whether the transaction is valid or not. Any transaction with a nonverifiable crosschain ID should be rejected.

The crosschain ID is not required to be signed into blockchain tx. For blockchains that do not cryptographically sign crosschain ID into the blocks, the crosschain ID cannot be verified with the blocks themselves and has to be verified with external smart contract address and offchain utilities implemented based on the crosschain ID specification.

To use the crosschainId, a service needs to be developed and deployed to a blockchain to register crosschain identities for different blockchains. This service should provide the following features:

- Allow a user to register a blockchain to the service

- Allow administrator or a group of administrators to approve or revoke a blockchain registered by a user

- Allow a user to modify the blockchain information before it is finalized

- Allow any user to list and retrieve crosschain IDs that are registered

- Allow lookup of crosschain ID through legacy chainId defined in EIP-155

Architecture

The architecture of the crosschain identity service is shown in the following diagram (Figure 11-4). The blockchain shown on the bottom layer provides security and immutability for the service. The middle layer is the smart contracts with functions such as adding crosschain ID, query ID, approve or revoke ID, modify ID, etc. The smart contract can query or save states to the blockchain through EVM. The top layer is the GUI layer that renders web pages, processes user inputs, and communicates with smart contracts with Web3 and MetaMask wallet. The Web3 layer will need to connect with an RPC node in order to access smart contracts.

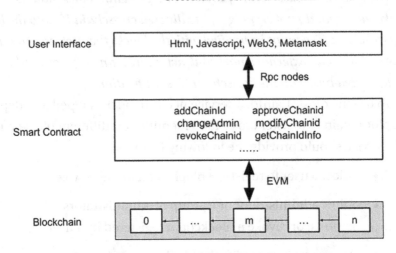

Figure 11-4. *Crosschain id service architecture*

Design the Smart Contract

When designing the smart contract, the following factors are considered: actors and roles, data structures, events, and functions.

Roles

Three roles are defined for the crosschain ID service smart contract. The owner is a role who deploys the smart contract. This owner owns the smart contract and has the privilege to assign an administrator for the smart contract. The administrator (admin) manages the crosschain IDs and can approve or revoke a crosschain ID. Then there are also regular users who can query crosschain IDs, add a new crosschain ID, or modify its information.

Events

When users perform operations on the smart contract, several kinds of events can be emitted so that client applications can query what has happened. Four events are defined:

> **AddChainId** – This event is emitted when a new crosschain ID is added to the service.
>
> **VerifyChainId** – This event is emitted when a crosschain ID has been verified and approved by the administrator.
>
> **RevokeChainId** – This event is emitted when a crosschain ID has been revoked by the administrator.
>
> **ModifyChainIdInfo** – This event is emitted when a registrator modifies metadata of a crosschain ID.

Data Structures

Several data structures have been defined. There is a chainidInfo data struct that contains manager address, long name, short name, category, and URL string of a blockchain. There is a Status enumeration with values of Pending, Verified, and Revoked. Pending is a status when a crosschain ID is just registered. Verified is a status when an administrator approves the crosschain ID. Revoked is a status when the administrator finds issues with the crosschain ID and rejects its registration. There are also several mapping data structures such as idStatus and idInfo that allow the smart contract to look up crosschain ID status and metadata information. And finally, there is a legacyIds that maps a legacy ID with a new crosschain ID.

Functions

The following functions are defined for the smart contract:

addChainId – This function adds a new crosschain ID to the service. It can be called by any user.

changeAdmin – This function changes the administrator of the service. It can be called by the owner of the smart contract.

apporveChainid – This function changes the status of the crosschain ID to Verified. It can only be called by the administrator of the smart contract service.

revokeChainid – This function changes the status of the crosschain ID to Revoked. It can only be called by the administrator of the smart contract service.

modifyChainidInfo – This function modified the metadata information of the crosschain ID. It can be called by the manager of a crosschain ID.

getChainIdStatus – This function returns the status of the crosschain ID.

getChainIdFromLegacyId – This function returns the crosschain ID associated with a legacy ID.

getChainIdInfo – This function returns the metadata information of a chainId.

UML of Smart Contract

To better visualize the crosschain id service smart contract, the following UML (Universal Modeling Language) diagram (Figure 11-5) is generated:

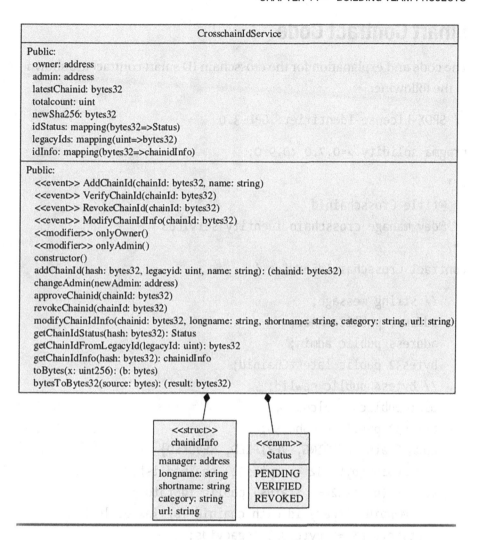

Figure 11-5. *UML diagram of crosschain id service smart contract*

Smart Contract Code

The code and explanation for the crosschain ID smart contract are shown in the following:

```solidity
// SPDX-License-Identifier: GPL-3.0

pragma solidity >=0.7.0 <0.9.0;

/**
 * @title CrosschainId
 * @dev manage crosschain identity services
 */
contract CrosschainIdService {

    // string message;
    address public owner;
    address public admin;
    bytes32 public latestChainid;
    // bytes4 public newIid;
    uint public totalcount;
    bytes32 public newSha256;
    enum Status{PENDING, VERIFIED, REVOKED}
    // mapping(bytes32 => bytes32) chainidlist;
    mapping(bytes32 => Status) public idStatus;
    //  mapping legacy id with chainid for faster lookup
    mapping(uint => bytes32) legacyIds;
    struct chainidInfo {
        address manager;
        string longname;
        string shortname;
        string category;
        string url;
    }
```

```
mapping(bytes32 => chainidInfo) idInfo;
event AddChainId(bytes32 indexed chainId, string name);
event VerifyChainId(bytes32 indexed chainId);
event RevokeChainId(bytes32 indexed chainId);
event ModifyChainIdInfo(bytes32 indexed chainId);

modifier onlyOwner() {
    require(msg.sender == owner);
    _;
}

modifier onlyAdmin() {
    require(msg.sender == admin);
    _;
}
//add common crosschain id such as Etherem mainnet.
constructor() {
    owner = msg.sender;
    admin = msg.sender;
    addChainId(0xd4e56740f876aef8c010b86a40d5f56745a118d090
    6a34e69aec8c0db1cb8fa3, 1, 'Ethereum Mainnet');
    modifyChainIdInfo(latestChainid, "Ethereum Mainnet",
    "eth", "mainnet", "www.etherscan.io");

    addChainId(0x6341fd3daf94b748c72ced5a5b26028f2474f5f0
    0d824504e4fa37a75767e177, 4, 'Ethereum Rinkeby');
    modifyChainIdInfo(latestChainid, "Ethereum Rinkeby",
    "rinkeby", "testnet", "rinkeby.etherscan.io");

}

// add a crosschainId
// @hash: The block hash for a genesis block or the first
forked block
```

```
// legacyid: Legacy chainid based on EIP-155
// name of the blockchain
function addChainId(bytes32 hash, uint legacyid, string
memory name) public returns (bytes32 chainid) {
    require(hash != 0x00);
    //require (check uniqueness, check oracle if needed)
    // trim the other 16 bytes
    hash = (hash >> 128) <<128;
    //get legacy chainid in bytes32 format
    bytes32 legacy_chainid = bytesToBytes32(toBytes(l
    egacyid));

    // reserve 8 bytes for legacy chainid. Merge with
    block hash
    hash = hash | (legacy_chainid << 64);

    // Calculate sha256 of the combined hash
    newSha256 = sha256(abi.encodePacked(hash));
    // merge the hash with first two bytes of sha256 as
    checksum
    hash = hash | (newSha256 >> 240);

    chainid = hash;

    //Check if chainid already registered. If idStatus is
    empty it has 0x00, revert and exit
    if(abi.encodePacked(idStatus[chainid]).length > 1) {
        revert();
     }

    if(legacyIds[legacyid] != bytes32(0)) {
        revert();
     }
```

```
    legacyIds[legacyid] = chainid;

    latestChainid = chainid;

    // set idStatus to PENDING
    idStatus[chainid] = Status.PENDING;

    // set chainid metadata (partial). The rest set with
    modifyChainIdInfo
    idInfo[chainid].manager = msg.sender;
    idInfo[chainid].longname = name;

    //increment totalcount
    totalcount++;

    emit  AddChainId(chainid, name);

}

//The owner changes the administrator of the service. The
admin can be a multisign address managed out of chain
function changeAdmin(address newAdmin) onlyOwner public {
    admin = newAdmin;
}

// require sender to be admin
// approve a chainid
function approveChainid(bytes32 chainId) onlyAdmin public {
    require(idStatus[chainId] == Status.PENDING);
    idStatus[chainId] = Status.VERIFIED;
    emit VerifyChainId(chainId);
}

// require sender to be admin
// revoke a chainid
function revokeChainid(bytes32 chainId) onlyAdmin public {
```

```
        require(idStatus[chainId] != Status.REVOKED); //Can
        revoke chainId in PENDING or VERIFIED status
        idStatus[chainId] = Status.REVOKED;
        emit RevokeChainId(chainId);
    }

    function modifyChainIdInfo(bytes32 chainid, string memory
    longname, string memory shortname, string memory category,
    string memory url) public {
        require(idStatus[chainid] == Status.PENDING);
        require(idInfo[chainid].manager == msg.sender);
        if(bytes(longname).length > 1) {
            idInfo[chainid].longname = longname;
        }
        if(bytes(shortname).length > 1) {
            idInfo[chainid].shortname = shortname;
        }
        if(bytes(category).length > 1) {
            idInfo[chainid].category = category;
        }
        if(bytes(url).length > 1) {
            idInfo[chainid].url = url;
        }
        emit ModifyChainIdInfo(chainid);
    }

    function getChainIdStatus(bytes32 hash) public view returns
    (Status) {
      return idStatus[hash];
    }

    function getChainIdFromLegacyId(uint legacyId) public view
    returns (bytes32) {
```

```
    return legacyIds[legacyId];
  }

  function getChainIdInfo(bytes32 hash) public view returns
  (chainidInfo memory) {
    return idInfo[hash];
  }

  //convert an integer to byte array
  function toBytes(uint256 x) public pure returns (bytes
  memory b) {
  b = new bytes(32);
  // b = abi.encodePacked(x);
  assembly { mstore(add(b, 32), x) }
}

//convert byte array to bytes32 fixed array
function bytesToBytes32(bytes memory source) public pure
returns (bytes32 result) {
    if (source.length == 0) {
        return 0x0;
    }
    assembly {
        result = mload(add(source, 32))
    }
  }
}
```

Client Considerations

In the preceding section, a smart contract is deployed to a blockchain that allows external programs to call the smart contract functions through transactions. These client programs can be in command-line interfaces or web applications. A popular client application is through a web-based browser to render the GUI and use MetaMask as a wallet to send the transactions. In the following, we demonstrate how to build web pages to interact with smart contracts.

Typically, a web page to interact with a smart contract contains the following components:

- HTML pages to render the GUI

- JavaScript to process user inputs and smart contract output

- Web3 for JavaScript and smart contract function calls

- MetaMask plug-in or extension for a wallet to sign transactions

In the case of crosschainId service, the following HTML pages are designed (Figure 11-6):

HTML page	Description	Input Parameters
addCrosschainid.html	A page for adding a crosschain ID to the service	The hash of block 0 Legacy ID A name for the chain
listCrosschainid.html	A page that shows registered crosschain IDs	None
showCrosschainid.html	Showing detailed information of a crosschain ID	crosschainId
editCrosschainidInfo.html	Edit the crosschain ID information in pending state	crosschainId
modifyCrosschainidStatus. html	Approve or Revoke a crosschain ID	crosschainId

Figure 11-6. Html files for the crosschain id service user interfacet

Each HTML page will have user input in the browser pages and also include JavaScript to handle the browser events and user interactions.

HTML Page Example

The following (Figure 11-7) is an example of an "Add crosschain id" GUI markup web page:

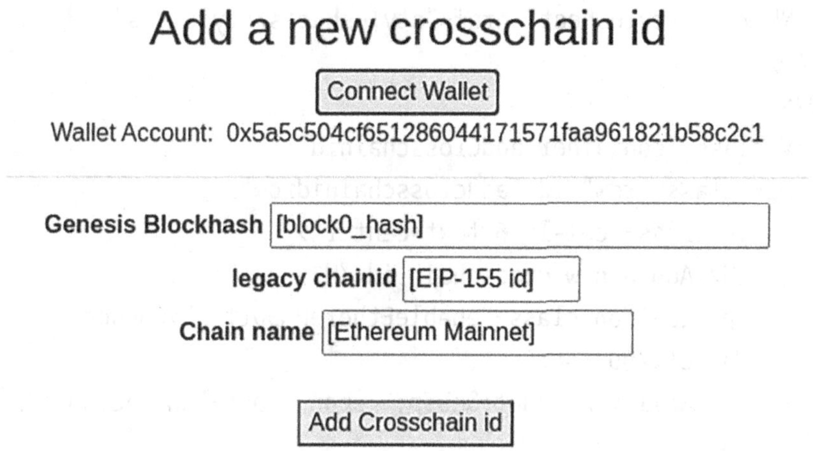

Add a new crosschain id

Connect Wallet

Wallet Account: 0x5a5c504cf651286044171571faa961821b58c2c1

Genesis Blockhash [block0_hash]

legacy chainid [EIP-155 id]

Chain name [Ethereum Mainnet]

Add Crosschain id

Figure 11-7. *Example of adding crosschain id GUI page*

To render this page, the following HTML is written with multiple clickable buttons and input fields. The "Connect Wallet" button allows that page to connect to a MetaMask wallet. The "Add Crosschain id" button triggers a call to crosschainId smart contract to add a chainId to the blockchain. To send transactions to smart contracts on a blockchain, several JavaScripts containing Web3, ABI, and APIs are included. The JavaScript codes are explained in the next section.

```
<!DOCTYPE html>
<HTML>
<HEAD>
```

```
<META name="generator" content=
"HTML Tidy for HTML5 for Linux version 5.6.0">
<META charset="utf-8">
<TITLE>CrosschainIdService</TITLE>
<BASE href="/">
<META name="viewport" content=
"width=device-width, initial-scale=1">
<LINK rel="stylesheet" href="stylesheets/bootstrap.min.css">
<LINK rel="stylesheet" href="stylesheets/style.css">
</HEAD>
<BODY>
  <DIV class="container addCrosschainid">
    <DIV class="row" id="addcrosschainidrow">
      <DIV class="col-lg-6 text-center">
        <H2>Add a new crosschain id</H2>
        <p> <button class="enableEthereumButton">Connect
        Wallet</button>
        <br>Wallet Account:  <span class="showAccount">
        <hr>
        <DIV class="blockhash">
          <LABEL for="blockhash"><B>Genesis Blockhash</B>
          </LABEL>
          <INPUT type="text" class="ignore-form-control" id=
          "blockhash" placeholder="" value="[block0_hash]"
          size="34"
          required="">
        </DIV>
        <DIV class="legacyid">
          <LABEL for="legacyid"><B>legacy chainid</B></LABEL>
          <INPUT type="text" class="ignore-form-control" id=
          "legacyid" placeholder="" value="[EIP-155 id]" size="10"
```

```
        required="">
      </DIV>
      <DIV class="chainname">
        <LABEL for="chainname"><B>Chain name</B></LABEL>
        <INPUT type="text" class="ignore-form-control" id=
        "chainname" placeholder="" value="[Ethereum Mainnet]"
        size="20"
        required="">
      </DIV>
      <br>
<div class="center-this" id="addChainidButton">
<button style="margin:0;" onclick="addChainid()"
id="addChainidButton">Add Crosschain id</button></div>
        <DIV id="addChainidValue"></DIV>
      </DIV>
    </DIV><!-- <hr class="featurette-divider"> -->
    <SCRIPT src="/scripts/web3.min.js"></SCRIPT>
    <SCRIPT src="/scripts/jquery-3.3.1.slim.min.js"></SCRIPT>
    <SCRIPT src="/scripts/jquery.min.js"></SCRIPT>
    <SCRIPT src="/scripts/enableEthereum.js"></SCRIPT>
    <SCRIPT src="/scripts/crosschainid_info.js"></SCRIPT>
    <SCRIPT src="/scripts/addCrosschainid.js"></SCRIPT>
  </DIV>
</BODY>
</HTML>
```

JavaScript Example

In the preceding addCrosschainid.html file, several JavaScript files are
included. The web3.min.js file is a JavaScript Web3 implementation for
browsers. This is an open source file that can be downloaded from the
Web. The enableEthereum.js file is to implement the "Connect Wallet"

button event. Clicking at this button will trigger a function call to get the wallet address connected to the browser. In this enableEthereum.js script, the ethereumButton object corresponds to the "Connect Wallet" button and is registered with a click event handler to call getAccount() function. The getAccount calls the Web3 function of eth_requestAccounts to retrieve the accounts in the MetaMask. The first account is assigned to account0 that can be referred to by other scripts. Here, the showAccount object is a Div object that will be populated with the account address retrieved from the getAccount() function call.

```
------------ enableEthereum.js ----------------------------
const ethereumButton = document.querySelector('.
enableEthereumButton');
const showAccount = document.querySelector('.showAccount');
var account0 = 0;

ethereumButton.addEventListener('click', () => {
  getAccount();
});

async function getAccount() {
  const accounts = await ethereum.request({ method: 'eth_
requestAccounts' });
  account0 = accounts[0];
  showAccount.innerHTML = account0;
}
```

Once enableEthereum.js retrieves the account, a user can enter block 0 hash, legacy chainId, and blockchain name and click the "Add crosschain id" button to register a new blockchain ID. This function is implemented in addCrosschainid.js JavaScript. In this script, the addChainid() function is called when "Add Crosschain id" button in the web page is clicked. This function first checks if the MetaMask wallet is enabled and connected. If not, the user will be prompted to install a MetaMask extension. If yes, a smart contract object named myContract will be constructed with a crosschain ID smart contract ABI and contract address. The ABI and contract address are specified in a separate crosschainid_info.js file. myContract object supports addChainId method that takes in parameters of block hash, legacyId, and chain name. These parameters are fetched through the input fields in the web page. There are multiple ways to call a smart contract function. In this example, the smart contract function call data is first calculated through the following code:

```
var chainidData = myContract.methods.addChainId(blockhash,
legacyid, chainname).encodeABI();
```

Then chainidData is sent to the smart contract through web3. eth.sendTransaction operation. The transaction receipt is returned and shown on the web page.

```
------------ addCrosschainid.js --------------------------
//addCrosschain.js implements the addChainid function call to
add a crosschain id to smart contract

var web3;

const ethEnabled = () => {
  if (typeof window.ethereum === 'undefined') {
    alert("You need a Dapp browser to get started. Please
    install metamask");
    return false;
  }
  web3 = new Web3(window.ethereum);

  return true;
}

function addChainid() {
  if (!ethEnabled()) {
```

```
    alert("Please install an Ethereum-compatible browser or
    extension like MetaMask to use this dApp!");
  }
  web3.eth.getAccounts(function(err, accounts) {
    var myContract = new web3.eth.Contract(crosschainid_abi,
    crosschainid_contract.toLowerCase());

    var blockhash = $('.blockhash input').val();
    var legacyid = $('.legacyid input').val();
    var chainname = $('.chainname input').val();
    var chainidData = myContract.methods.addChainId(blockhash,
    legacyid, chainname).encodeABI();

    var tx_chainid = web3.eth.sendTransaction({
      from: accounts[0].toLowerCase(),
      to: crosschainid_contract.toLowerCase(),
      data: chainidData
    }, function(err, transactionHash) {
      document.getElementById("addChainidValue").innerHTML =
      "addChainid tx:" + transactionHash;
    })

  })

}

$(document).ready(function() {
  if (!ethEnabled()) {
    alert("Please install an Ethereum-compatible browser or
extension like MetaMask to use this dApp!");
  }
});
```

The preceding example shows how to build an add crosschain ID web page to interact with a deployed smart contract. Similar pages can be built for other functions for listing crosschain IDs, modifying chainId information, approving or revoking crosschain IDs, etc.

Security Review

There are many factors to be considered for security. The security guideline in Chapter 8 should be followed. Each function in the smart contract should have a privilege check. For example, when modifying the crosschain ID information, there should be a check on the requester to ensure that it is the original registrator of the crosschain ID. The second check is that the status of the crosschain ID should be in "Pending" state. If the crosschain ID is in "Verified" or "Revoked" state, its information cannot be modified.

Another important item is to ensure that only the administrator can approve or revoke a crosschain ID registration. This administrator can be a single account or a multisign account from a consortium. An administrator can transfer its ownership to another account.

Besides security for the smart contract, the web pages security should also be evaluated. For a service to be deployed for production, it is a best practice to have a security audit and white box testing to ensure that there is no major security vulnerability.

Deploy to Testnet

When writing the code for smart contract and web GUI, developers can have a development system and a local web service to test the project. Once local development is completed, it can be deployed to public testnet for external users to test it. There are several options for Ethereum testnet. For the Ethereum blockchain, there are four popular testnets that are available, including Ropsten, Kovan, Rinkeby, and Goerli testnets. All the testnets mentioned here use proof-of-authority (POA) consensus and are faster than the mainnet. To use these testnets, first connect the MetaMask wallet to the testnet you want the smart contract to be deployed to (Figure 11-8). The testnets have been added to the MetaMask already. If you cannot see the testnet listed, simply click at show/hide testnets to open up the configuration widget and set "show the testnets" to "on."

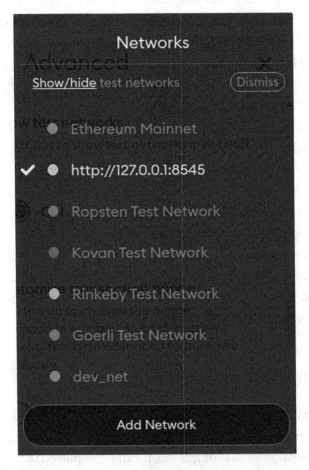

Figure 11-8. Connecting to the Ethereum mainnet or testnet through MetaMask

Once the MetaMask wallet is set to the designed testnet, testers need to get some testing ether to test the dApp. These testnets all provide a small amount of ether for testing purposes through dedicated faucets. The faucet addresses and block browser URLs are shown in the following (Figure 11-9):

Testnet	Faucet Address	Block Explorer Address
Rinkeby	https://faucet.rinkeby.io/	https://rinkeby.etherscan.io
Ropsten	https://faucet.ropsten.be/	https://ropsten.etherscan.io
Kovan	https://faucet.kovan.network/	https://kovan.etherscan.io
Goerli	https://goerli.etherscan.io/	https://goerli.etherscan.io

Figure 11-9. *Ethereum testnet faucet addresses*

Once a smart contract is deployed to testnet and the web pages are set up to access the smart contract, the project team can announce alpha or beta test programs to the users. The testing program is to involve community members to try out the decentralized applications and report issues found in the project. Normally, bounties are given to users who report issues found in the project. Due to the immutability of blockchain, it is critical that the dApps are tested thoroughly in testnet before being deployed to the mainnet.

Deploy to Mainnet

Once the dApp is thoroughly tested in testnet, it can be deployed to the Ethereum mainnet. The tools and methods for deploying a smart contract to a production network are the same as the testnet. There is no faucet for the production network. The ether used for deploying smart contracts will need to be purchased. Deployment requires noncustodial accounts where developers actually hold private keys. The custodial accounts hosted by companies such as Coinbase and PayPal cannot be used. Developers need to own the private key of an account in order to deploy a smart contract. In addition, there are several factors to consider for the deployment to the mainnet.

First and foremost is security. Deployment of smart contracts is done by sending a transaction to the address 0 of the blockchain. The smart contract address is generated through hashing only the sender address and the nonce of that transaction. The data field of the transaction will be the bytecode of the smart contract and saved to the calculated address on the blockchain. Once a smart contract is deployed, the owner of the smart contract is the sender that sends the transaction. This sender may be assigned privileges to make modifications to the blockchain. It is very important to safeguard the smart contract owner address. Sometimes, a smart contract owner can call a function to denounce the ownership or transfer the ownership to another EOA (external owner account).

Secondly, the smart contract address will need to be published in a trusted media. Users interact with smart contracts by sending transactions to the smart contract address. If users send the transactions to a smart contract with the wrong address, the fake smart contract may intercept the funds sent to faked smart contracts.

Thirdly, the token associated with the project smart contract will need to be added from the users' wallet. The instructions should be provided to the users. For most of the crypto wallet, the tokens are not automatically added to the wallet. Users need to add a token to the wallet by adding a smart contract, token symbol, decimal value, etc. This information will come from the project team and should be published to the users.

Fourthly, a stable RPC node should be selected and connected to the MetaMask or other wallets. An RPC node is an Ethereum client node that syncs all blocks to a system and opens connection to Web3 clients. The RPC node can be owned by a third party or by the project team itself. In either case, the RPC node should be safeguarded and prevented from the attacks.

And lastly, the web pages and smart contract should be properly integrated. In the web pages, the Web3 object constructs transactions and sends the request to the blockchain. It is important to evaluate the Web3 and other scripts to make sure that they will not be tempered.

Once the smart contracts are deployed to mainnet, it is open to the world. Besides the interfaces such as web portal and CLI provided by the project team, third-party developers can also write applications to access the smart contract. Due to the "openness," "decentralization," and "immutability" of blockchain, the operation of decentralized apps is more challenging than regular applications and will need to be discussed further.

Operation and Upgrade Consideration

Since decentralized applications are not supposed to have centralized owner and management, there is a need to build a community that can govern the operation and upgrade of decentralized applications. Many projects build voting mechanisms to decide on project operation and upgrade. Project team issues governing tokens and distributes them to community members. The voting power is proportional to the amount of governing tokens. The community members can earn governing tokens to increase their voting capacity. When a new feature or upgrade is proposed, it is sent to a voting system, and each community member can vote to adopt or reject the proposal. The accepted proposals are implemented by developers as open source and then deployed to the mainnet.

One major challenge is to upgrade the deployed smart contract if security vulnerability is found. Since there is no central authority, the community will need to vote for an upgrade. However, since blockchain is immutable, the deployed smart contract cannot be patched or upgraded.

In this case, the smart contract will need to be redeployed. When redeploying a new smart contract, the tokens governed by the old smart contract will need to be ported to the new smart contract. When the new smart contract is deployed, all web pages and Web3 interface should point to the new smart contract address. This is a very tedious and error-prone process.

Sometimes, it would be good to write upgradable smart contracts. This is to separate a smart contract into two or multiple smart contracts. The first smart contract is an entry smart contract with very simple functionality such as receiving an address and calling a target smart contract at that address. The target smart contract is the one with the majority of functions implemented. If the target smart contract has security vulnerability and needs to be upgraded, a new target smart contract can be deployed, and the new address can be sent to the entry smart contract. When the entry smart contract receives the new target smart contract address, it will call the new target smart contract. With this upgradable smart contract design, the web pages and CLI does not need to be reconfigured as the entry smart contract address does not change.

To optimally operate a decentralized application, it is essential to build some services to monitor key parameters. For example, the total minted token should be monitored to ensure that no additional tokens are minted by hackers. The transaction throughput and gas fees can also be monitored to ensure that that dApp is in healthy operational state. In addition, the EVM upgrades and Ethereum hark forks should also be monitored to ensures there is no negative impacts to the decentralized applications.

And finally, a vibrant community is the key for a successful operation of decentralized applications. Building a dApp is unseparable from building a community. Only with active enrollments of community, decentralized applications can sustain, grow, and survive severe attacks.

Index

A

Abstract class, 295
Address type, 258, 259
Alternate currencies, 37
Application Bytecode Interface
(ABI), 236, 246, 310
Application design decisions
consensus, 132, 133
data, 130–132
development stack, 135–138
smart contracts, 128, 129
stakeholder
organization, 133–135
tokens, 124–127
transactions, 122–124
Application themes
data sovereignty, 117
payments, 117
transparency, 117
Arbitration, 224
Arithmetic operations, 280, 281,
370, 400
Assert() function, 279
Assert violation, 279
Asset management tools, 221
Asymmetric key cryptography,
48, 49, 55

Atomic value exchanges, 16
Auditors, 329
Authorization through tx.origin,
282, 283
Automated Market Maker (AMM)
mechanism, 224, 386

B

Backward compatible, 412
Beacon chain, 371
Bitcoin, 12, 13, 164, 209
block, 167, 175
block header fields, 176
blocks, 177
coinbase transaction, 172
components, 167
consensus mechanism, 184–187
design decision, 181
distributed ledger software, 169
economics, 182–184
fields, 174
hash Merkle root of
transactions, 177
inputs and outputs structure, 170
miners, 166
mining node, 166
mining reward, 197

C

Printed in the United States
by Baker & Taylor Publisher Services